ALIEN 3

THE UNPRODUCED SCREENPLAY

A L I E N 3

THE UNPRODUCED SCREENPLAY

WILLIAM GIBSON
JOHNNIE CHRISTMAS
TAMRA BONVILLAIN

LETTERS BY NATE PIEKOS OF BLAMBOT®

COVER BY JOHNNIE CHRISTMAS
WITH TAMRA BONVILLAIN

DARK HORSE BOOKS

PRESIDENT & PUBLISHER
MIKE RICHARDSON

EDITOR
DANIEL CHABON

ASSISTANT EDITORS
BRETT ISRAEL AND CHUCK HOWITT

DESIGNER
JUSTIN COUCH

DIGITAL ART TECHNICIAN
JOSIE CHRISTENSEN

Library of Congress Cataloging-in-Publication Data

Names: Gibson, William, 1948- author. I Christmas, Johnnie, artist, author. I
  Bonvillain, Tamra, colourist, cover artist. I Piekos, Nate, letterer.
Title: William Gibson's Alien 3 : the unproduced screenplay / story, William
  Gibson ; adaptation script and art, Johnnie Christmas ; color art, Tamra
  Bonvillain ; letters, Nate Piekos of Blambot ; cover, Johnnie Christmas
  with Tamra Bonvillain.
Description: First edition. I Milwaukie, OR : Dark Horse Books, July 2019. I
  "Collects issues #1–#5 of the Dark Horse Comics series William Gibson's
  Alien 3"
Identifiers: LCCN 2019003649 I ISBN 9781506708119 (paperback)
Subjects: LCSH: Comic books, strips, etc. I BISAC: COMICS & GRAPHIC NOVELS /
  Media Tie-In. I COMICS & GRAPHIC NOVELS / Horror. I COMICS & GRAPHIC
  NOVELS / Science Fiction.
Classification: LCC PN6728.A463 G56 2019 I DDC 741.5/973--dc23
LC record available at https://lccn.loc.gov/2019003649

Published by
DARK HORSE BOOKS
A division of Dark Horse Comics LLC
10956 SE Main Street, Milwaukie, OR 97222

DarkHorse.com   I   To find a comics shop in your area, visit comicshoplocator.com

First edition: August 2019
ISBN 978-1-50670-811-9

10 9 8 7 6 5 4 3 2 1
Printed in China

Collects issues #1–#5 of the Dark Horse Comics series *William Gibson's Alien 3*

Neil Hankerson, Executive Vice President · Tom Weddle, Chief Financial Officer · Randy Stradley, Vice President of Publishing · Nick McWhort-
er, Chief Business · Development Officer · Dale LaFountain, Chief Information Officer · Matt Parkinson, Vice President of Marketing · Cara
Niece, Vice President of Production and Scheduling · Mark Bernardi, Vice President of Book Trade and Digital Sales · Ken Lizzi, General Coun-
sel · Dave Marshall, Editor in Chief · Davey Estrada, Editorial Director Chris Warner, Senior Books Editor · Cary Grazzini, Director of Specialty
Projects · Lia Ribacchi, Art Director · Vanessa Todd-Holmes, Director of Print Purchasing · Matt Dryer, Director of Digital Art and Prepress ·
Michael Gombos, Senior Director of Licensed Publications · Kari Yadro, Director of Custom Programs · Kari Torson, Director of International
Licensing · Sean Brice, Director of Trade Sales

WORK FOR HIRE

The screenplay this series was based on was my first attempt at writing one, something I'd never considered prior to it being commissioned by the *Alien* franchise's three producers. It was also my first experience of executing "a work for hire," a piece of fiction (of sorts) to order, that wouldn't be my intellectual property.

I'm fairly certain that I'd never read a screenplay before being sent the shooting scripts of the first two *Alien* films. I certainly hadn't read a treatment before, and I was sent one of those as well, quite detailed, written by the producers (Walter Hill, David Giler, and Gordon Carroll).

I wasn't a member of the Writers Guild, but as a non-member you're allowed to write a single, first contract screenplay, to a Guild-approved contract, it being understood that your next one will be written as a member. All of this seemed a nicely paid break from what seemed then to be becoming my day job, the writing of prose fiction.

I read the two screenplays and the treatment, met with the producers, and went home to write. Almost immediately, the Writers Guild went rather spectacularly on strike. As a sort of honorary member, I gathered I was expected to down tools (not that I had yet picked any up) and not communicate with my employers. Which I did, though I then found myself with an indefinite amount of time in which to study those screenplays, which proved crucial.

It seemed to me that if I considered those as the first two volumes of a trilogy, and attempted to write a third "like" them, I'd have my best shot at not looking like someone who'd never before imagined writing a screenplay. Not that I intended to wrap anything up, to provide the end of any grand arc, but simply that I wanted to write something that would feel as much as possible like the missing third of a triangle.

The other thing I had in my favor, I felt, was that I was very much a fan of both previous films. They'd both affected my sense of what SF prose could do, let alone SF film (as had *Blade Runner* and *Escape From New York*).

And the treatment, the "screen story," was very carefully and thoroughly written. I wouldn't, given my druthers, have written Ripley out, though the treatment did. On the other hand, the whole Space Marxists aspect was something I wouldn't have thought of, but which I took to enthusiastically. After Ripley, my favorite character in the first two films had been Bishop, so I decided to crank my Bishop up for Volume Three.

And eventually I did, hand-formatting the whole thing on my brand-new Apple II-C (a hideous chore) as I had no idea of Final Draft (if indeed that even existed then). Having submitted the result, and receiving a response, I then, to terms of my contract, produced a second draft. And thereafter, for whatever reasons, ceased to be involved.

I've since read that the producers had given it to me not in hope getting a serviceable screenplay, but hoping for a certain amount of what might be called cyberpunk flash, which might then be laminated into someone else's actual screenplay. But I confounded their expectations doubly, first by turning in what they seem to have regarded, to their surprise, as a somewhat serviceable screenplay, but also by turning in one devoid of whatever exciting new flavor they were hoping for.

They simply hadn't, I imagine in retrospect, expected me to be quite so big an *Alien(s)* fanboy.

Much later (some thirty draft screenplays?) when the Writers Guild was going through the process of formally assigning writing credits to the eventual film, all I could find that remained of my work, in the shooting script, was a barcode tattoo.

And there things sat, for literal decades, until Dark Horse decided to publish a series based on that screenplay, something that would never have occurred to me, not least because the screenplay isn't my intellectual property.

This brought on board the remarkable Johnnie Christmas, whose adaptation of the screenplay to his medium is no doubt far more sensitive to the screenplay's intentions than any feature film would likely ever have been. It's been a really peculiar pleasure, watching this story unfold as drawn by Johnnie Christmas (who also literally adapted it, from screenplay to comic script). It looks better than I imagined it. The characters are more emotionally expressive that I imagined them (quite hauntingly so) and it moves in a way that far exceeds any expectations I may have had for it as a film (which had always seemed quite a long shot anyway).

Thank you, Johnnie, and thank you, Dark Horse.

The work for hire has finally found a home.

WM.GIBSON

Vancouver, BC
January 23, 2019

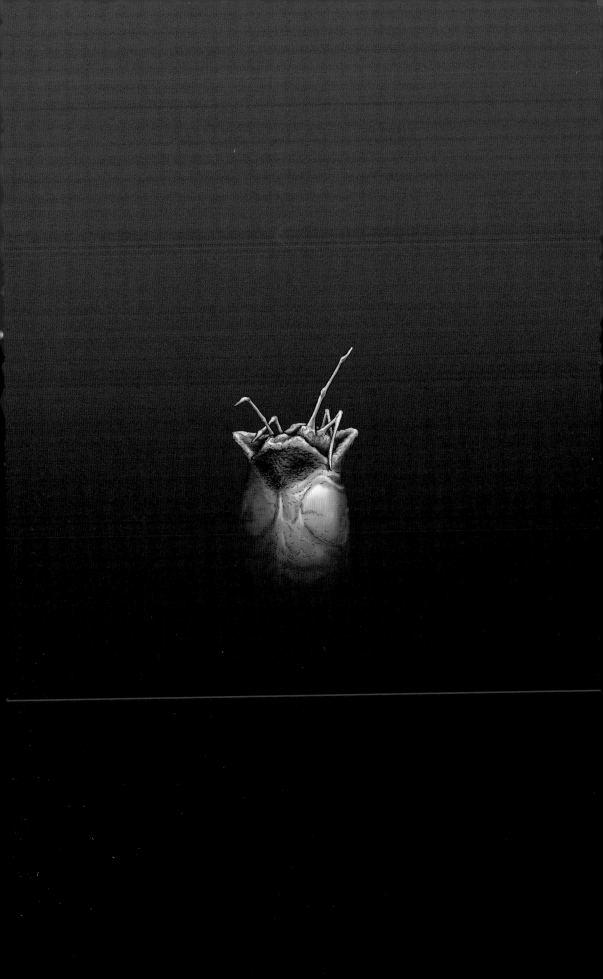

U.S.S. SULACO.

HYPERSLEEP VAULT.

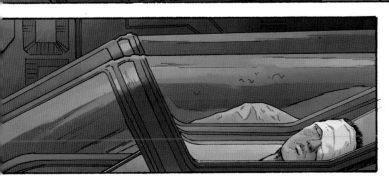

AAAAACK AAAAAACK

DUE TO NAVIGATIONAL SOFTWARE FAILURE, SULACO HAS ENTERED TERRITORY CLAIMED BY THE UNION OF PROGRESSIVE PEOPLES. AUXILIARY SYSTEMS ARE NOW ONLINE.

TROOP TRANSPORT
SULACO

CMC 846A/BETA>
GATEWAY

MISSION/LV-426/
RETURN

+++STATUS RED+++

COURSE FOR GATEWAY HAS BEEN CANCELLED IN FAVOR OF DOCKING-- INTERCEPT WITH ANCHORPOINT CLUSTER.

HARDWIRED PROTOCOLS PREVENT, REPEAT, PREVENT ARMING OF NUCLEAR WARHEADS IN THE ABSENCE OF DIPLOMATIC OVERRIDE, DECRYPTION STANDARD CHARLIE NINE.

TREATY VIOLATION
REF: #99AG558L5

CAUSE:
NAVIGATIONAL ERROR

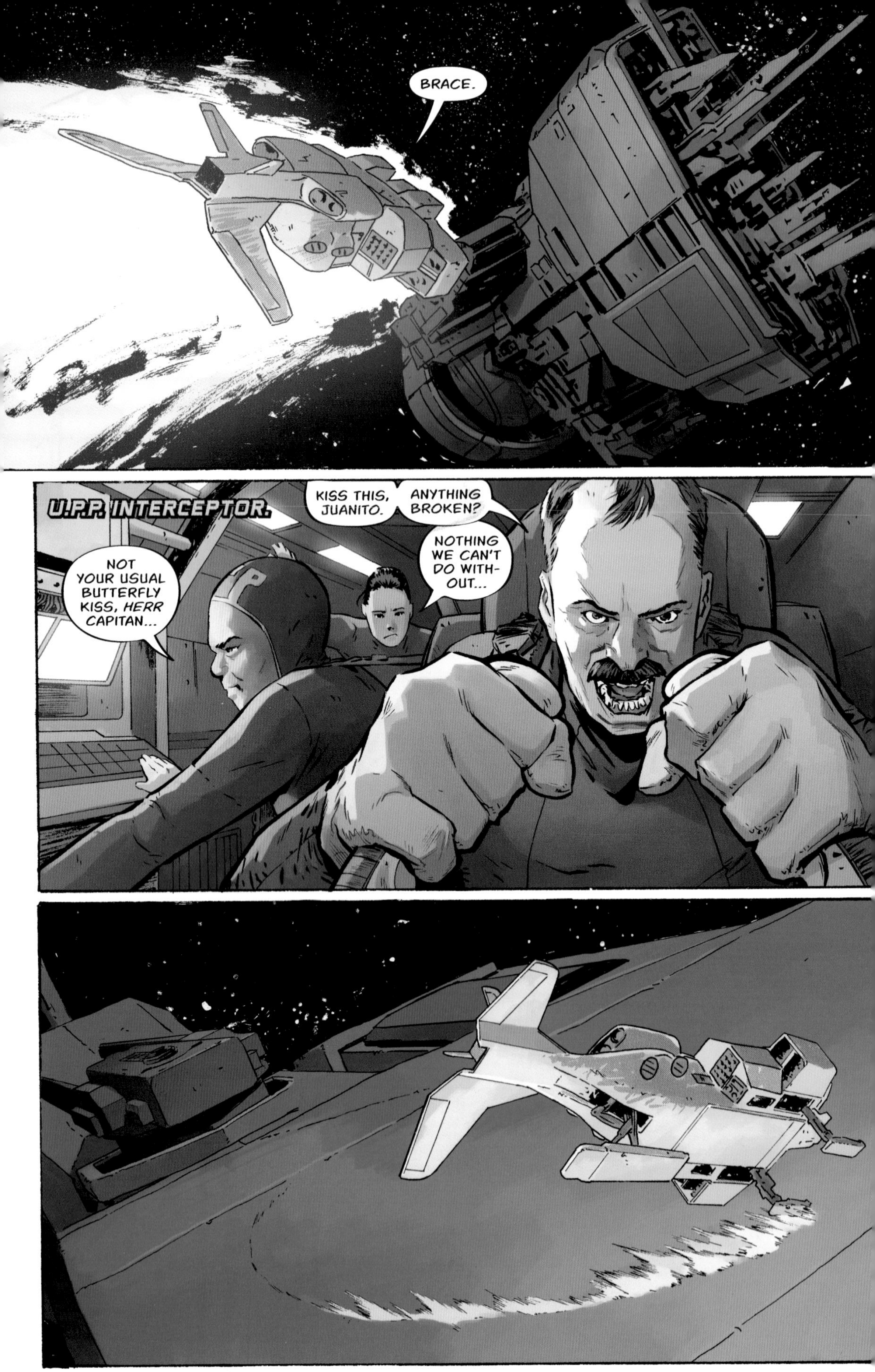
BRACE.
U.P.P. INTERCEPTOR.
NOT YOUR USUAL BUTTERFLY KISS, *HERR CAPITAN*...
KISS THIS, JUANITO.
ANYTHING BROKEN?
NOTHING WE CAN'T DO WITH-OUT...

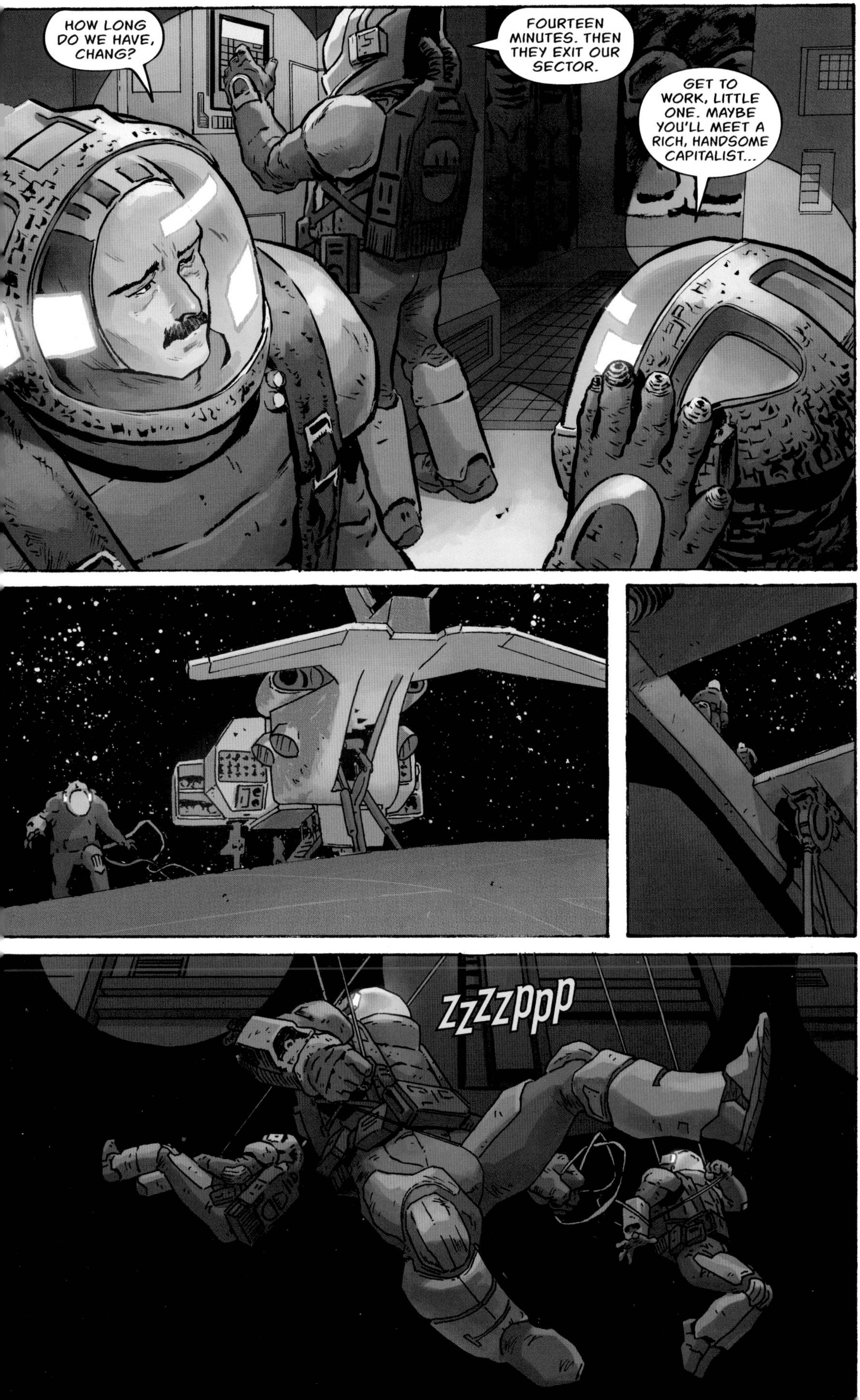
HOW LONG DO WE HAVE, CHANG?
FOURTEEN MINUTES. THEN THEY EXIT OUR SECTOR.
GET TO WORK, LITTLE ONE. MAYBE YOU'LL MEET A RICH, HANDSOME CAPITALIST...
ZZZZPPP

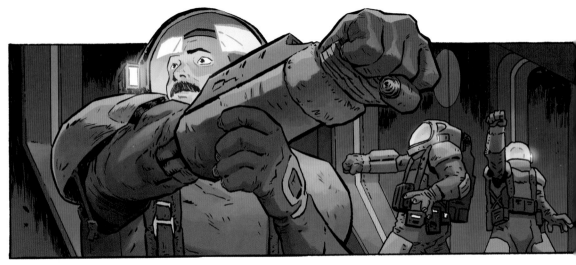

CAPTAIN...

ATTENTION. INTEGRITY BREACH, CARGO LOCK 3. SECURITY ALERT. INTEGRITY BREACH, B DECK...

PUTA MADRE...

THE HYPERSLEEP VAULT.

GOT A CAPSULE MALFUNCTION OVER HERE.

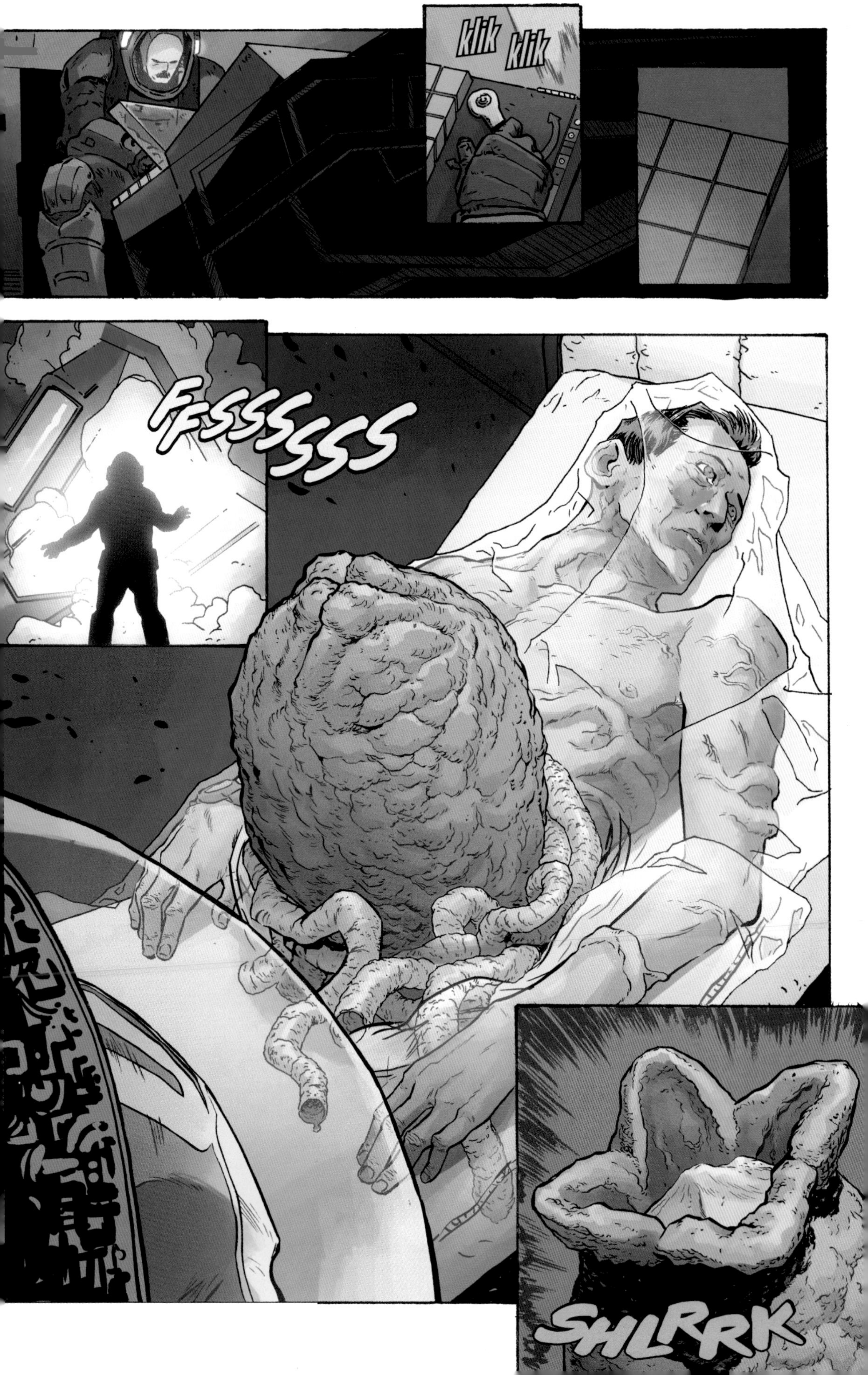
klik klik
FFSSSSSSS
SHLRRK

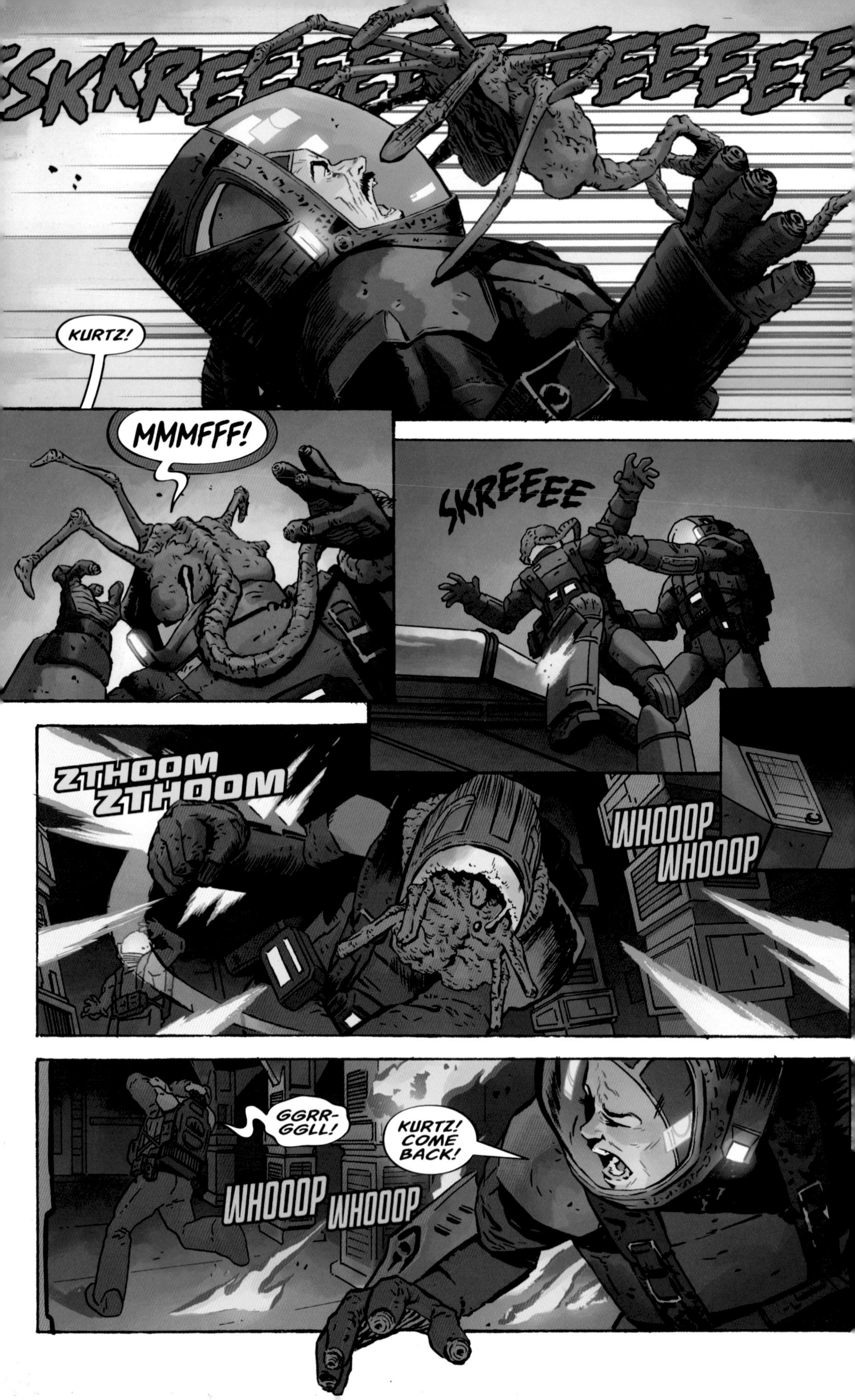
SKKREEEEEEEEEEEEE
KURTZ!
MMMFFF!
SKREEEE
ZTHOOM
ZTHOOM
WHOOOP
WHOOOP
GGRR-GGLL!
KURTZ! COME BACK!
WHOOOP
WHOOOP

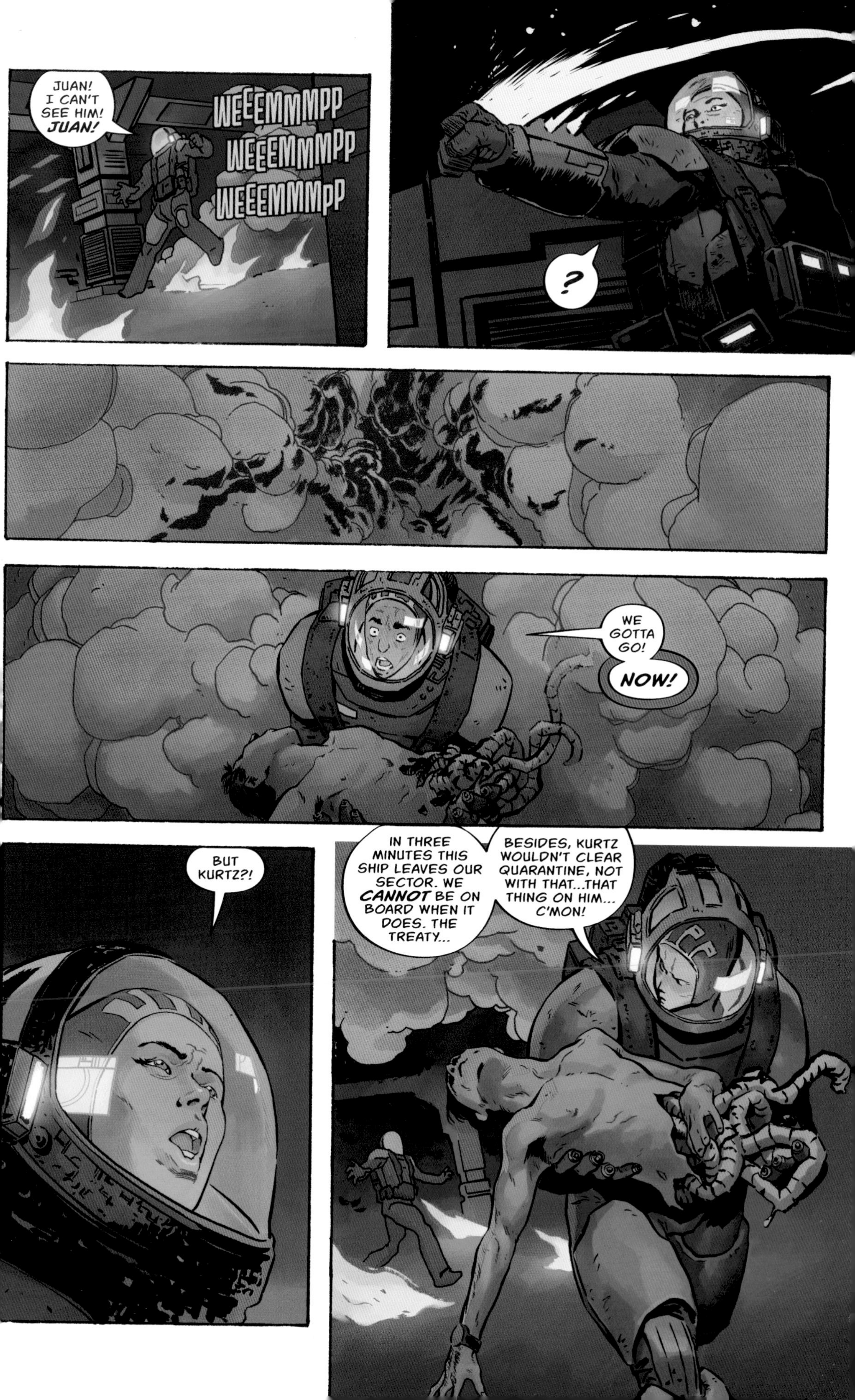

JUAN! I CAN'T SEE HIM! ***JUAN!***
WEEEMMMPP
WEEEMMMPP
WEEEMMMPP
?
WE GOTTA GO!
NOW!
BUT KURTZ?!
IN THREE MINUTES THIS SHIP LEAVES OUR SECTOR. WE ***CANNOT*** BE ON BOARD WHEN IT DOES. THE TREATY...
BESIDES, KURTZ WOULDN'T CLEAR QUARANTINE, NOT WITH THAT...THAT THING ON HIM... C'MON!

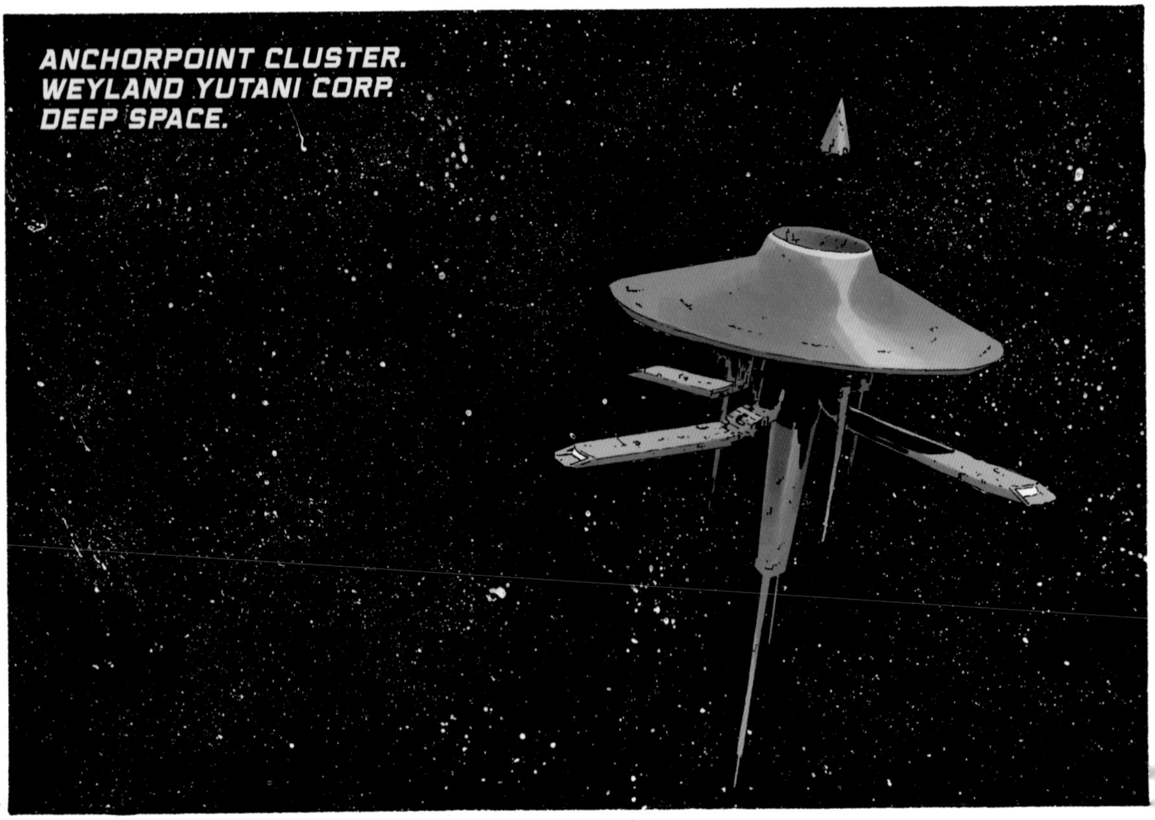
ANCHORPOINT CLUSTER.
WEYLAND YUTANI CORP.
DEEP SPACE.

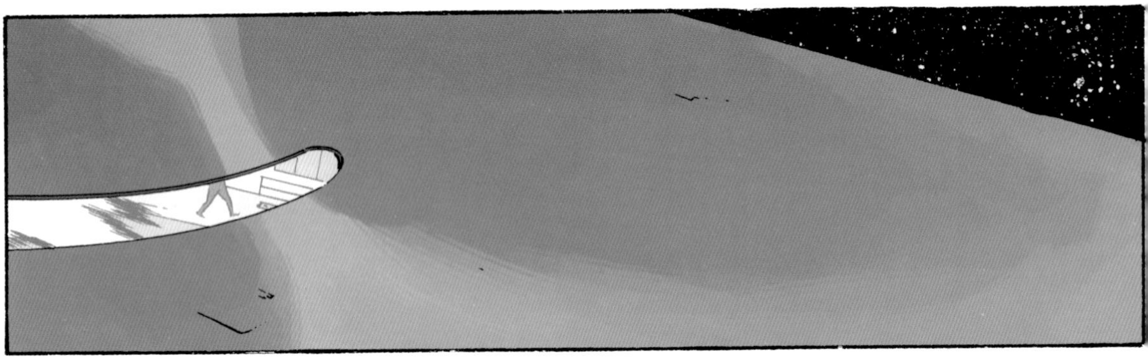

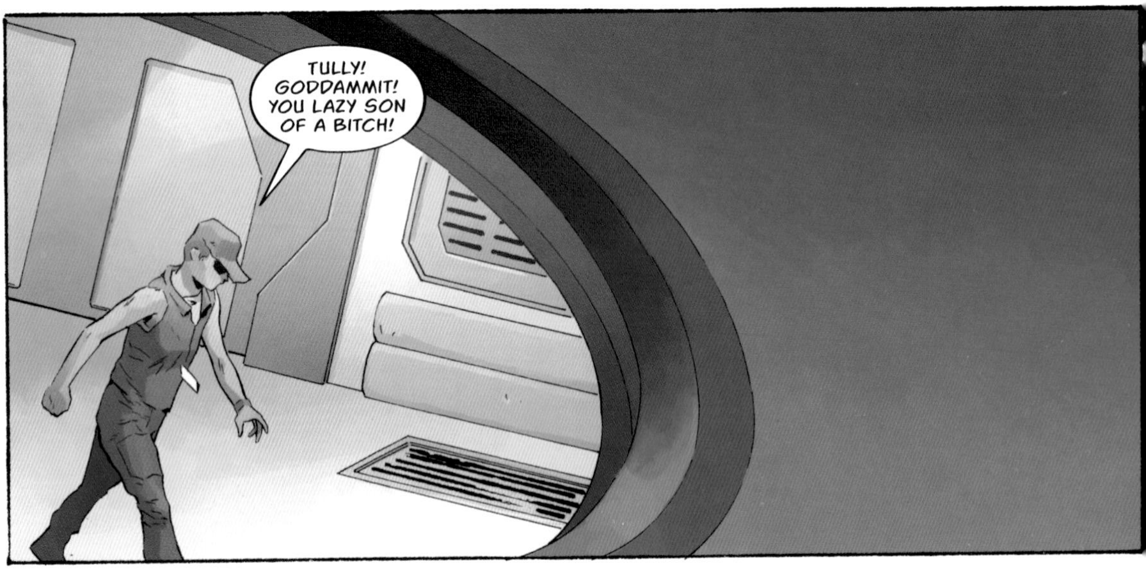
TULLY! GODDAMMIT! YOU LAZY SON OF A BITCH!

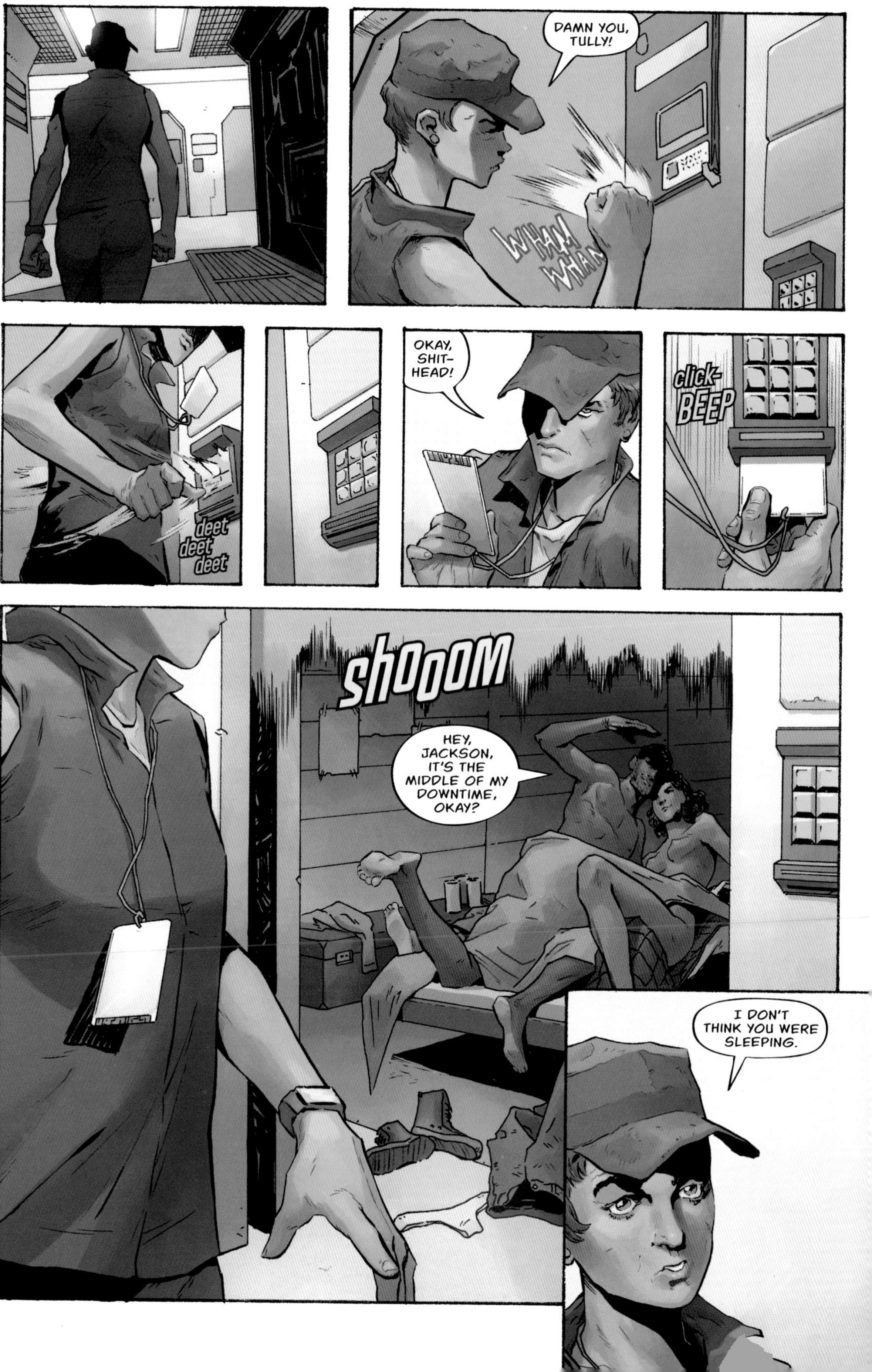
DAMN YOU, TULLY!
WHAM WHAM
deet deet deet
OKAY, SHIT-HEAD!
click-BEEP
shOOOM
HEY, JACKSON, IT'S THE MIDDLE OF MY DOWNTIME, OKAY?
I DON'T THINK YOU WERE SLEEPING.

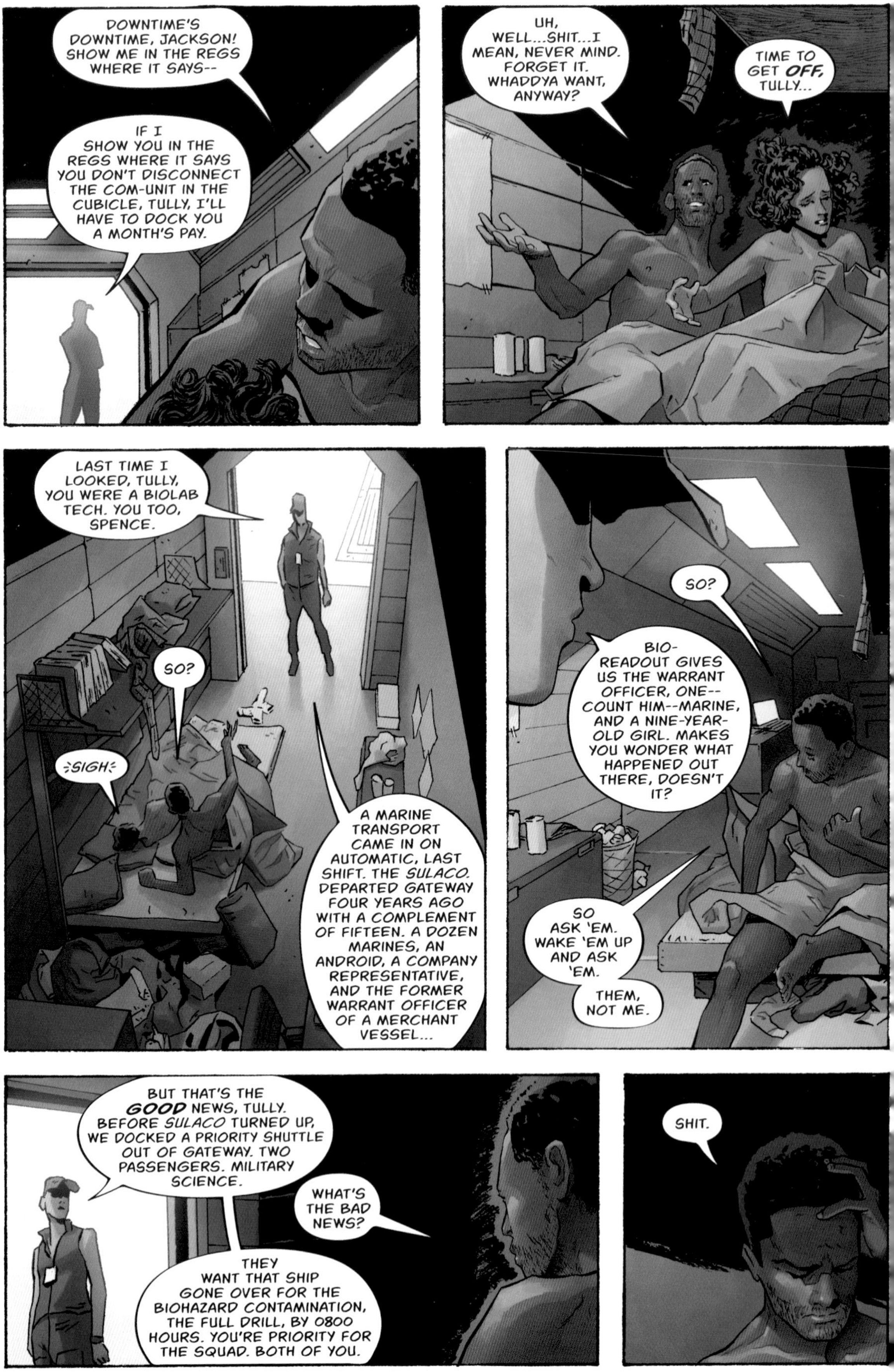
DOWNTIME'S DOWNTIME, JACKSON! SHOW ME IN THE REGS WHERE IT SAYS--
IF I SHOW YOU IN THE REGS WHERE IT SAYS YOU DON'T DISCONNECT THE COM-UNIT IN THE CUBICLE, TULLY, I'LL HAVE TO DOCK YOU A MONTH'S PAY.
UH, WELL...SHIT...I MEAN, NEVER MIND. FORGET IT. WHADDYA WANT, ANYWAY?
TIME TO GET *OFF,* TULLY...
LAST TIME I LOOKED, TULLY, YOU WERE A BIOLAB TECH. YOU TOO, SPENCE.
SO?
SIGH
A MARINE TRANSPORT CAME IN ON AUTOMATIC, LAST SHIFT. THE *SULACO.* DEPARTED GATEWAY FOUR YEARS AGO WITH A COMPLEMENT OF FIFTEEN. A DOZEN MARINES, AN ANDROID, A COMPANY REPRESENTATIVE, AND THE FORMER WARRANT OFFICER OF A MERCHANT VESSEL...
SO?
BIO-READOUT GIVES US THE WARRANT OFFICER, ONE--COUNT HIM--MARINE, AND A NINE-YEAR-OLD GIRL. MAKES YOU WONDER WHAT HAPPENED OUT THERE, DOESN'T IT?
SO ASK 'EM. WAKE 'EM UP AND ASK 'EM.
THEM, NOT ME.
BUT THAT'S THE *GOOD* NEWS, TULLY. BEFORE *SULACO* TURNED UP, WE DOCKED A PRIORITY SHUTTLE OUT OF GATEWAY. TWO PASSENGERS. MILITARY SCIENCE.
WHAT'S THE BAD NEWS?
THEY WANT THAT SHIP GONE OVER FOR THE BIOHAZARD CONTAMINATION, THE FULL DRILL, BY 0800 HOURS. YOU'RE PRIORITY FOR THE SQUAD. BOTH OF YOU.
SHIT.

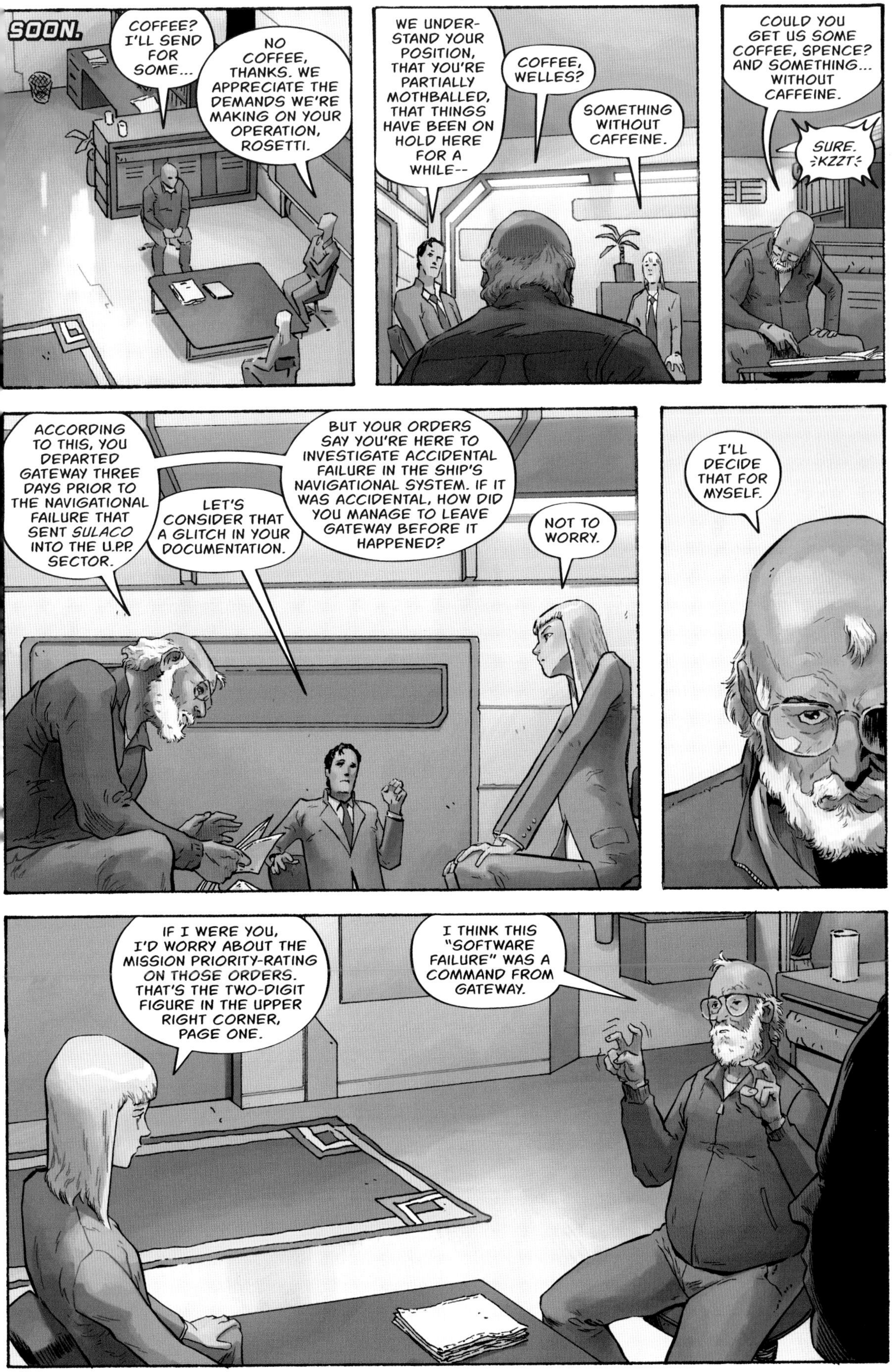
SOON.
COFFEE? I'LL SEND FOR SOME...
NO COFFEE, THANKS. WE APPRECIATE THE DEMANDS WE'RE MAKING ON YOUR OPERATION, ROSETTI.
WE UNDERSTAND YOUR POSITION, THAT YOU'RE PARTIALLY MOTHBALLED, THAT THINGS HAVE BEEN ON HOLD HERE FOR A WHILE--
COFFEE, WELLES?
SOMETHING WITHOUT CAFFEINE.
COULD YOU GET US SOME COFFEE, SPENCE? AND SOMETHING... WITHOUT CAFFEINE.
SURE. KZZT
ACCORDING TO THIS, YOU DEPARTED GATEWAY THREE DAYS PRIOR TO THE NAVIGATIONAL FAILURE THAT SENT SULACO INTO THE U.P.P. SECTOR.
BUT YOUR ORDERS SAY YOU'RE HERE TO INVESTIGATE ACCIDENTAL FAILURE IN THE SHIP'S NAVIGATIONAL SYSTEM. IF IT WAS ACCIDENTAL, HOW DID YOU MANAGE TO LEAVE GATEWAY BEFORE IT HAPPENED?
LET'S CONSIDER THAT A GLITCH IN YOUR DOCUMENTATION.
NOT TO WORRY.
I'LL DECIDE THAT FOR MYSELF.
IF I WERE YOU, I'D WORRY ABOUT THE MISSION PRIORITY-RATING ON THOSE ORDERS. THAT'S THE TWO-DIGIT FIGURE IN THE UPPER RIGHT CORNER, PAGE ONE.
I THINK THIS "SOFTWARE FAILURE" WAS A COMMAND FROM GATEWAY.

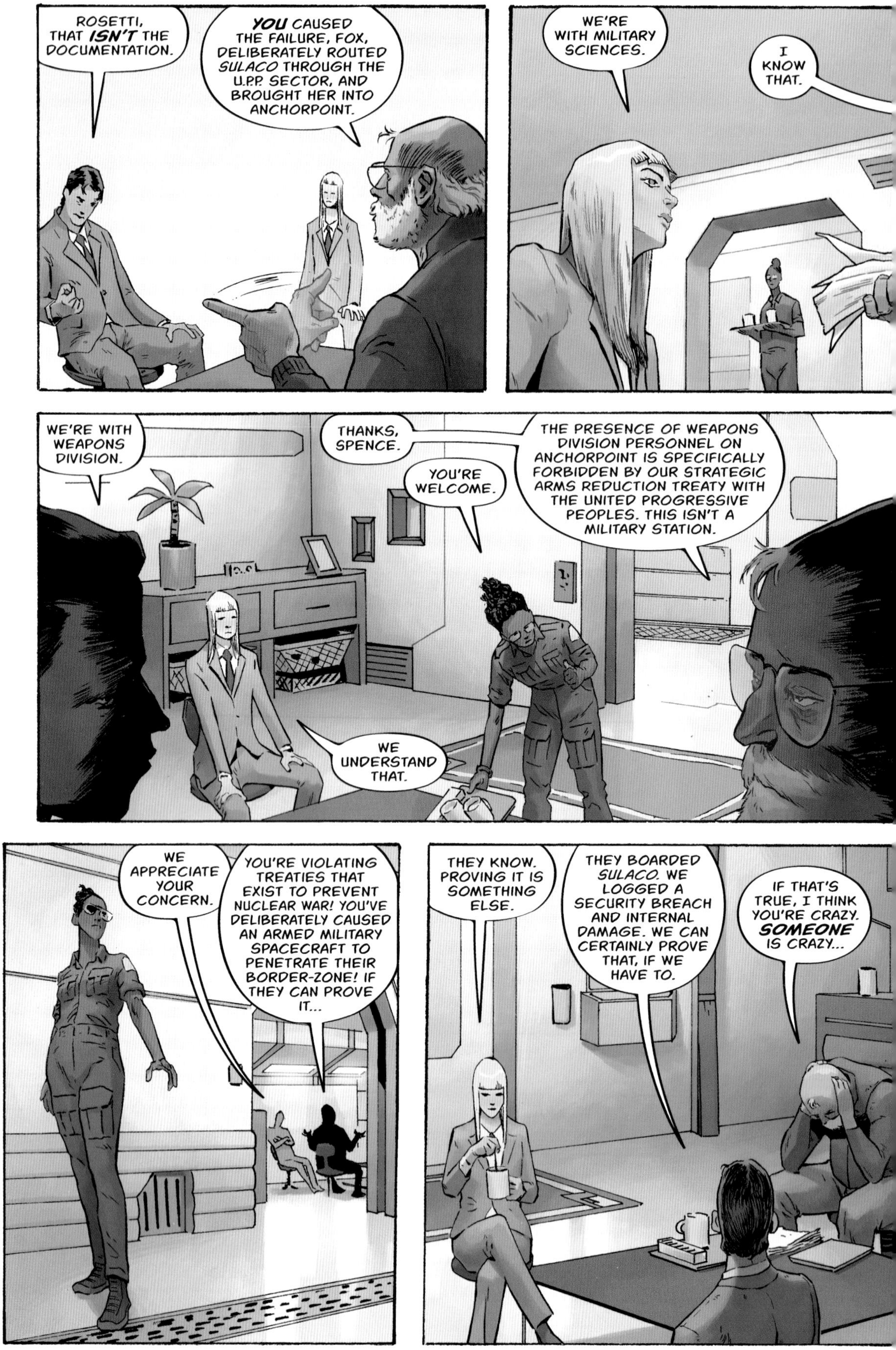
ROSETTI, THAT ISN'T THE DOCUMENTATION.
YOU CAUSED THE FAILURE, FOX, DELIBERATELY ROUTED SULACO THROUGH THE U.P.P. SECTOR, AND BROUGHT HER INTO ANCHORPOINT.
WE'RE WITH MILITARY SCIENCES.
I KNOW THAT.
WE'RE WITH WEAPONS DIVISION.
THANKS, SPENCE.
YOU'RE WELCOME.
THE PRESENCE OF WEAPONS DIVISION PERSONNEL ON ANCHORPOINT IS SPECIFICALLY FORBIDDEN BY OUR STRATEGIC ARMS REDUCTION TREATY WITH THE UNITED PROGRESSIVE PEOPLES. THIS ISN'T A MILITARY STATION.
WE UNDERSTAND THAT.
WE APPRECIATE YOUR CONCERN.
YOU'RE VIOLATING TREATIES THAT EXIST TO PREVENT NUCLEAR WAR! YOU'VE DELIBERATELY CAUSED AN ARMED MILITARY SPACECRAFT TO PENETRATE THEIR BORDER-ZONE! IF THEY CAN PROVE IT...
THEY KNOW. PROVING IT IS SOMETHING ELSE.
THEY BOARDED SULACO. WE LOGGED A SECURITY BREACH AND INTERNAL DAMAGE. WE CAN CERTAINLY PROVE THAT, IF WE HAVE TO.
IF THAT'S TRUE, I THINK YOU'RE CRAZY. SOMEONE IS CRAZY...

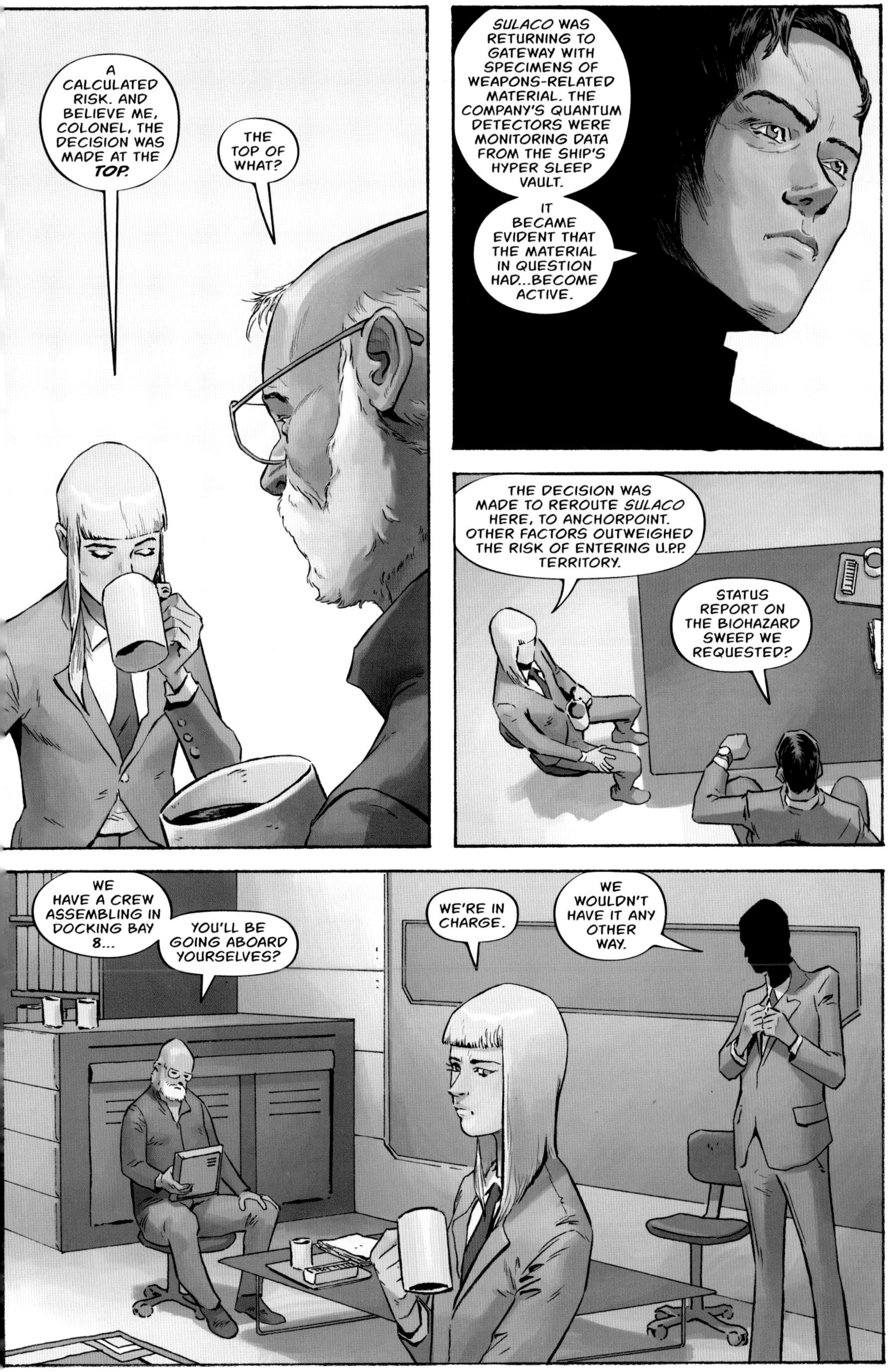
A CALCULATED RISK. AND BELIEVE ME, COLONEL, THE DECISION WAS MADE AT THE *TOP*.
THE TOP OF WHAT?
SULACO WAS RETURNING TO GATEWAY WITH SPECIMENS OF WEAPONS-RELATED MATERIAL. THE COMPANY'S QUANTUM DETECTORS WERE MONITORING DATA FROM THE SHIP'S HYPER SLEEP VAULT.
IT BECAME EVIDENT THAT THE MATERIAL IN QUESTION HAD...BECOME ACTIVE.
THE DECISION WAS MADE TO REROUTE *SULACO* HERE, TO ANCHORPOINT. OTHER FACTORS OUTWEIGHED THE RISK OF ENTERING U.P.P. TERRITORY.
STATUS REPORT ON THE BIOHAZARD SWEEP WE REQUESTED?
WE HAVE A CREW ASSEMBLING IN DOCKING BAY 8...
YOU'LL BE GOING ABOARD YOURSELVES?
WE'RE IN CHARGE.
WE WOULDN'T HAVE IT ANY OTHER WAY.

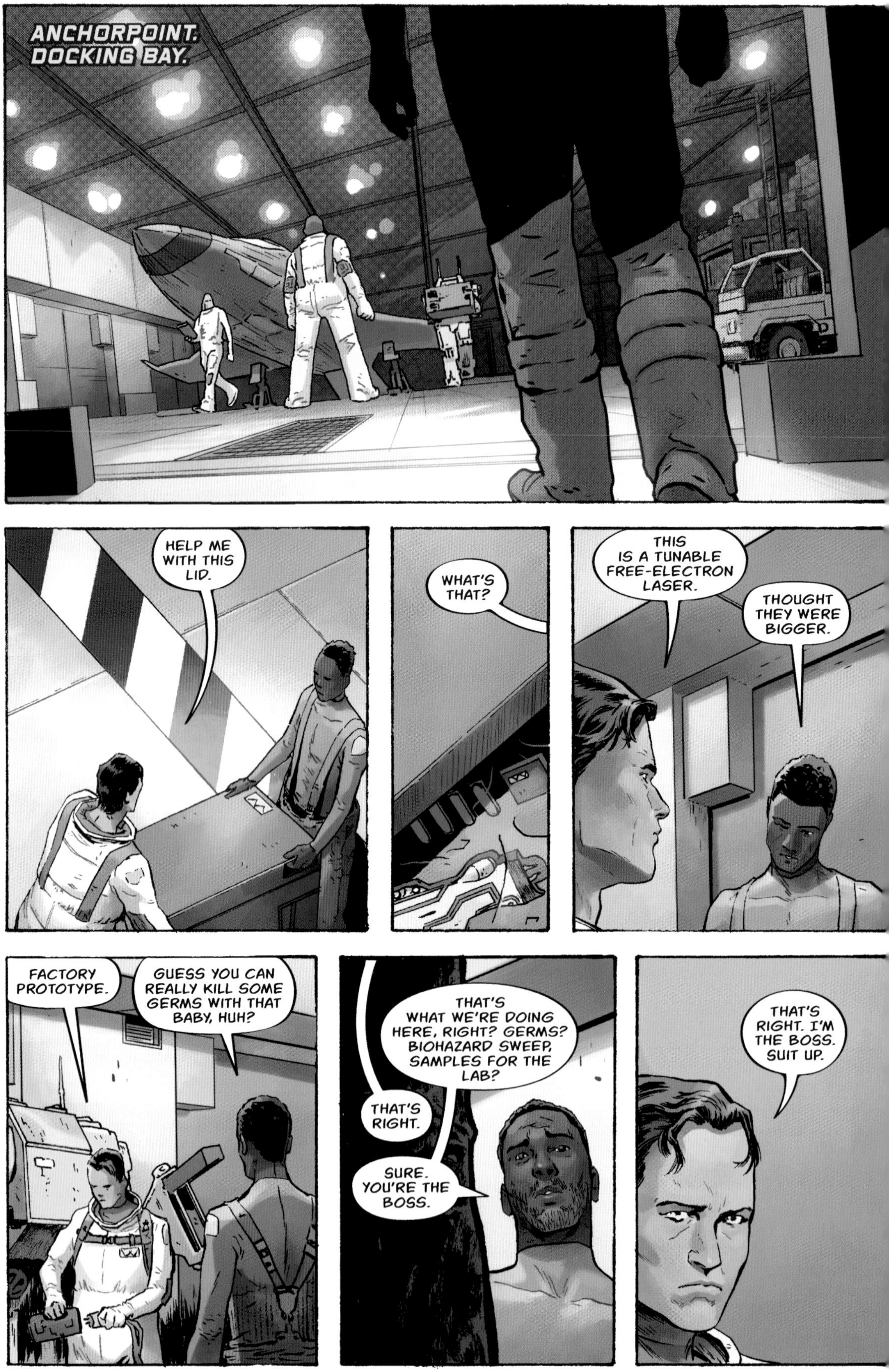
ANCHORPOINT. DOCKING BAY.
HELP ME WITH THIS LID.
WHAT'S THAT?
THIS IS A TUNABLE FREE-ELECTRON LASER.
THOUGHT THEY WERE BIGGER.
FACTORY PROTOTYPE.
GUESS YOU CAN REALLY KILL SOME GERMS WITH THAT BABY, HUH?
THAT'S WHAT WE'RE DOING HERE, RIGHT? GERMS? BIOHAZARD SWEEP, SAMPLES FOR THE LAB?
THAT'S RIGHT.
SURE. YOU'RE THE BOSS.
THAT'S RIGHT. I'M THE BOSS. SUIT UP.

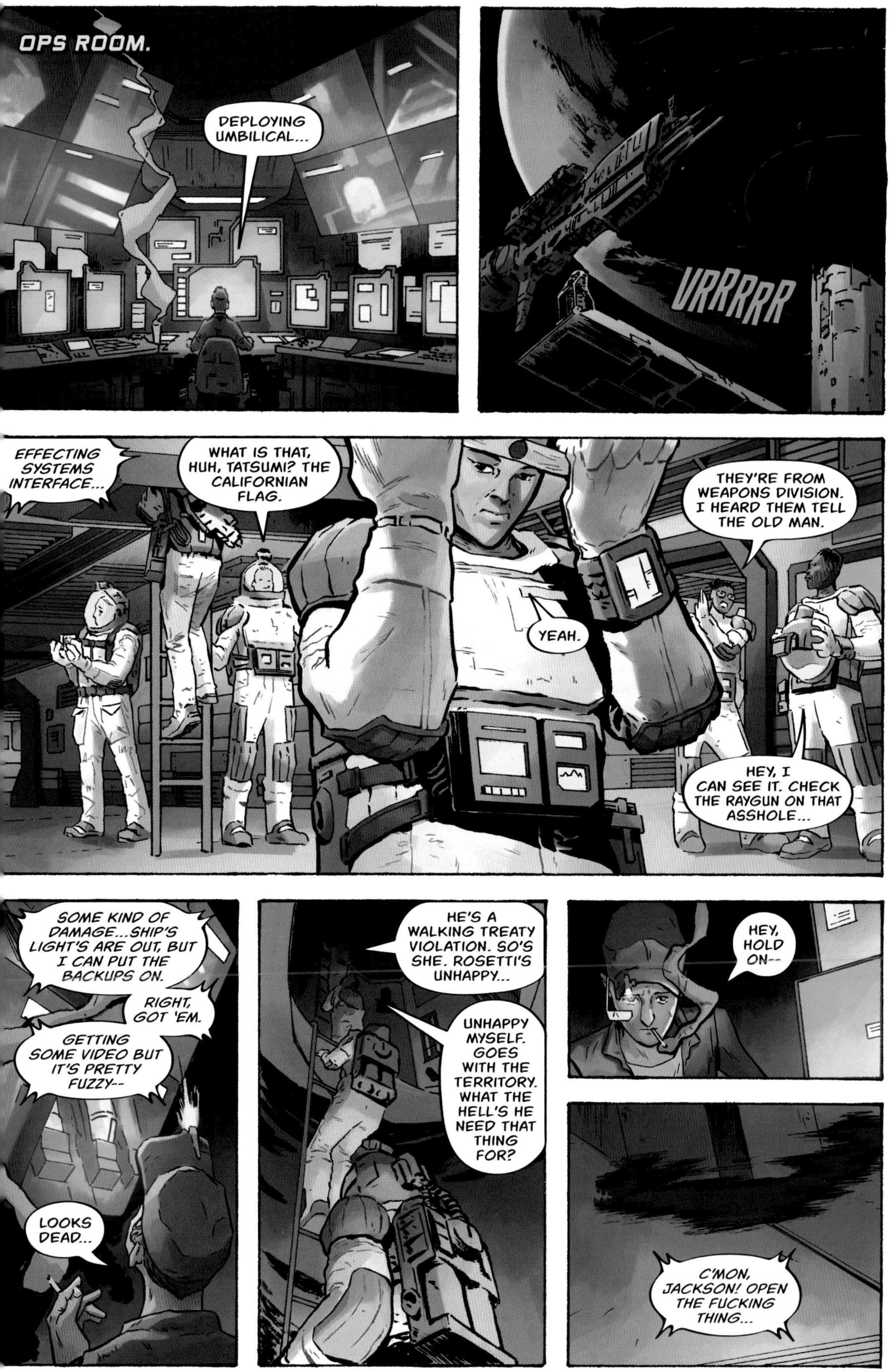
OPS ROOM.
DEPLOYING UMBILICAL...
URRRRR
EFFECTING SYSTEMS INTERFACE...
WHAT IS THAT, HUH, TATSUMI? THE CALIFORNIAN FLAG.
YEAH.
THEY'RE FROM WEAPONS DIVISION. I HEARD THEM TELL THE OLD MAN.
HEY, I CAN SEE IT. CHECK THE RAYGUN ON THAT ASSHOLE...
SOME KIND OF DAMAGE...SHIP'S LIGHT'S ARE OUT, BUT I CAN PUT THE BACKUPS ON.
RIGHT, GOT 'EM.
GETTING SOME VIDEO BUT IT'S PRETTY FUZZY--
LOOKS DEAD...
HE'S A WALKING TREATY VIOLATION. SO'S SHE. ROSETTI'S UNHAPPY...
UNHAPPY MYSELF. GOES WITH THE TERRITORY. WHAT THE HELL'S HE NEED THAT THING FOR?
HEY, HOLD ON--
C'MON, JACKSON! OPEN THE FUCKING THING...

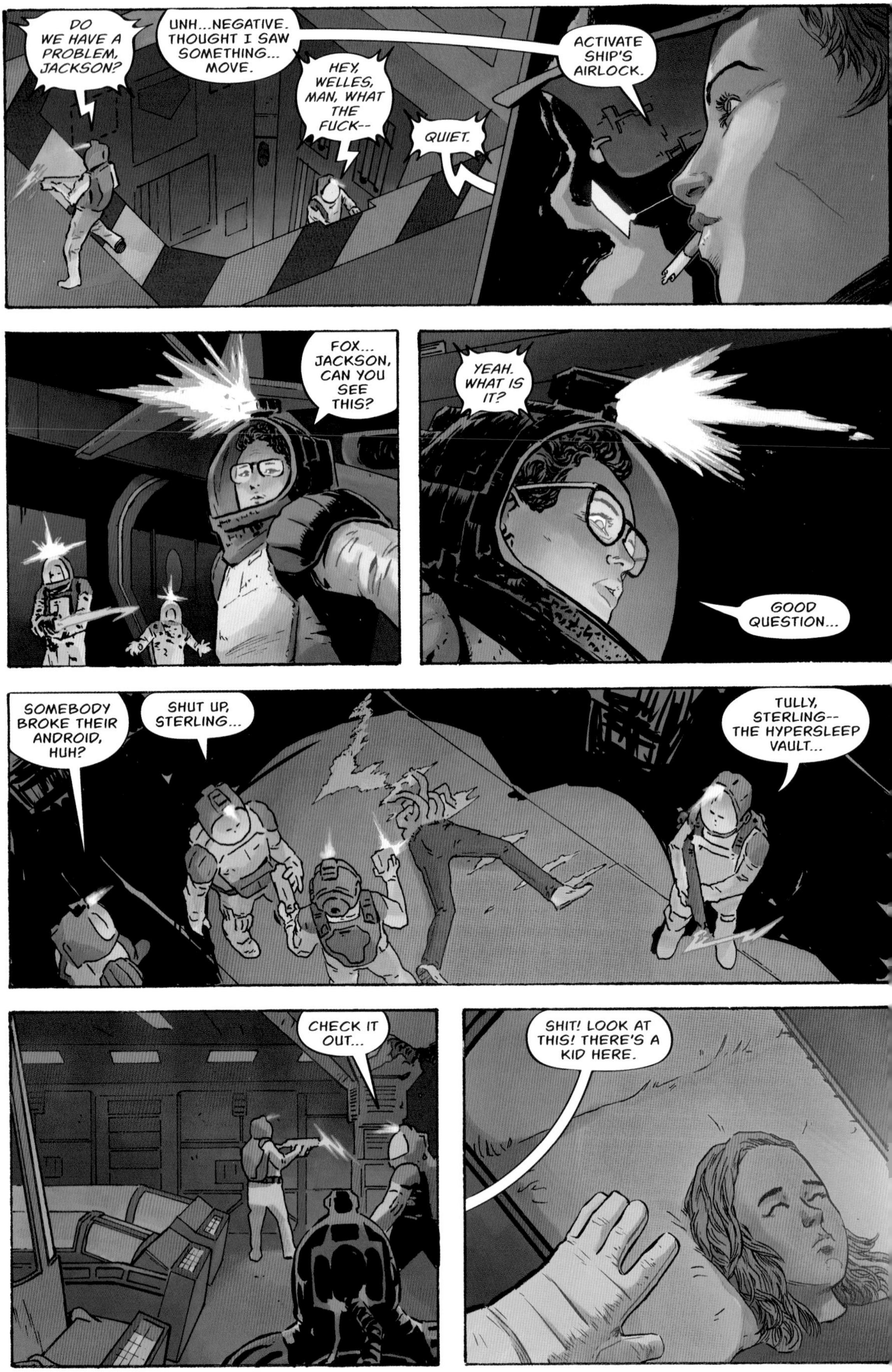
DO WE HAVE A PROBLEM, JACKSON?
UNH...NEGATIVE. THOUGHT I SAW SOMETHING... MOVE.
HEY, WELLES, MAN, WHAT THE FUCK--
ACTIVATE SHIP'S AIRLOCK.
QUIET.
FOX... JACKSON, CAN YOU SEE THIS?
YEAH. WHAT IS IT?
GOOD QUESTION...
SOMEBODY BROKE THEIR ANDROID, HUH?
SHUT UP, STERLING...
TULLY, STERLING-- THE HYPERSLEEP VAULT...
CHECK IT OUT...
SHIT! LOOK AT THIS! THERE'S A KID HERE.

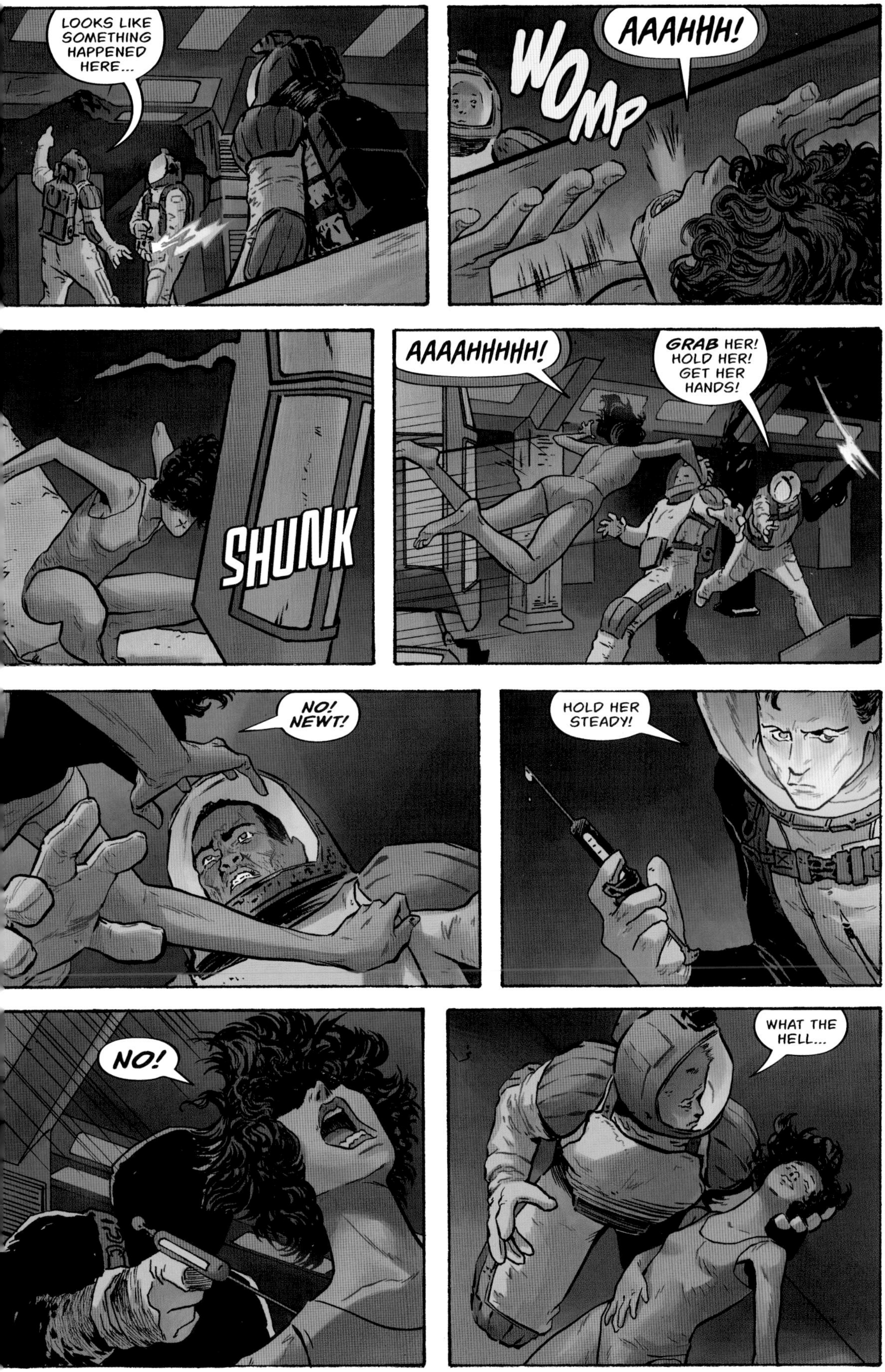
LOOKS LIKE SOMETHING HAPPENED HERE...
AAAHHH!
WOMP
SHUNK
AAAAHHHH!
GRAB HER! HOLD HER! GET HER HANDS!
NO! NEWT!
HOLD HER STEADY!
NO!
WHAT THE HELL...

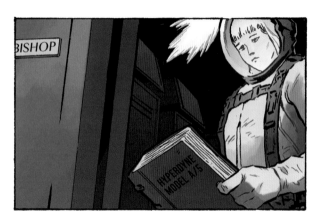

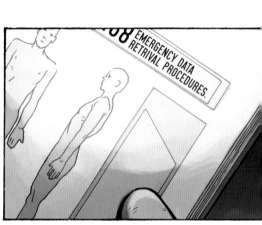

BISHOP
HYPERDYNE MODEL A/5
EMERGENCY DATA RETRIVAL PROCEDURES.
FOX, I'M IN OFFICERS' QUARTERS, C DECK. GET DOWN HERE.
SOON.
DON'T TRY TO MOVE HIM.
HE'S U.P.P. SOMETIMES THEY BOOBYTRAP 'EM. I SAW THAT ON TITAN IN THE THREE-DAY WAR...
THOUGHT YOU MIGHT NEED HELP, WELLES.
YOU AREN'T REQUIRED HERE, STERLING.
RIPLEY
DIDN'T YOU HEAR HER?
MR. STERLING, GO BACK TO THE CARGO LOCK. WE'LL HAVE A TALK LATER, ABOUT CERTAIN CLAUSES IN YOUR CONTRACT WITH THE CORPORATION...
HEY! NO PROBLEM! I JUST--
JESUS...

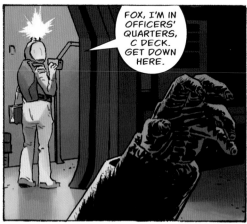

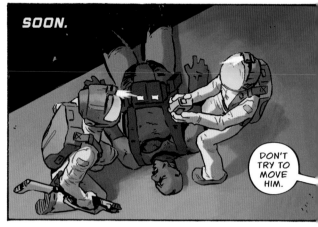

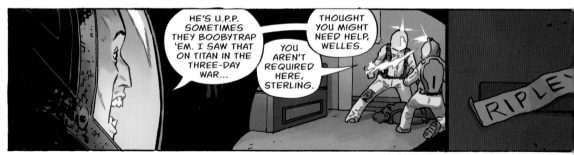

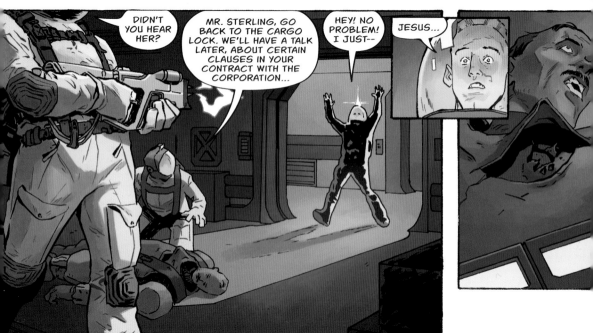

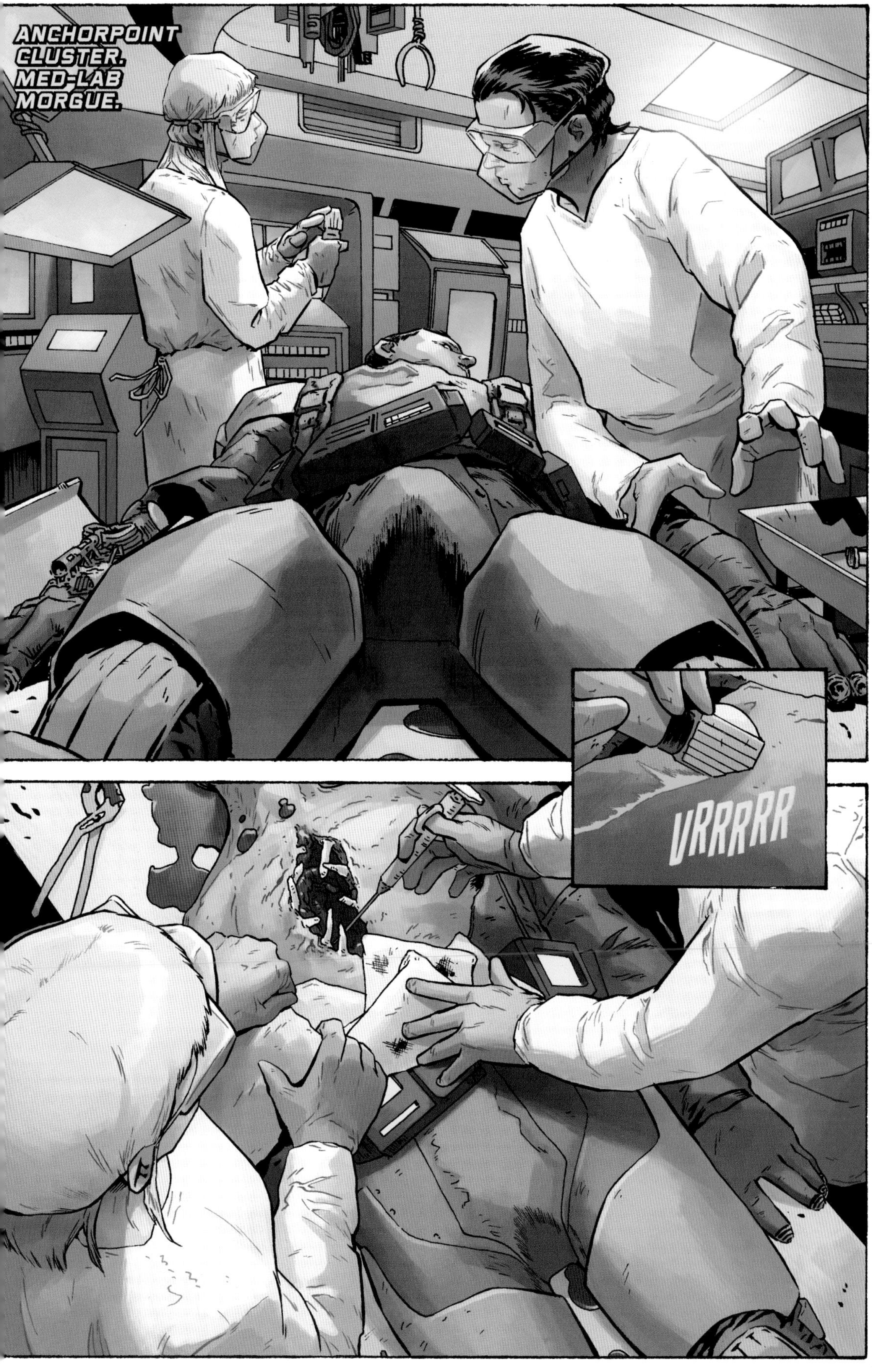
ANCHORPOINT CLUSTER. MED-LAB MORGUE.
VRRRRR

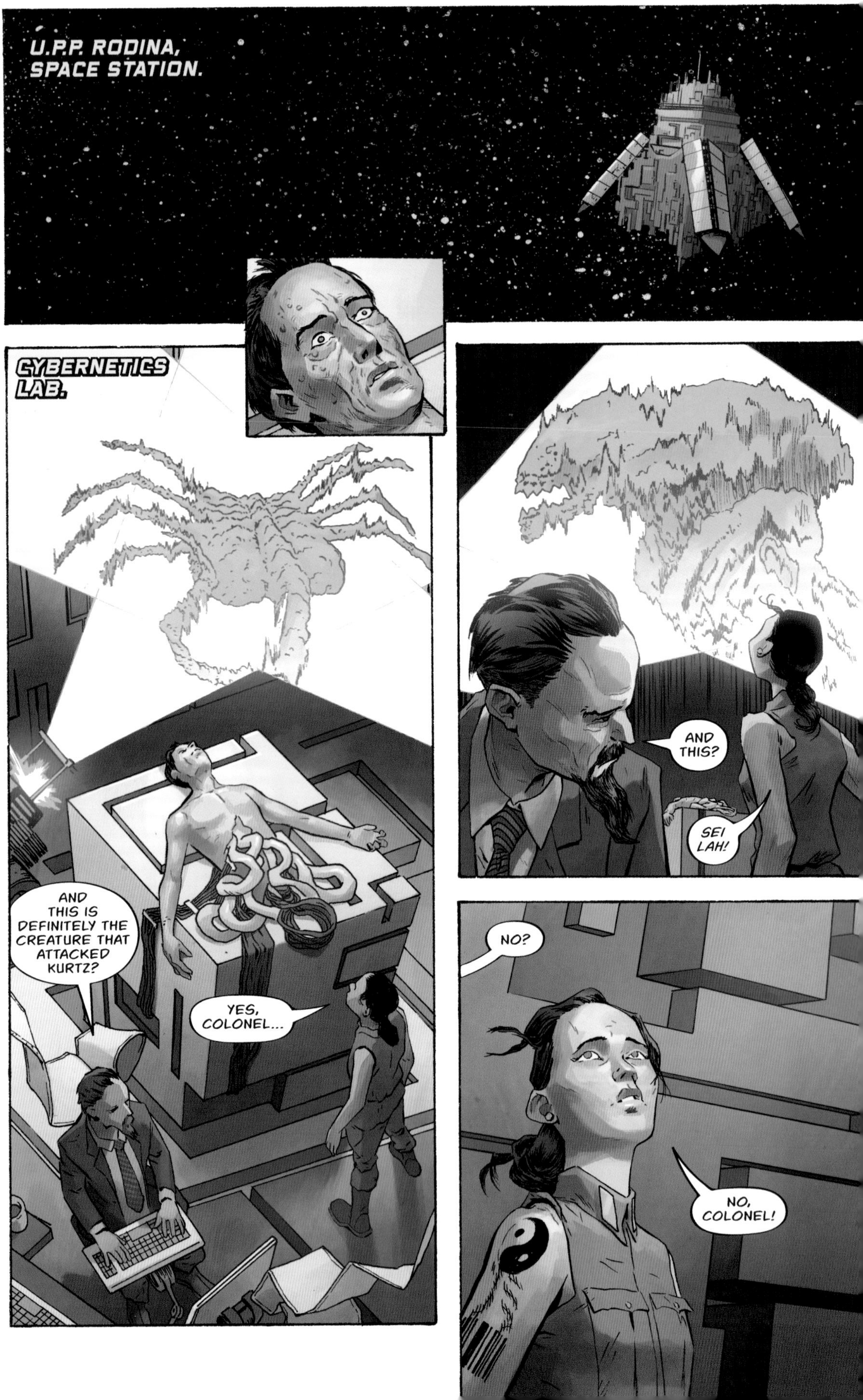
U.P.P. RODINA, SPACE STATION.
CYBERNETICS LAB.
AND THIS IS DEFINITELY THE CREATURE THAT ATTACKED KURTZ?
YES, COLONEL...
AND THIS?
SEI LAH!
NO?
NO, COLONEL!

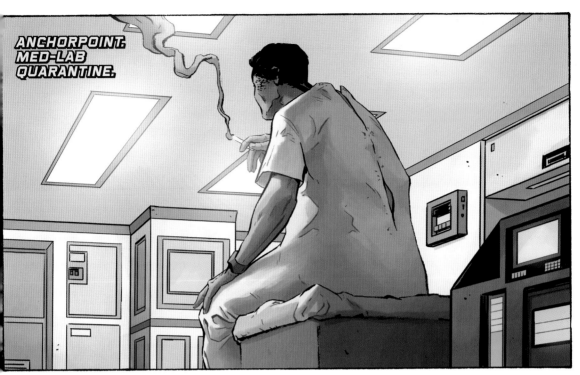

ANCHORPOINT:
MED-LAB
QUARANTINE.

NO SMOKING IN HERE, MARINE.

fffffft

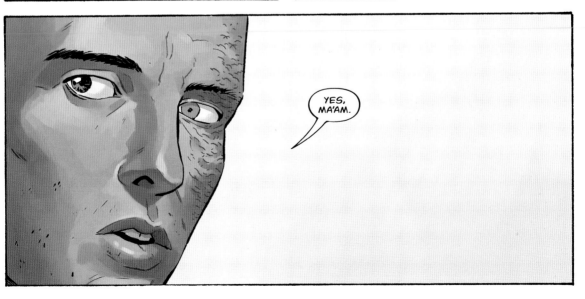

YES, MA'AM.

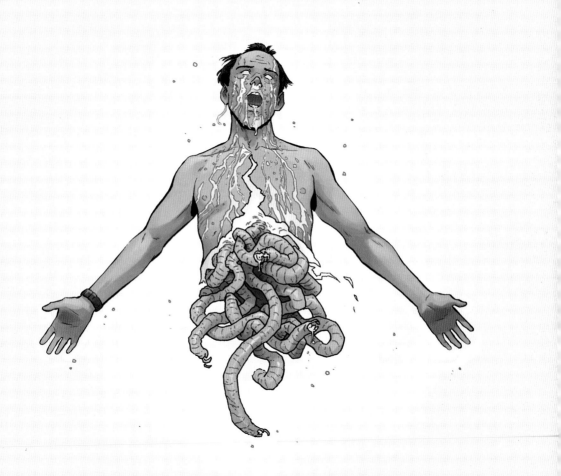

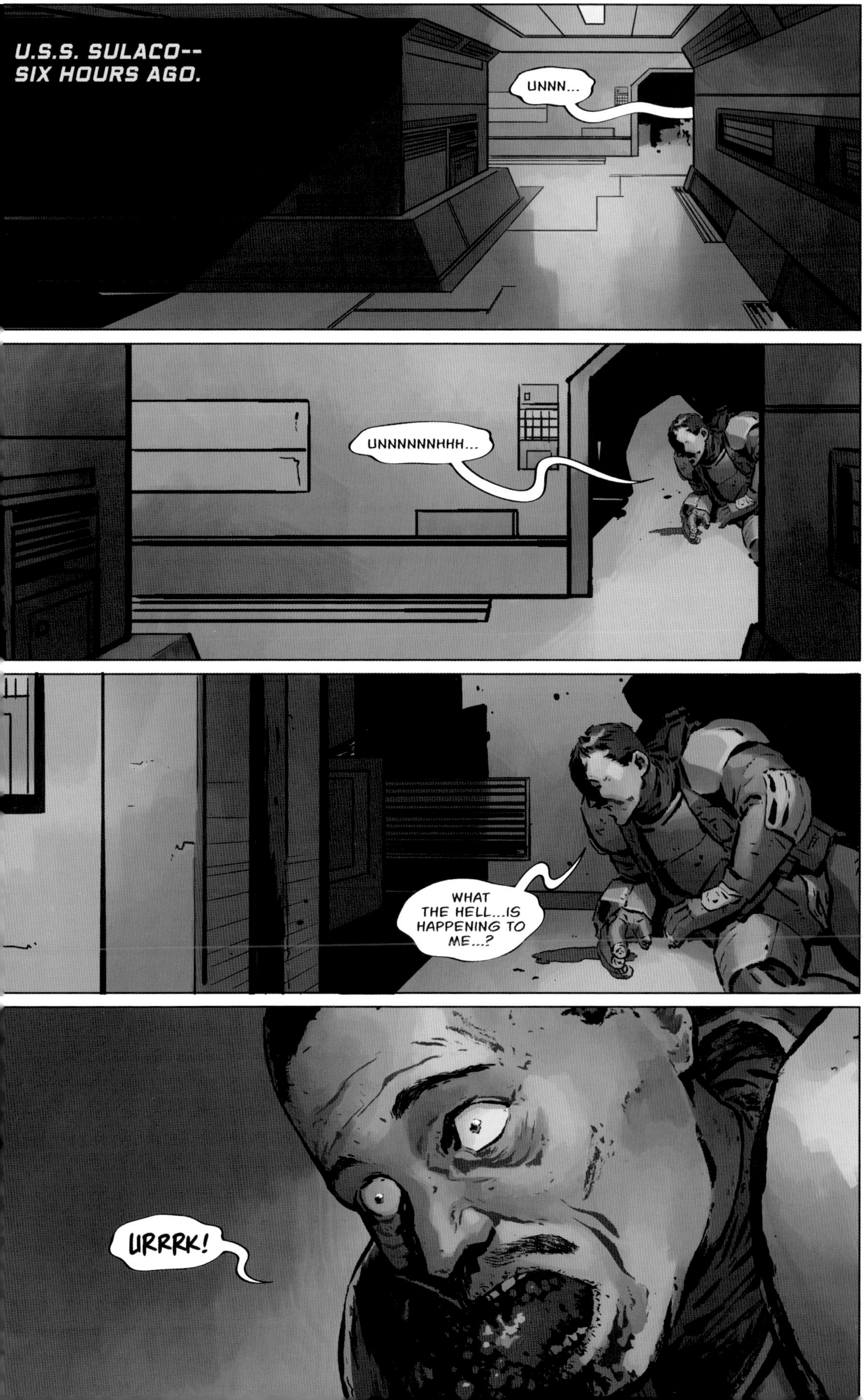
U.S.S. SULACO--
SIX HOURS AGO.
UNNN...
UNNNNNNHHH...
WHAT THE HELL...IS HAPPENING TO ME...?
URRRK!

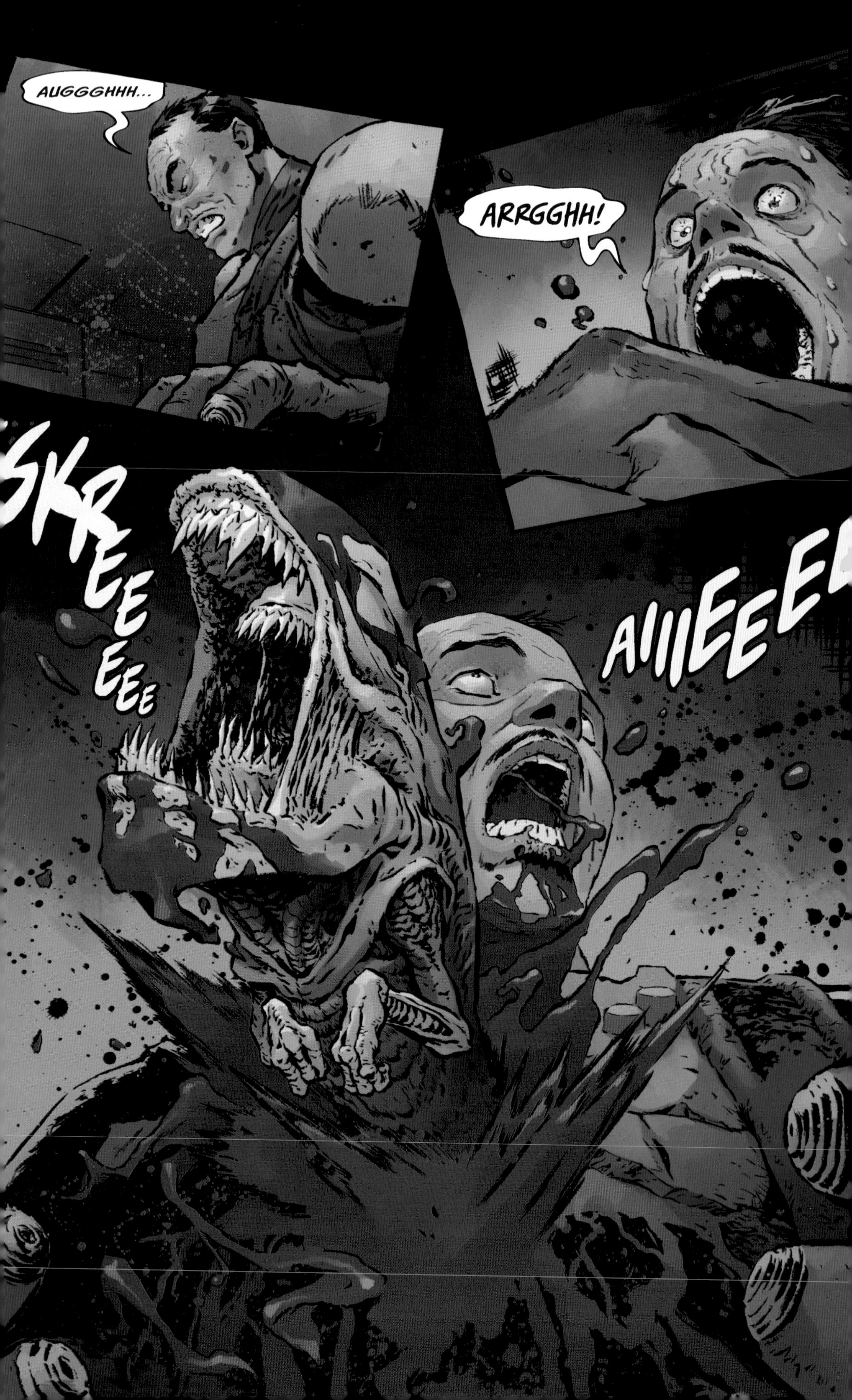
AUGGGHHH...
ARRGGHH!
SKREEEEEE
AIIIEEEEE

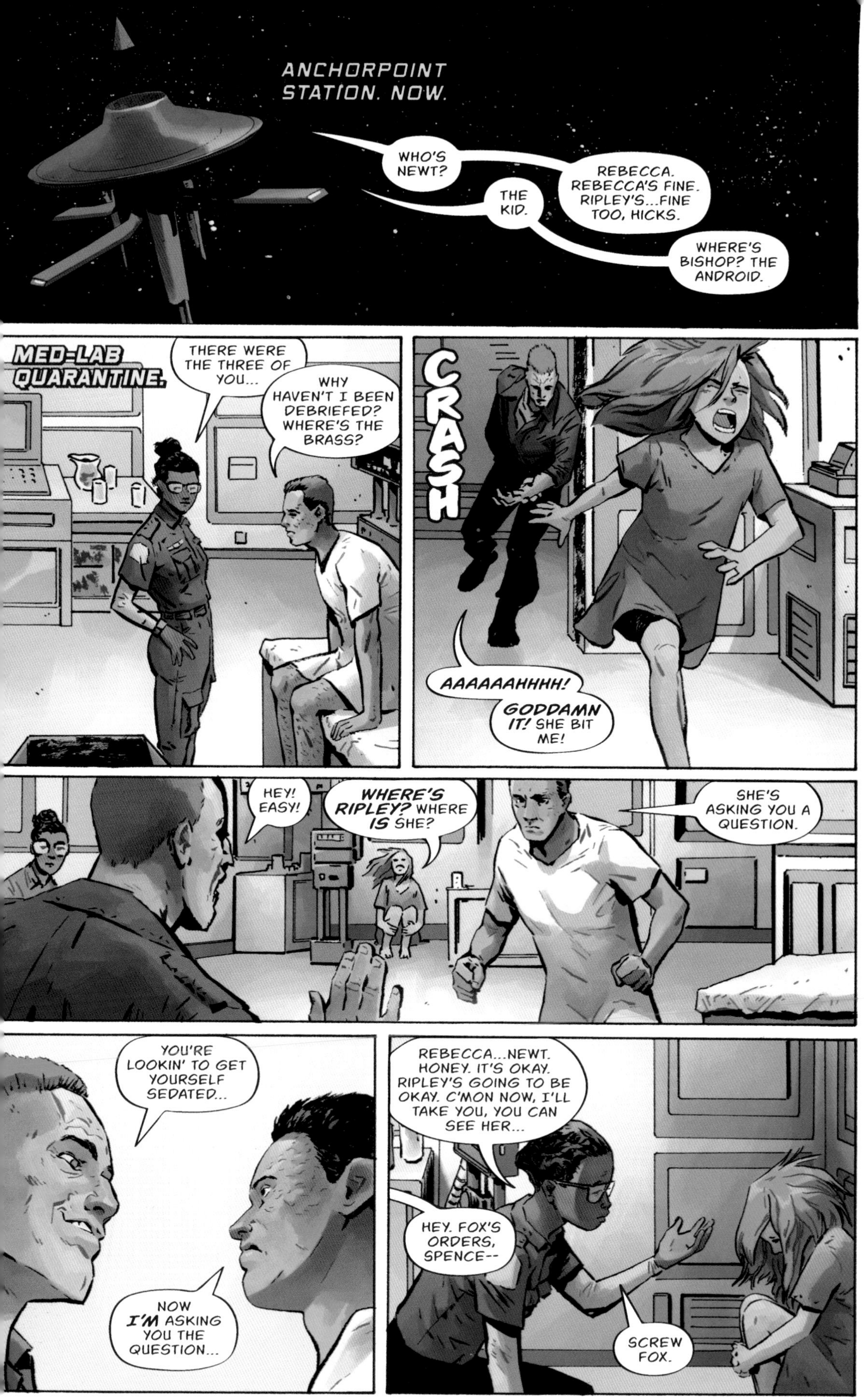

ANCHORPOINT STATION. NOW.
WHO'S NEWT?
REBECCA. REBECCA'S FINE. RIPLEY'S...FINE TOO, HICKS.
THE KID.
WHERE'S BISHOP? THE ANDROID.
MED-LAB QUARANTINE.
THERE WERE THE THREE OF YOU...
WHY HAVEN'T I BEEN DEBRIEFED? WHERE'S THE BRASS?
CRASH
AAAAAAHHHH!
GODDAMN IT! SHE BIT ME!
HEY! EASY!
WHERE'S RIPLEY? WHERE IS SHE?
SHE'S ASKING YOU A QUESTION.
YOU'RE LOOKIN' TO GET YOURSELF SEDATED...
NOW I'M ASKING YOU THE QUESTION...
REBECCA...NEWT. HONEY. IT'S OKAY. RIPLEY'S GOING TO BE OKAY. C'MON NOW, I'LL TAKE YOU, YOU CAN SEE HER...
HEY. FOX'S ORDERS, SPENCE--
SCREW FOX.

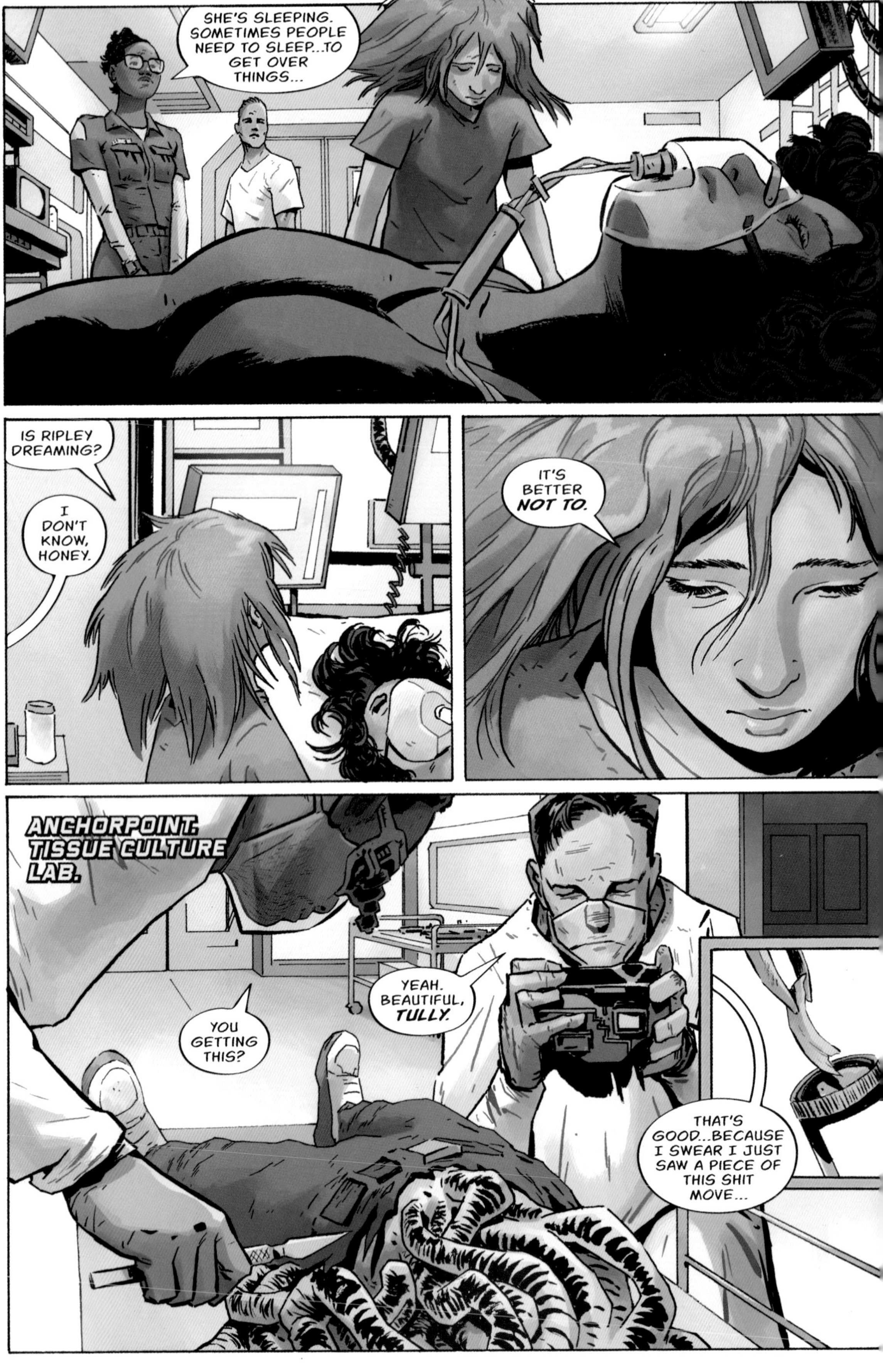
SHE'S SLEEPING. SOMETIMES PEOPLE NEED TO SLEEP...TO GET OVER THINGS...
IS RIPLEY DREAMING?
I DON'T KNOW, HONEY.
IT'S BETTER *NOT TO.*
ANCHORPOINT. TISSUE CULTURE LAB.
YOU GETTING THIS?
YEAH. BEAUTIFUL, *TULLY.*
THAT'S GOOD...BECAUSE I SWEAR I JUST SAW A PIECE OF THIS SHIT MOVE...

OPS ROOM.

LV-426
COMBINED
TERRAFORMING/
MINING
OPERATION,
POP. 158

bleeeeep

FILES DELETED

AUTHORITY WEYLAND
YUTANI SECURITY
EXECUTIVE

(cont.)
INCOMING TRANSMISSION
SOURCE: GATEWAY
TRANSIT TIME: 4.7
HOURS
TO: FIRST OFFICER
ROSETTI
>>NOW DECODING>>

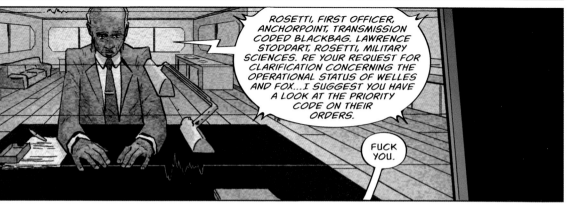

ROSETTI, FIRST OFFICER, ANCHORPOINT, TRANSMISSION CODED BLACKBAG. LAWRENCE STODDART, ROSETTI, MILITARY SCIENCES. RE YOUR REQUEST FOR CLARIFICATION CONCERNING THE OPERATIONAL STATUS OF WELLES AND FOX...I SUGGEST YOU HAVE A LOOK AT THE PRIORITY CODE ON THEIR ORDERS.

FUCK YOU.

YOU DON'T NEED TO CHECK YOUR BRIEF AS FIRST OFFICER TO KNOW THAT WE EXPECT YOU TO PROVIDE EVERY POSSIBLE DEGREE OF ASSISTANCE. TO PUT IT ANOTHER WAY, YOUR PRIMARY RESPONSIBILITY IS TO THE CORPORATION--

AND YOUR INTERIOR DECORATOR.

--NOW CONSISTS OF SEEING THAT WELLES AND FOX IMPLEMENT THEIR ORDERS UNDER CONDITIONS OF OPTIMUM SECURITY.

AS YOU KNOW, CONTINUED FUNDING OF THE ANCHORPOINT PROJECT IS CURRENTLY IN QUESTION--

bleep

DON'T YOU WANT TO HEAR THE WHOLE THING?

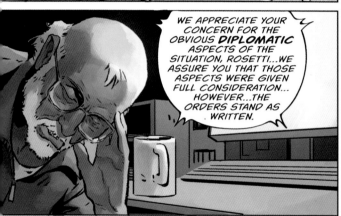

WE APPRECIATE YOUR CONCERN FOR THE OBVIOUS **DIPLOMATIC** ASPECTS OF THE SITUATION, ROSETTI...WE ASSURE YOU THAT THOSE ASPECTS WERE GIVEN FULL CONSIDERATION... HOWEVER...THE ORDERS STAND AS WRITTEN.

KLACK

NO.

YOU'RE MISSING THE GOOD PART, *ROSETTI,* THE PART WHERE HE TELLS YOU THEY'LL KEEP ANCHORPOINT OPERATIVE IF WEAPONS DIVISION MAKES IT COST EFFECTIVE.

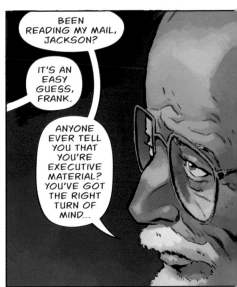

BEEN READING MY MAIL, JACKSON?

IT'S AN EASY GUESS, FRANK.

ANYONE EVER TELL YOU THAT YOU'RE EXECUTIVE MATERIAL? YOU'VE GOT THE RIGHT TURN OF MIND...

COME ON, FRANK. I'M NOT TELLING YOU ANYTHING YOU DON'T ALREADY KNOW. YOU'VE BEEN OUT HERE WHAT, FIVE YEARS? YOU WERE ON THE ORIGINAL DESIGN TEAM, WEREN'T YOU? IT'S YOUR BABY, IT'S NOT HAPPENING. YOU'D LIKE TO SEE IT HAPPEN...

WOULDN'T YOU?

NOT IF IT MEANS LETTING THEM TURN IT INTO A GERM WARFARE LAB.

YOU THINK THAT'S IT?

WHAT'S IT LOOK LIKE TO YOU?

TISSUE CULTURE LAB.

GET ANY SLEEP, TULLY?

NO. YOU?

HOW ARE THEY, SPENCE?

SACKED OUT IN A SPARE BERTH IN MED-LAB. THEY KEPT ME UP TRIMMING CUTICLE OFF SLEEPING BEAUTY AND HER FRIENDS, RUNNING BIOPSIES.

Peck

SHE'S GONE INTO CATATONIC SHOCK. THE AUTO-DOC'S HEDGING ITS PROGNOSIS, BUT VITAL SIGNS ARE OKAY...NEWT SEEMS OKAY EXCEPT FOR THIS *LOOK* SHE GETS, SOMETIMES. AND SHE WON'T SAY A THING ABOUT WHAT HAPPENED, EXCEPT THAT HER PARENTS ARE DEAD AND RIPLEY'S HER FRIEND...

NEWT WHO?

NEWT. THE LITTLE GIRL. REBECCA.

HOW ABOUT THE MARINE?

HICKS. HE'S A MARINE, WHAT DO YOU EXPECT? KEEPS ASKING WHEN HE'S GOING TO BE DEBRIEFED. NAME, RANK, SERIAL NUMBER. WONDER HOW MANY PLANETARY SPECIES HE'S HELPED EXTERMINATE?

I ALWAYS FORGET, YOU'RE AN ECOLOGIST.

WHAT'S THAT?

SOME CRAP TATSUMI AND I SCRAPED UP... WELLES WANTS IT PREPARED FOR--

HEY SPENCE, C'MERE...

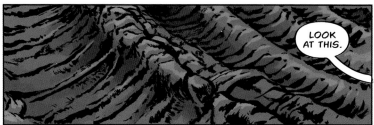

LOOK AT THIS.

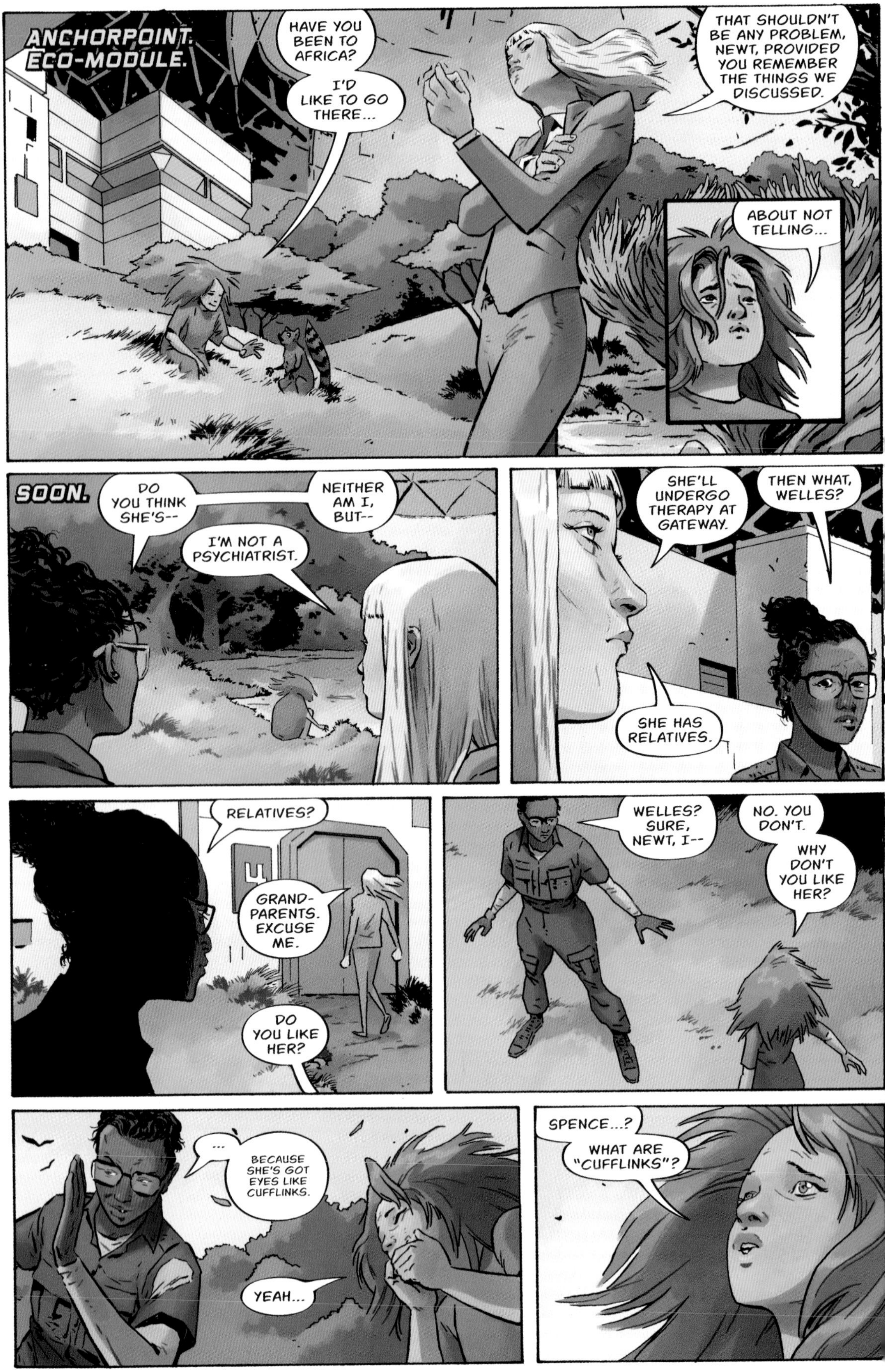
ANCHORPOINT. ECO-MODULE.
HAVE YOU BEEN TO AFRICA?
I'D LIKE TO GO THERE...
THAT SHOULDN'T BE ANY PROBLEM, NEWT, PROVIDED YOU REMEMBER THE THINGS WE DISCUSSED.
ABOUT NOT TELLING...
SOON.
DO YOU THINK SHE'S--
I'M NOT A PSYCHIATRIST.
NEITHER AM I, BUT--
SHE'LL UNDERGO THERAPY AT GATEWAY.
THEN WHAT, WELLES?
SHE HAS RELATIVES.
RELATIVES?
GRAND-PARENTS. EXCUSE ME.
DO YOU LIKE HER?
WELLES? SURE, NEWT, I--
NO. YOU DON'T.
WHY DON'T YOU LIKE HER?
...
BECAUSE SHE'S GOT EYES LIKE CUFFLINKS.
YEAH...
SPENCE...?
WHAT ARE "CUFFLINKS"?

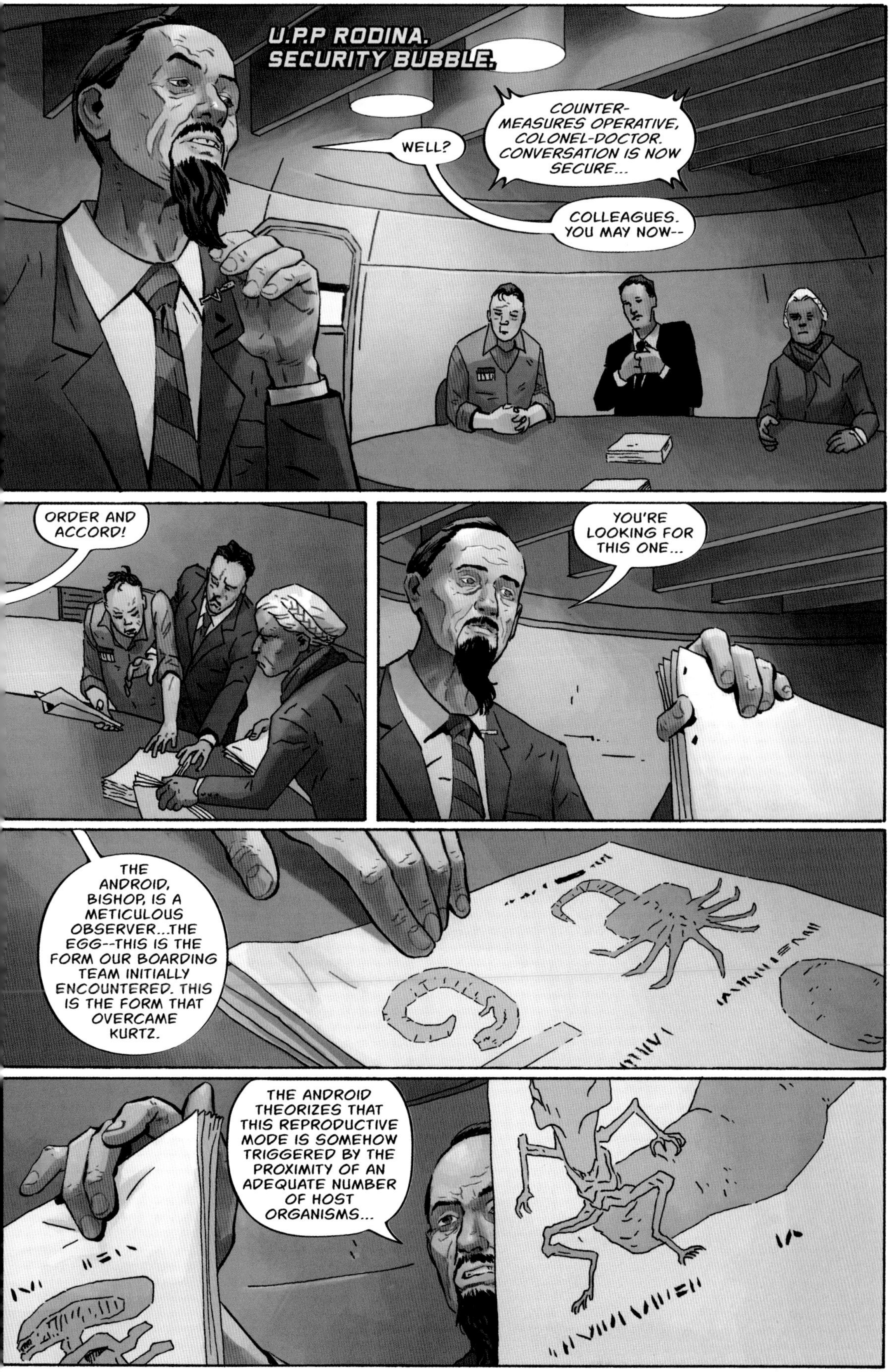
U.P.P RODINA.
SECURITY BUBBLE.
COUNTER-MEASURES OPERATIVE, COLONEL-DOCTOR. CONVERSATION IS NOW SECURE...
WELL?
COLLEAGUES. YOU MAY NOW--
ORDER AND ACCORD!
YOU'RE LOOKING FOR THIS ONE...
THE ANDROID, BISHOP, IS A METICULOUS OBSERVER...THE EGG--THIS IS THE FORM OUR BOARDING TEAM INITIALLY ENCOUNTERED. THIS IS THE FORM THAT OVERCAME KURTZ.
THE ANDROID THEORIZES THAT THIS REPRODUCTIVE MODE IS SOMEHOW TRIGGERED BY THE PROXIMITY OF AN ADEQUATE NUMBER OF HOST ORGANISMS...

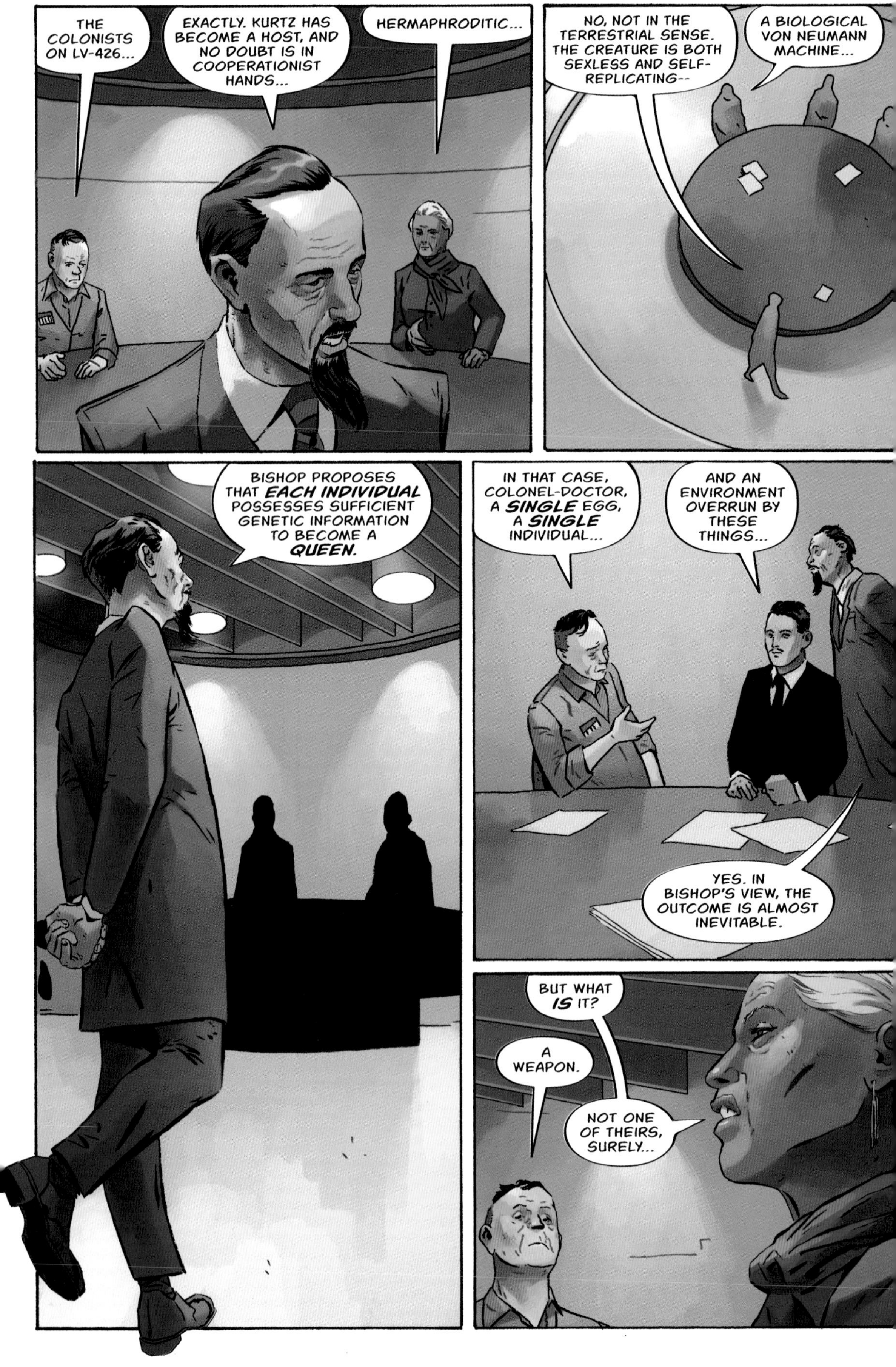
THE COLONISTS ON LV-426...
EXACTLY. KURTZ HAS BECOME A HOST, AND NO DOUBT IS IN COOPERATIONIST HANDS...
HERMAPHRODITIC...
NO, NOT IN THE TERRESTRIAL SENSE. THE CREATURE IS BOTH SEXLESS AND SELF-REPLICATING--
A BIOLOGICAL VON NEUMANN MACHINE...
BISHOP PROPOSES THAT EACH INDIVIDUAL POSSESSES SUFFICIENT GENETIC INFORMATION TO BECOME A QUEEN.
IN THAT CASE, COLONEL-DOCTOR, A SINGLE EGG, A SINGLE INDIVIDUAL...
AND AN ENVIRONMENT OVERRUN BY THESE THINGS...
YES. IN BISHOP'S VIEW, THE OUTCOME IS ALMOST INEVITABLE.
BUT WHAT IS IT?
A WEAPON.
NOT ONE OF THEIRS, SURELY...

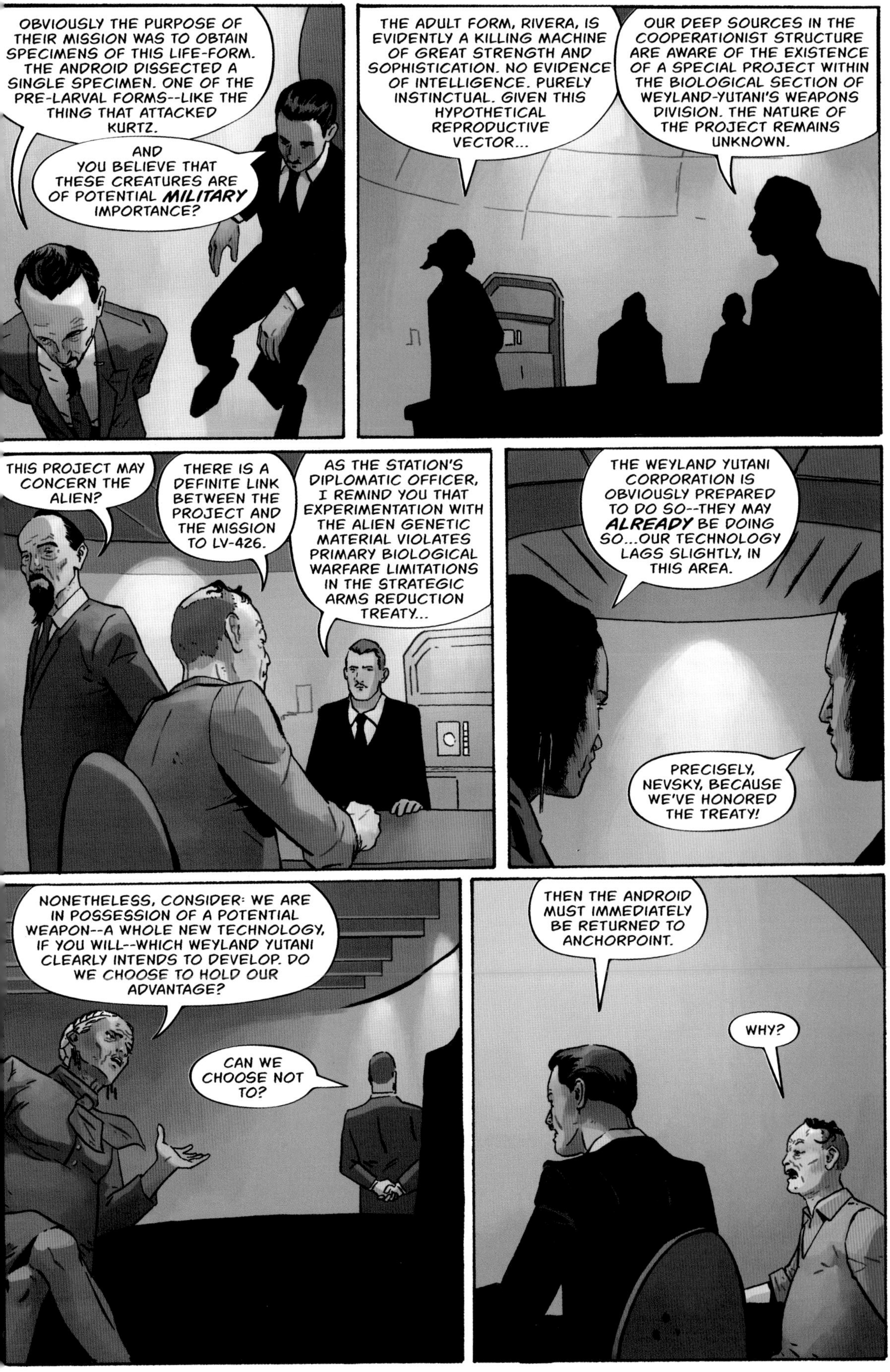
OBVIOUSLY THE PURPOSE OF THEIR MISSION WAS TO OBTAIN SPECIMENS OF THIS LIFE-FORM. THE ANDROID DISSECTED A SINGLE SPECIMEN. ONE OF THE PRE-LARVAL FORMS--LIKE THE THING THAT ATTACKED KURTZ.
AND YOU BELIEVE THAT THESE CREATURES ARE OF POTENTIAL MILITARY IMPORTANCE?
THE ADULT FORM, RIVERA, IS EVIDENTLY A KILLING MACHINE OF GREAT STRENGTH AND SOPHISTICATION. NO EVIDENCE OF INTELLIGENCE. PURELY INSTINCTUAL. GIVEN THIS HYPOTHETICAL REPRODUCTIVE VECTOR...
OUR DEEP SOURCES IN THE COOPERATIONIST STRUCTURE ARE AWARE OF THE EXISTENCE OF A SPECIAL PROJECT WITHIN THE BIOLOGICAL SECTION OF WEYLAND-YUTANI'S WEAPONS DIVISION. THE NATURE OF THE PROJECT REMAINS UNKNOWN.
THIS PROJECT MAY CONCERN THE ALIEN?
THERE IS A DEFINITE LINK BETWEEN THE PROJECT AND THE MISSION TO LV-426.
AS THE STATION'S DIPLOMATIC OFFICER, I REMIND YOU THAT EXPERIMENTATION WITH THE ALIEN GENETIC MATERIAL VIOLATES PRIMARY BIOLOGICAL WARFARE LIMITATIONS IN THE STRATEGIC ARMS REDUCTION TREATY...
THE WEYLAND YUTANI CORPORATION IS OBVIOUSLY PREPARED TO DO SO--THEY MAY ALREADY BE DOING SO...OUR TECHNOLOGY LAGS SLIGHTLY, IN THIS AREA.
PRECISELY, NEVSKY, BECAUSE WE'VE HONORED THE TREATY!
NONETHELESS, CONSIDER: WE ARE IN POSSESSION OF A POTENTIAL WEAPON--A WHOLE NEW TECHNOLOGY, IF YOU WILL--WHICH WEYLAND YUTANI CLEARLY INTENDS TO DEVELOP. DO WE CHOOSE TO HOLD OUR ADVANTAGE?
CAN WE CHOOSE NOT TO?
THEN THE ANDROID MUST IMMEDIATELY BE RETURNED TO ANCHORPOINT.
WHY?

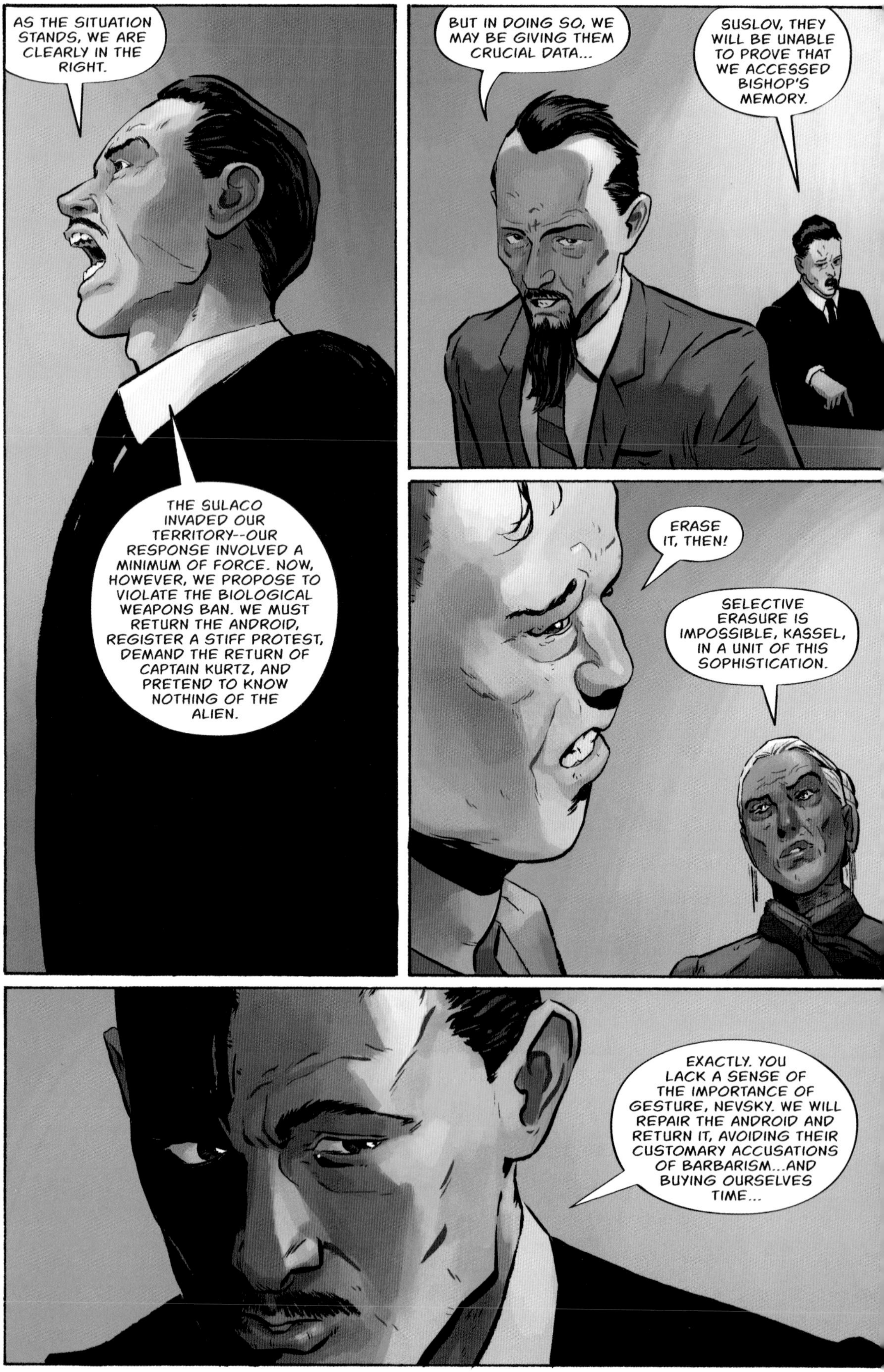

AS THE SITUATION STANDS, WE ARE CLEARLY IN THE RIGHT.
THE SULACO INVADED OUR TERRITORY--OUR RESPONSE INVOLVED A MINIMUM OF FORCE. NOW, HOWEVER, WE PROPOSE TO VIOLATE THE BIOLOGICAL WEAPONS BAN. WE MUST RETURN THE ANDROID, REGISTER A STIFF PROTEST, DEMAND THE RETURN OF CAPTAIN KURTZ, AND PRETEND TO KNOW NOTHING OF THE ALIEN.
BUT IN DOING SO, WE MAY BE GIVING THEM CRUCIAL DATA...
SUSLOV, THEY WILL BE UNABLE TO PROVE THAT WE ACCESSED BISHOP'S MEMORY.
ERASE IT, THEN!
SELECTIVE ERASURE IS IMPOSSIBLE, KASSEL, IN A UNIT OF THIS SOPHISTICATION.
EXACTLY. YOU LACK A SENSE OF THE IMPORTANCE OF GESTURE, NEVSKY. WE WILL REPAIR THE ANDROID AND RETURN IT, AVOIDING THEIR CUSTOMARY ACCUSATIONS OF BARBARISM...AND BUYING OURSELVES TIME...

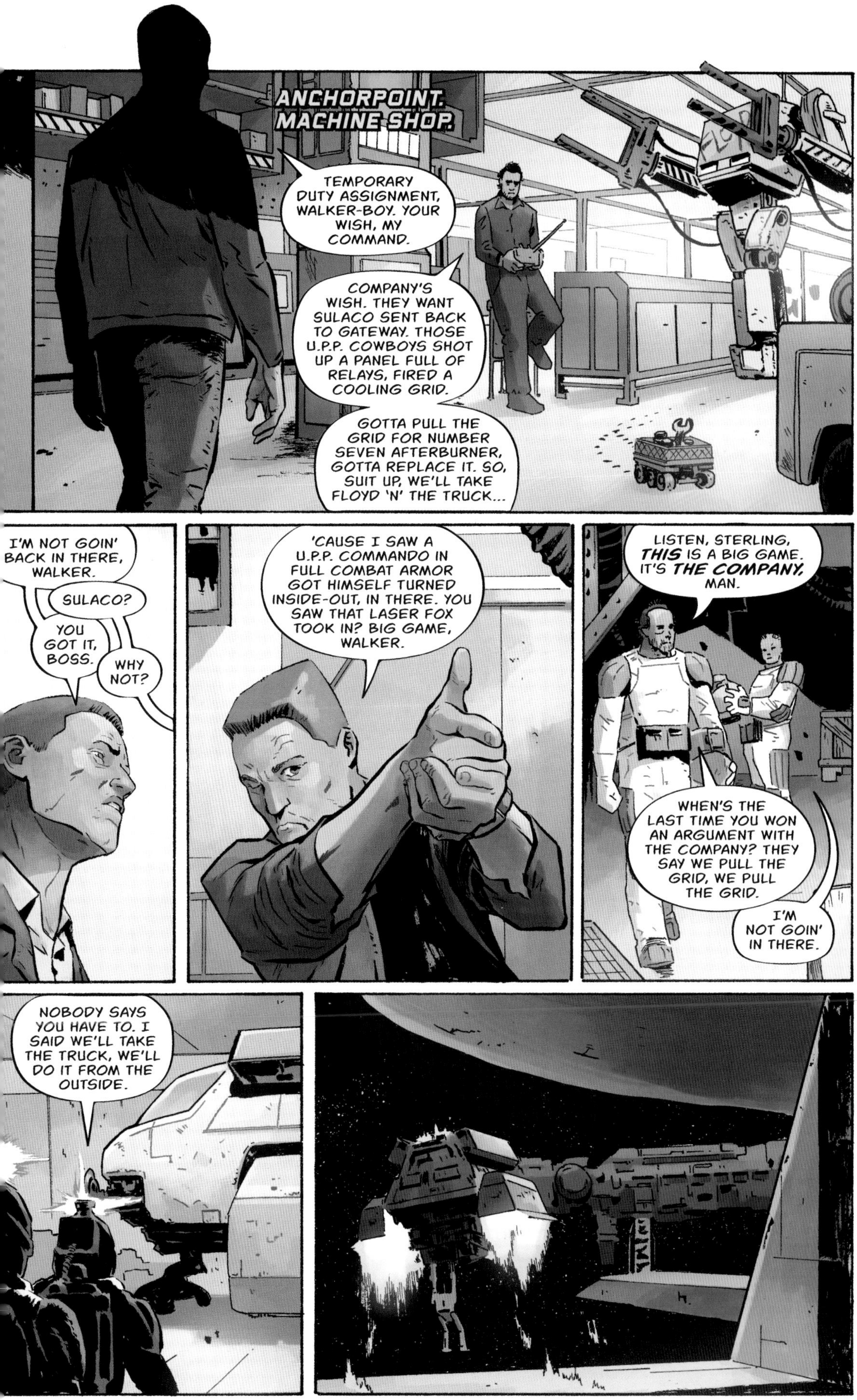
ANCHORPOINT. MACHINE SHOP.
TEMPORARY DUTY ASSIGNMENT, WALKER-BOY. YOUR WISH, MY COMMAND.
COMPANY'S WISH. THEY WANT SULACO SENT BACK TO GATEWAY. THOSE U.P.P. COWBOYS SHOT UP A PANEL FULL OF RELAYS, FIRED A COOLING GRID.
GOTTA PULL THE GRID FOR NUMBER SEVEN AFTERBURNER, GOTTA REPLACE IT. SO, SUIT UP, WE'LL TAKE FLOYD 'N' THE TRUCK...
I'M NOT GOIN' BACK IN THERE, WALKER.
SULACO?
YOU GOT IT, BOSS.
WHY NOT?
'CAUSE I SAW A U.P.P. COMMANDO IN FULL COMBAT ARMOR GOT HIMSELF TURNED INSIDE-OUT, IN THERE. YOU SAW THAT LASER FOX TOOK IN? BIG GAME, WALKER.
LISTEN, STERLING, THIS IS A BIG GAME. IT'S THE COMPANY, MAN.
WHEN'S THE LAST TIME YOU WON AN ARGUMENT WITH THE COMPANY? THEY SAY WE PULL THE GRID, WE PULL THE GRID.
I'M NOT GOIN' IN THERE.
NOBODY SAYS YOU HAVE TO. I SAID WE'LL TAKE THE TRUCK, WE'LL DO IT FROM THE OUTSIDE.

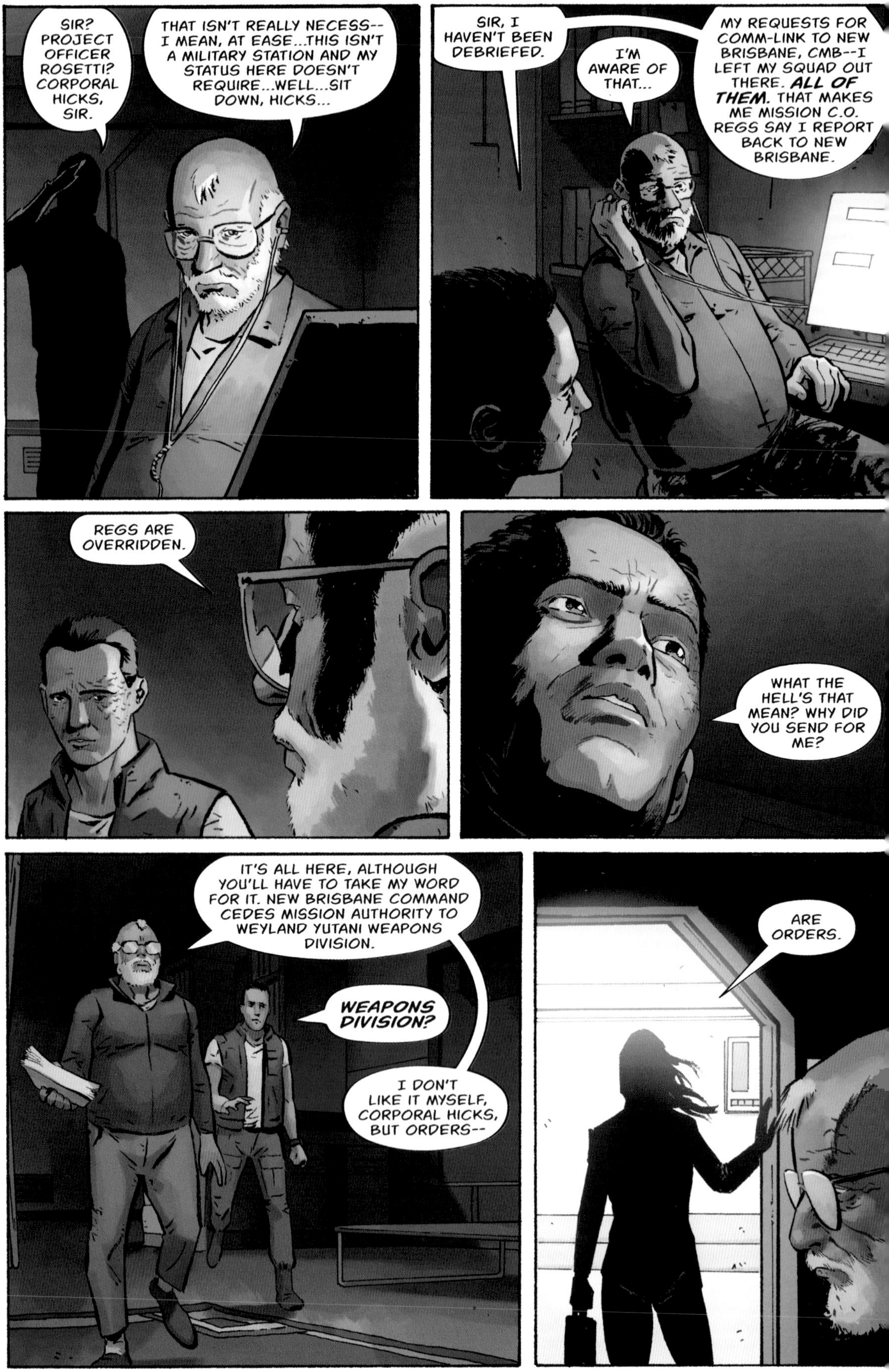
SIR? PROJECT OFFICER ROSETTI? CORPORAL HICKS, SIR.
THAT ISN'T REALLY NECESS-- I MEAN, AT EASE...THIS ISN'T A MILITARY STATION AND MY STATUS HERE DOESN'T REQUIRE...WELL...SIT DOWN, HICKS...
SIR, I HAVEN'T BEEN DEBRIEFED.
I'M AWARE OF THAT...
MY REQUESTS FOR COMM-LINK TO NEW BRISBANE, CMB--I LEFT MY SQUAD OUT THERE. **ALL OF THEM.** THAT MAKES ME MISSION C.O. REGS SAY I REPORT BACK TO NEW BRISBANE.
REGS ARE OVERRIDDEN.
WHAT THE HELL'S THAT MEAN? WHY DID YOU SEND FOR ME?
IT'S ALL HERE, ALTHOUGH YOU'LL HAVE TO TAKE MY WORD FOR IT. NEW BRISBANE COMMAND CEDES MISSION AUTHORITY TO WEYLAND YUTANI WEAPONS DIVISION.
WEAPONS DIVISION?
I DON'T LIKE IT MYSELF, CORPORAL HICKS, BUT ORDERS--
ARE ORDERS.

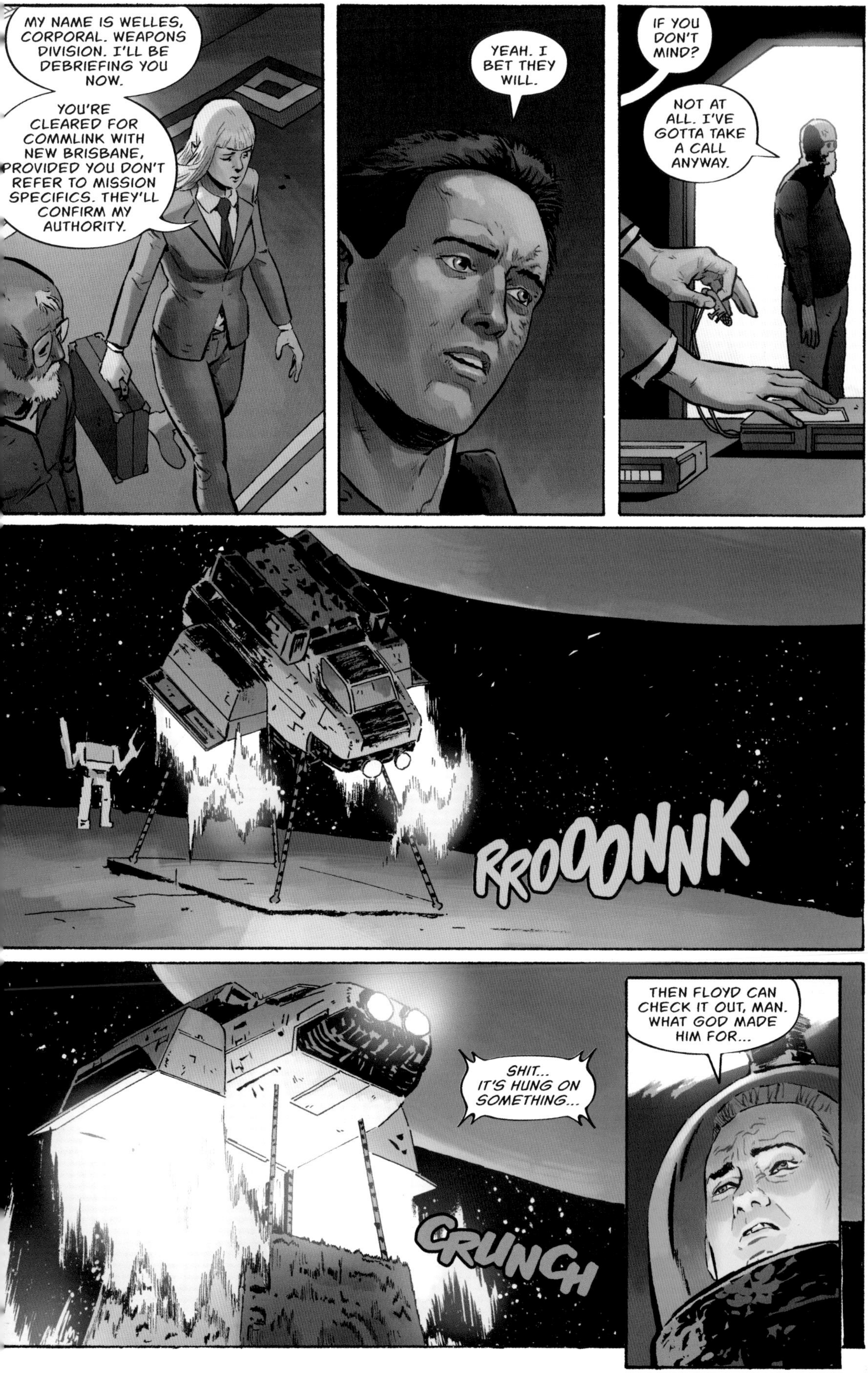

MY NAME IS WELLES, CORPORAL. WEAPONS DIVISION. I'LL BE DEBRIEFING YOU NOW.
YOU'RE CLEARED FOR COMMLINK WITH NEW BRISBANE, PROVIDED YOU DON'T REFER TO MISSION SPECIFICS. THEY'LL CONFIRM MY AUTHORITY.
YEAH. I BET THEY WILL.
IF YOU DON'T MIND?
NOT AT ALL. I'VE GOTTA TAKE A CALL ANYWAY.
RROOONNK
SHIT... IT'S HUNG ON SOMETHING...
CRUNCH
THEN FLOYD CAN CHECK IT OUT, MAN. WHAT GOD MADE HIM FOR...

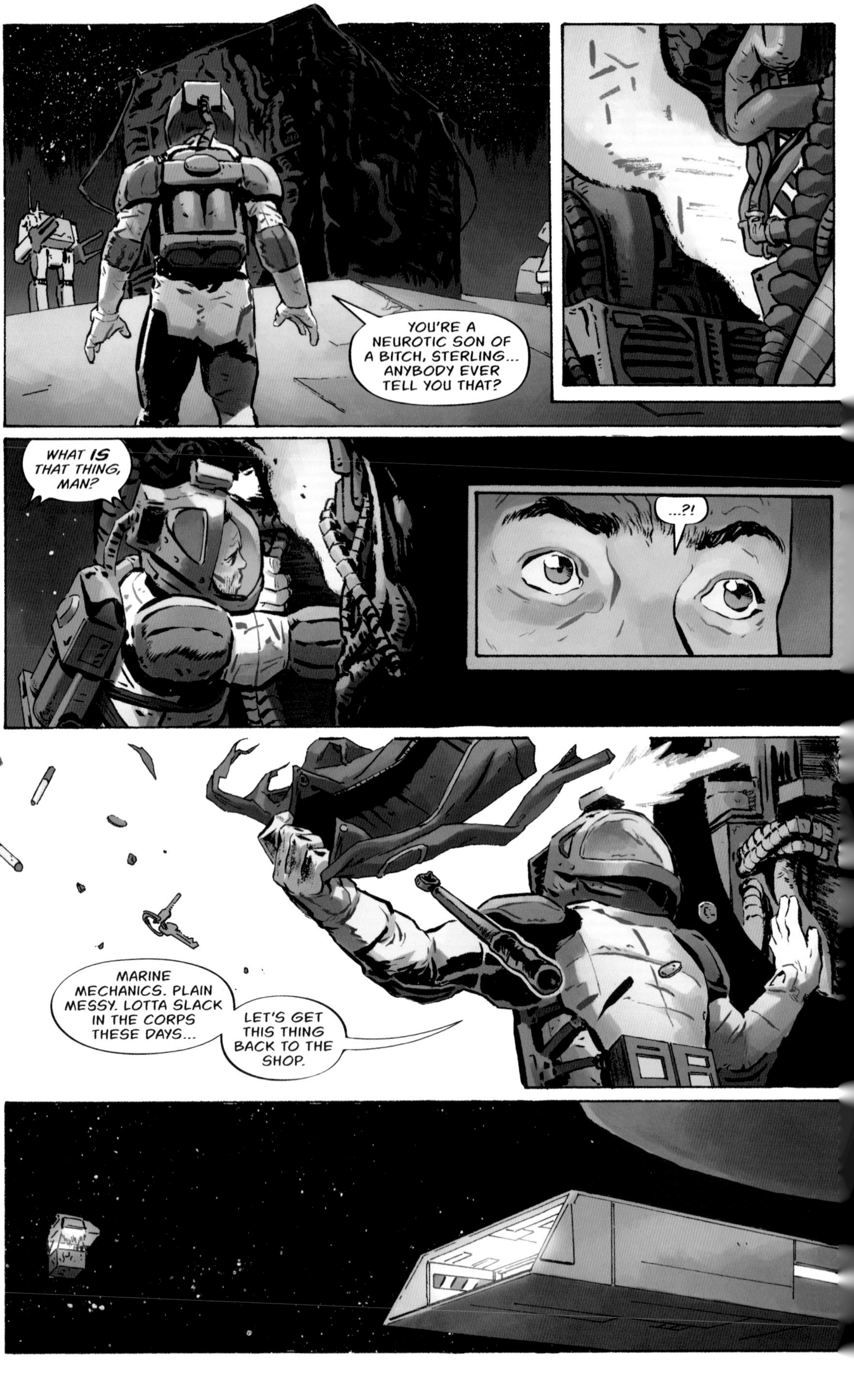
YOU'RE A NEUROTIC SON OF A BITCH, STERLING... ANYBODY EVER TELL YOU THAT?
WHAT *IS* THAT THING, MAN?
...?!
MARINE MECHANICS. PLAIN MESSY. LOTTA SLACK IN THE CORPS THESE DAYS...
LET'S GET THIS THING BACK TO THE SHOP.

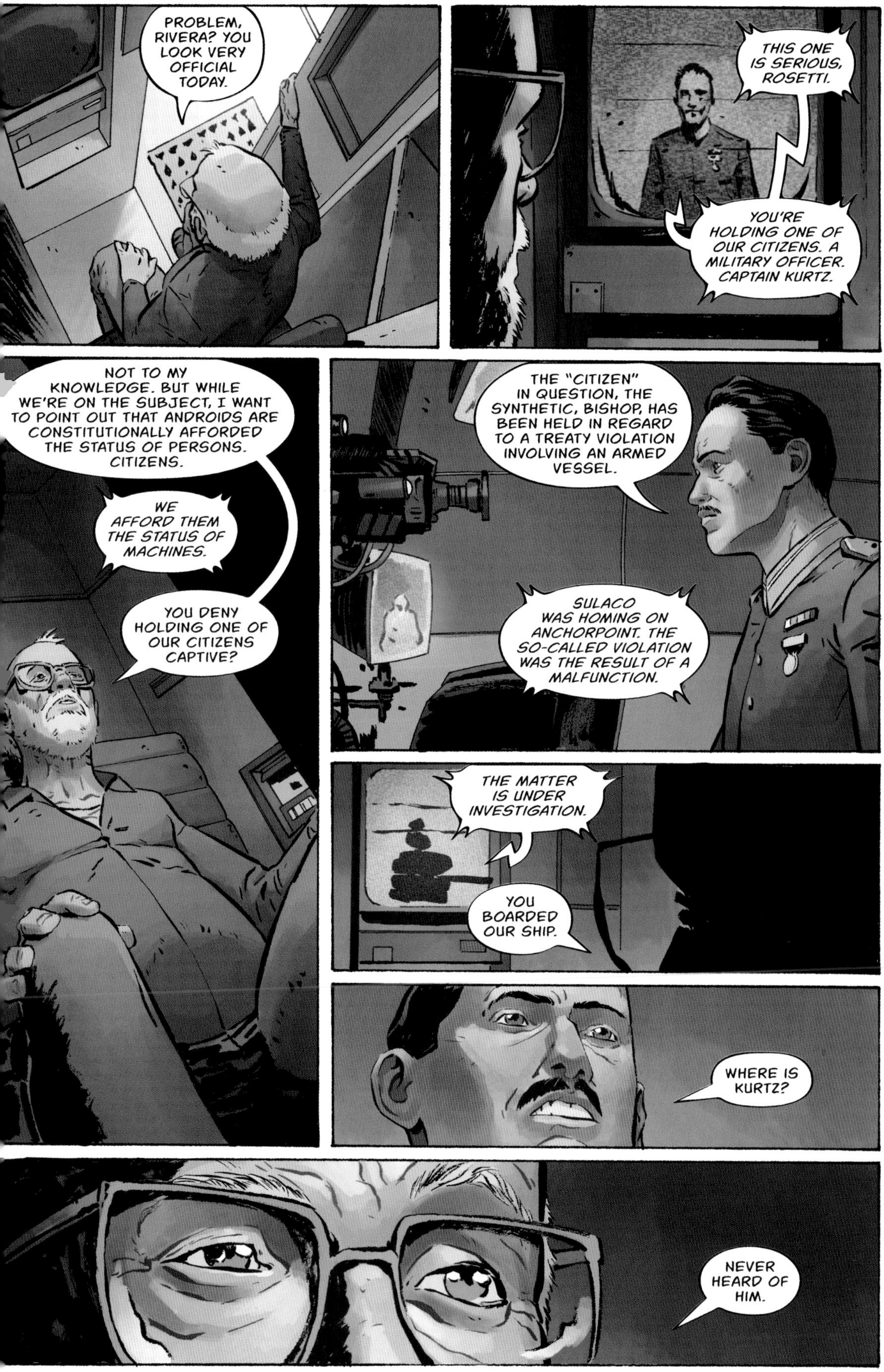
PROBLEM, RIVERA? YOU LOOK VERY OFFICIAL TODAY.
THIS ONE IS SERIOUS, ROSETTI.
YOU'RE HOLDING ONE OF OUR CITIZENS. A MILITARY OFFICER. CAPTAIN KURTZ.
NOT TO MY KNOWLEDGE. BUT WHILE WE'RE ON THE SUBJECT, I WANT TO POINT OUT THAT ANDROIDS ARE CONSTITUTIONALLY AFFORDED THE STATUS OF PERSONS. CITIZENS.
WE AFFORD THEM THE STATUS OF MACHINES.
YOU DENY HOLDING ONE OF OUR CITIZENS CAPTIVE?
THE "CITIZEN" IN QUESTION, THE SYNTHETIC, BISHOP, HAS BEEN HELD IN REGARD TO A TREATY VIOLATION INVOLVING AN ARMED VESSEL.
SULACO WAS HOMING ON ANCHORPOINT. THE SO-CALLED VIOLATION WAS THE RESULT OF A MALFUNCTION.
THE MATTER IS UNDER INVESTIGATION.
YOU BOARDED OUR SHIP.
WHERE IS KURTZ?
NEVER HEARD OF HIM.

THE INCIDENT IS BEING INVESTIGATED WITH REGARD TO VIOLATIONS OF THE STRATEGIC ARMS REDUCTION TREATY.

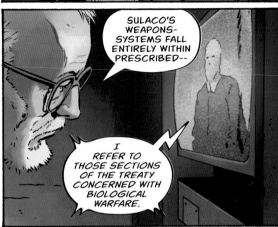

SULACO'S WEAPONS-SYSTEMS FALL ENTIRELY WITHIN PRESCRIBED--

I REFER TO THOSE SECTIONS OF THE TREATY CONCERNED WITH BIOLOGICAL WARFARE.

A BASELESS ALLEGATION, JORGE. WHO'S PUTTING YOU UP TO THIS? SUSLOV? I'D THINK HE KNEW BETTER...

THERE ARE NO FORMAL ALLEGATIONS AT THIS TIME. THE MATTER IS UNDER INVESTIGATION. BISHOP, HOWEVER, IS OF NO FURTHER USE IN THE INQUIRY, SO WE ARE RETURNING HIM TO YOU.

YOU ARE?

LEAVING YOU NO GROUNDS WHATEVER FOR DETAINING KURTZ.

blink

TULLY? YOU PUT A CALL FOR ME THROUGH OPS?

SURE DID...

WELL?

YOU ORDERED US TO RUN TEST-SERIES 10-C ON THE MATERIAL RECOVERED FROM--

YES?

WELL, THAT INCLUDES A STANDARD COMPATIBILITY-RUN ON HUMAN DNA, STANDARD RECOMBINANT--

THEN DO IT, TULLY.

DID IT.

IMPOSSIBLE. MINIMUM CULTIVATION PERIOD IS FIFTY-THREE HOURS.

I WANT YOU TO SEE SOMETHING, FOX.

CLICK

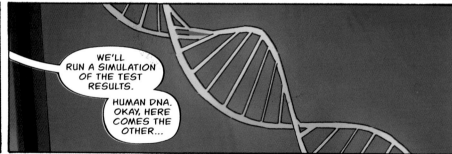

WE'LL RUN A SIMULATION OF THE TEST RESULTS.

HUMAN DNA. OKAY, HERE COMES THE OTHER...

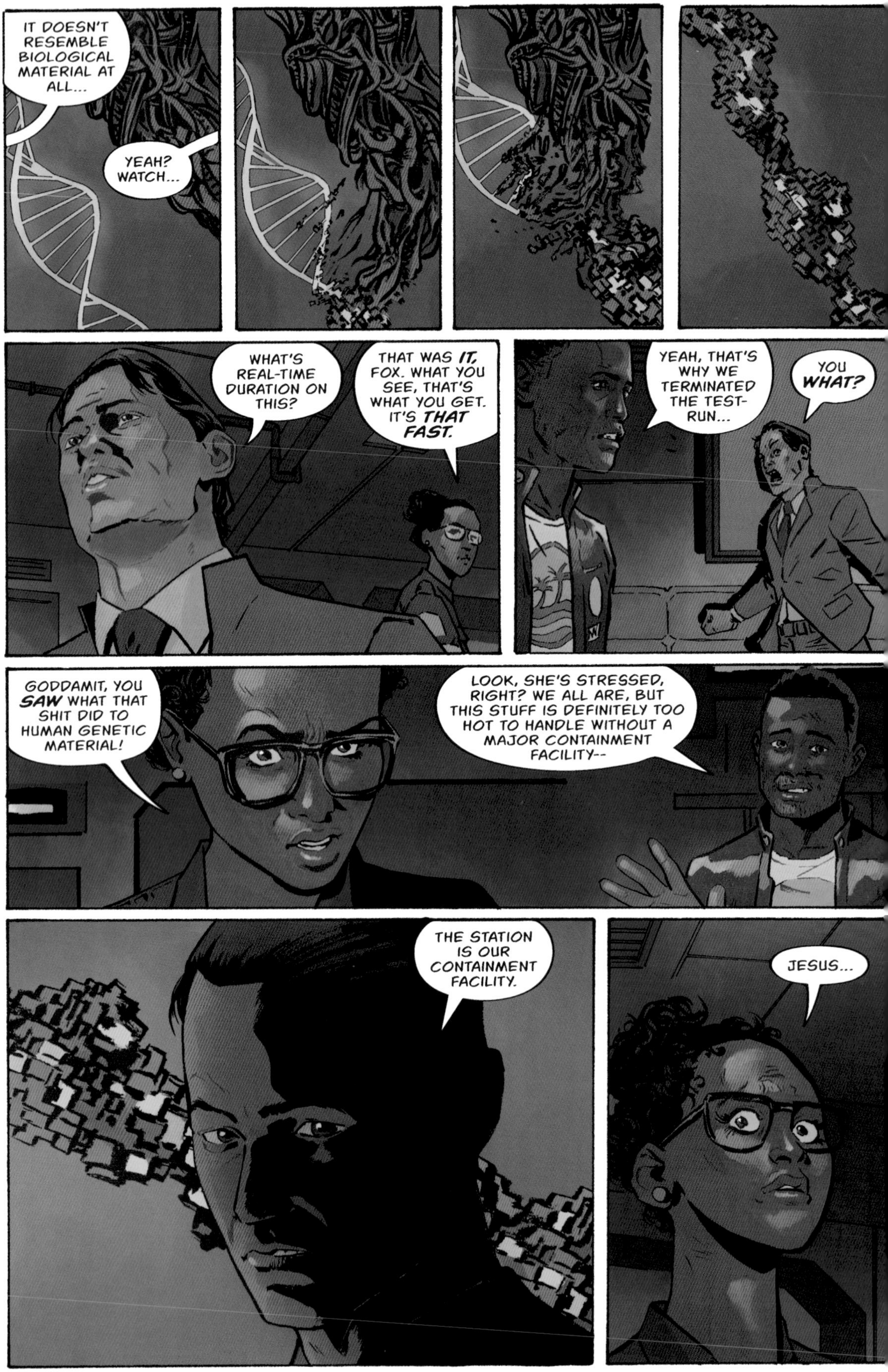
IT DOESN'T RESEMBLE BIOLOGICAL MATERIAL AT ALL...
YEAH? WATCH...
WHAT'S REAL-TIME DURATION ON THIS?
THAT WAS IT, FOX. WHAT YOU SEE, THAT'S WHAT YOU GET. IT'S THAT FAST.
YEAH, THAT'S WHY WE TERMINATED THE TEST-RUN...
YOU WHAT?
GODDAMIT, YOU SAW WHAT THAT SHIT DID TO HUMAN GENETIC MATERIAL!
LOOK, SHE'S STRESSED, RIGHT? WE ALL ARE, BUT THIS STUFF IS DEFINITELY TOO HOT TO HANDLE WITHOUT A MAJOR CONTAINMENT FACILITY--
THE STATION IS OUR CONTAINMENT FACILITY.
JESUS...

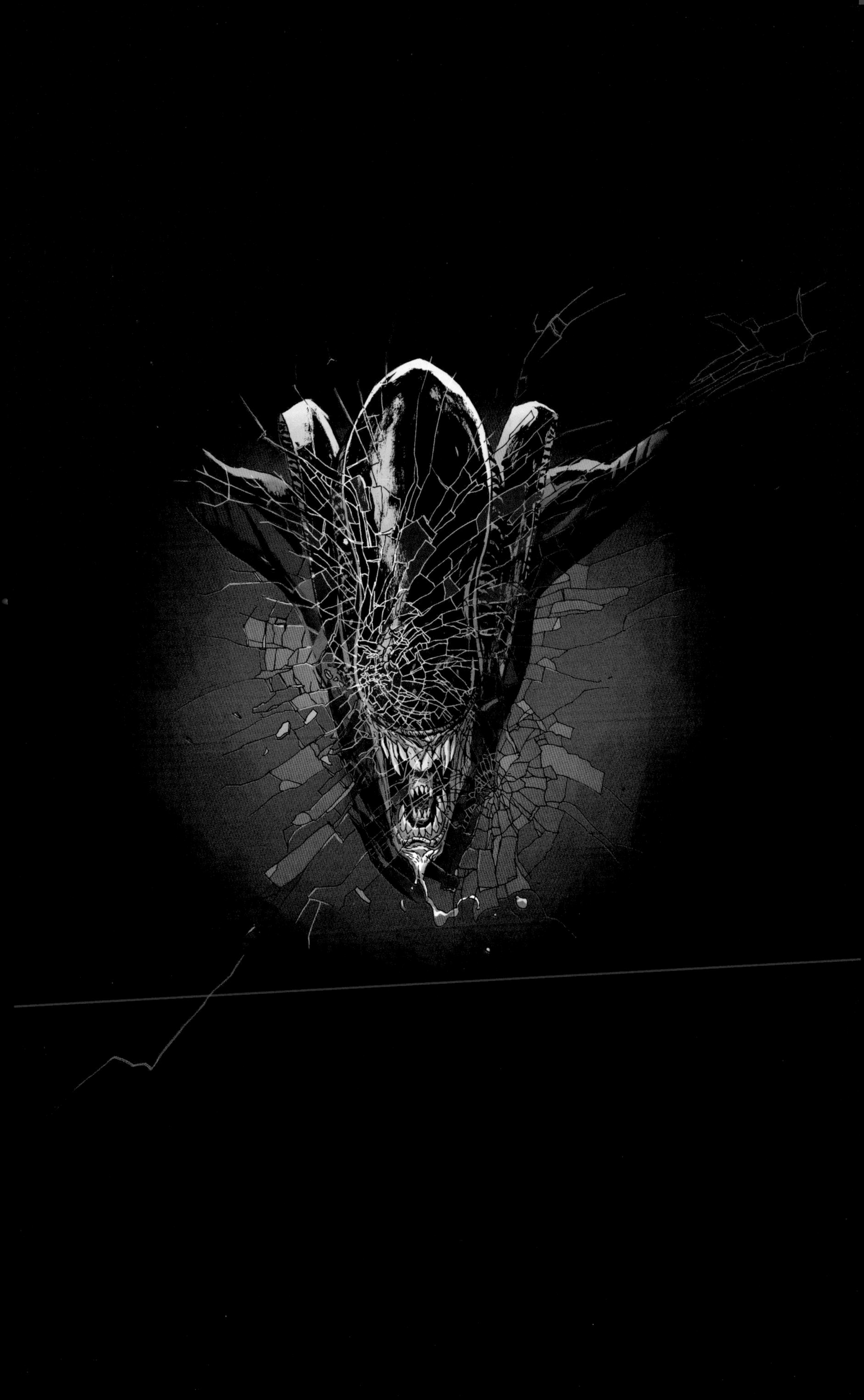

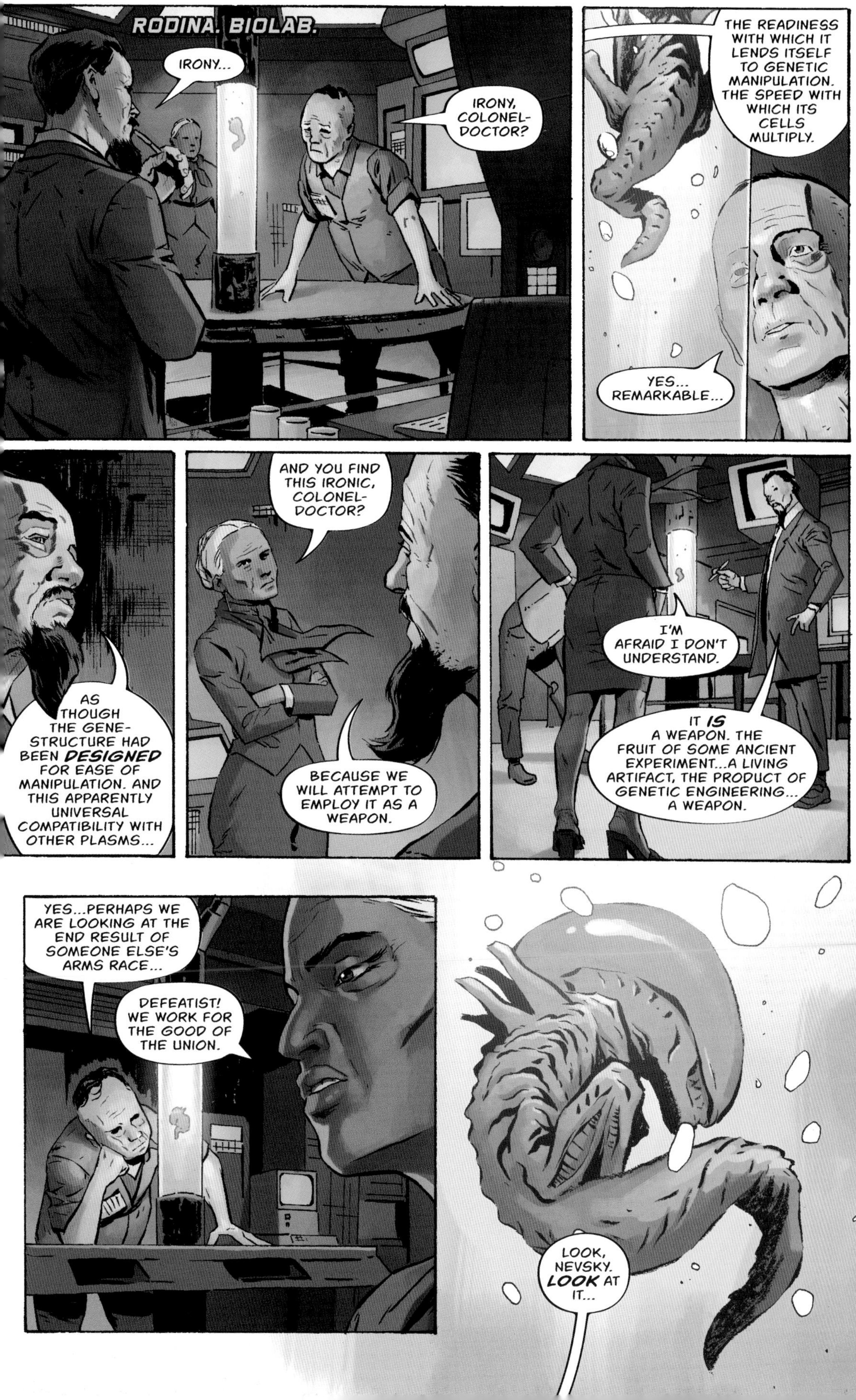
RODINA. BIOLAB.
IRONY...
IRONY, COLONEL-DOCTOR?
THE READINESS WITH WHICH IT LENDS ITSELF TO GENETIC MANIPULATION. THE SPEED WITH WHICH ITS CELLS MULTIPLY.
YES... REMARKABLE...
AS THOUGH THE GENE-STRUCTURE HAD BEEN DESIGNED FOR EASE OF MANIPULATION. AND THIS APPARENTLY UNIVERSAL COMPATIBILITY WITH OTHER PLASMS...
AND YOU FIND THIS IRONIC, COLONEL-DOCTOR?
BECAUSE WE WILL ATTEMPT TO EMPLOY IT AS A WEAPON.
I'M AFRAID I DON'T UNDERSTAND.
IT IS A WEAPON. THE FRUIT OF SOME ANCIENT EXPERIMENT...A LIVING ARTIFACT, THE PRODUCT OF GENETIC ENGINEERING... A WEAPON.
YES...PERHAPS WE ARE LOOKING AT THE END RESULT OF SOMEONE ELSE'S ARMS RACE...
DEFEATIST! WE WORK FOR THE GOOD OF THE UNION.
LOOK, NEVSKY. LOOK AT IT...

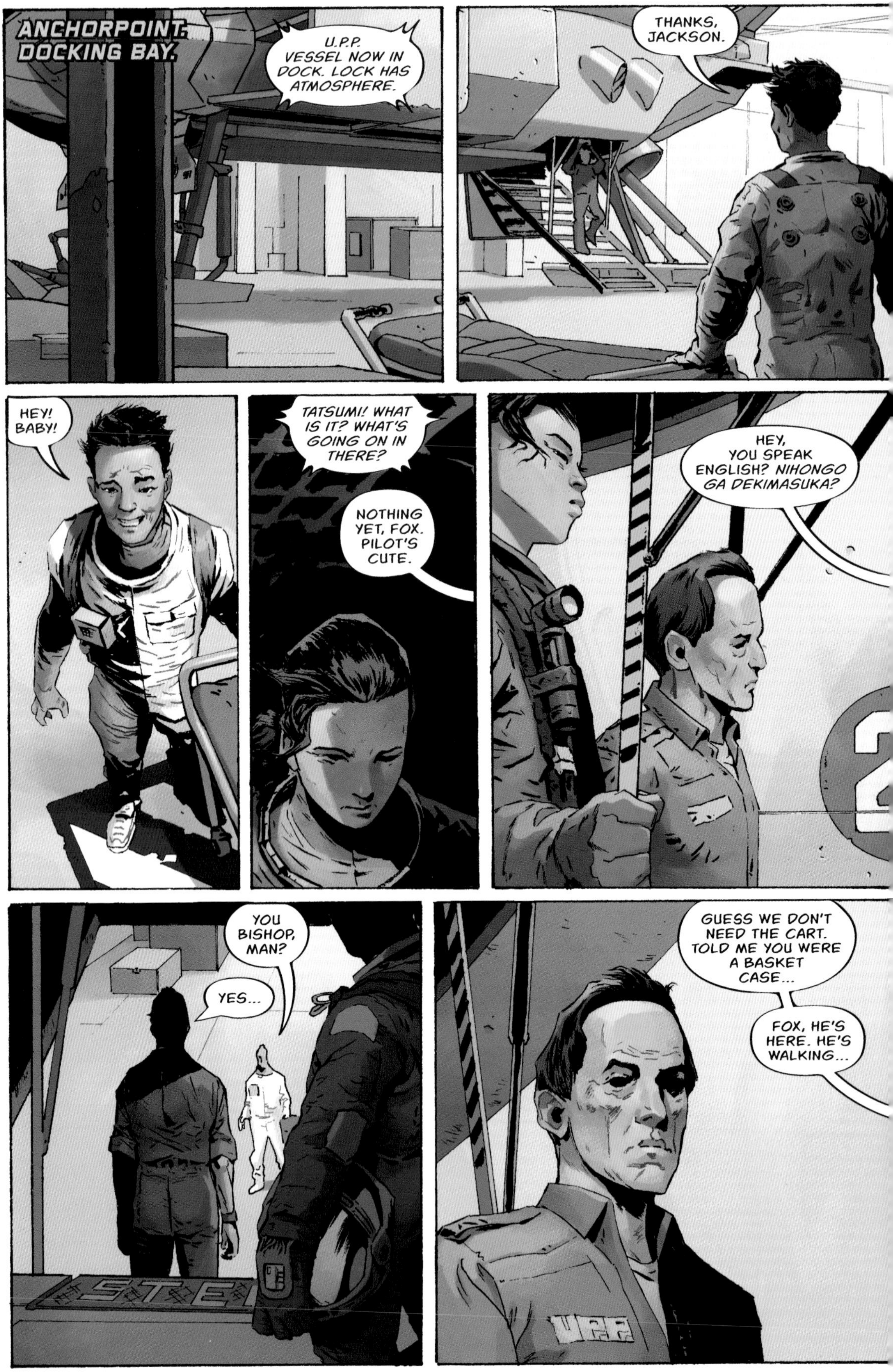
ANCHORPOINT: DOCKING BAY.
U.P.P. VESSEL NOW IN DOCK. LOCK HAS ATMOSPHERE.
THANKS, JACKSON.
HEY! BABY!
TATSUMI! WHAT IS IT? WHAT'S GOING ON IN THERE?
NOTHING YET, FOX. PILOT'S CUTE.
HEY, YOU SPEAK ENGLISH? NIHONGO GA DEKIMASUKA?
YOU BISHOP, MAN?
YES...
GUESS WE DON'T NEED THE CART. TOLD ME YOU WERE A BASKET CASE...
FOX, HE'S HERE. HE'S WALKING...

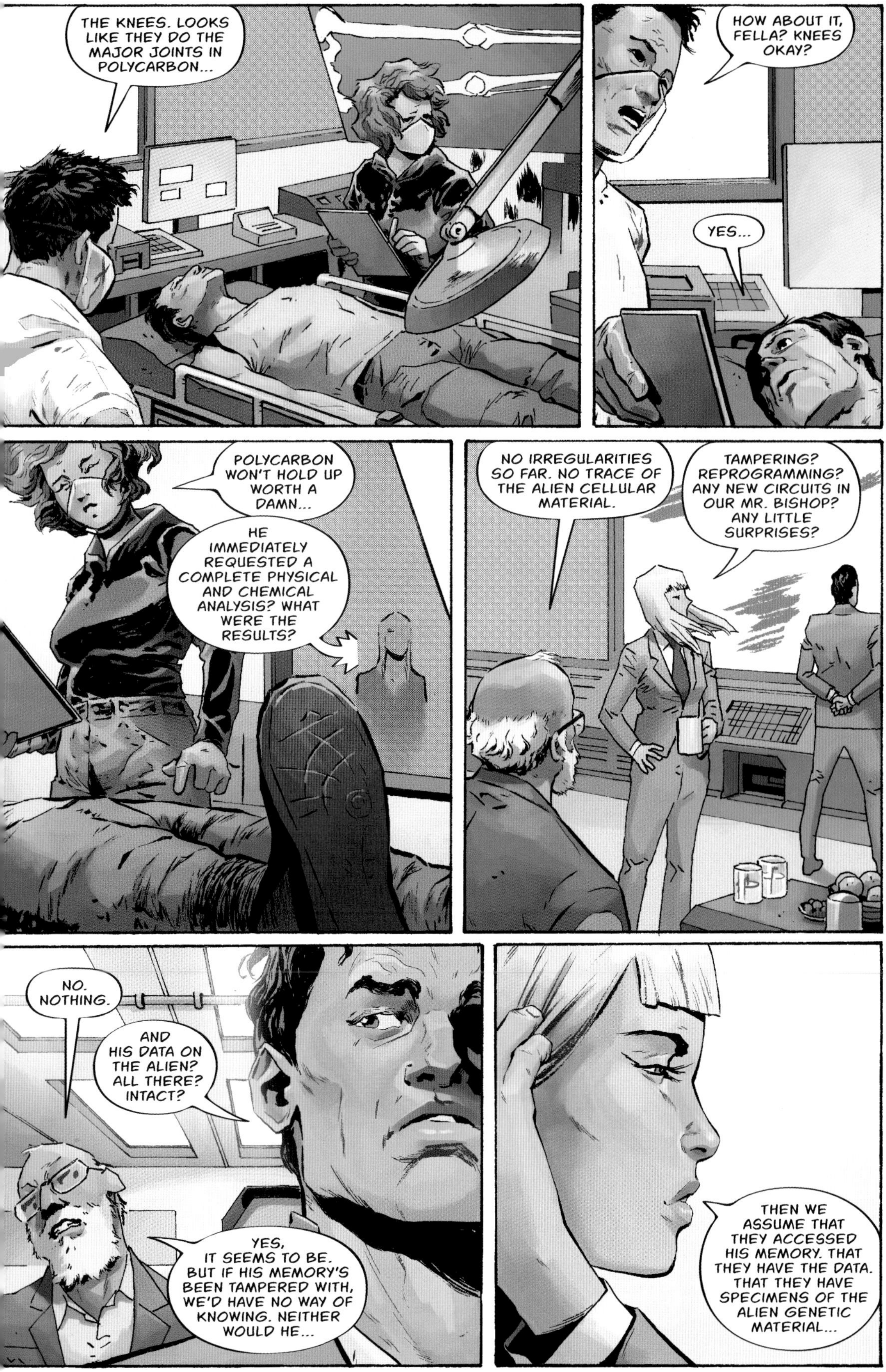
THE KNEES. LOOKS LIKE THEY DO THE MAJOR JOINTS IN POLYCARBON...
HOW ABOUT IT, FELLA? KNEES OKAY?
YES...
POLYCARBON WON'T HOLD UP WORTH A DAMN...
HE IMMEDIATELY REQUESTED A COMPLETE PHYSICAL AND CHEMICAL ANALYSIS? WHAT WERE THE RESULTS?
NO IRREGULARITIES SO FAR. NO TRACE OF THE ALIEN CELLULAR MATERIAL.
TAMPERING? REPROGRAMMING? ANY NEW CIRCUITS IN OUR MR. BISHOP? ANY LITTLE SURPRISES?
NO. NOTHING.
AND HIS DATA ON THE ALIEN? ALL THERE? INTACT?
YES, IT SEEMS TO BE. BUT IF HIS MEMORY'S BEEN TAMPERED WITH, WE'D HAVE NO WAY OF KNOWING. NEITHER WOULD HE...
THEN WE ASSUME THAT THEY ACCESSED HIS MEMORY. THAT THEY HAVE THE DATA. THAT THEY HAVE SPECIMENS OF THE ALIEN GENETIC MATERIAL...

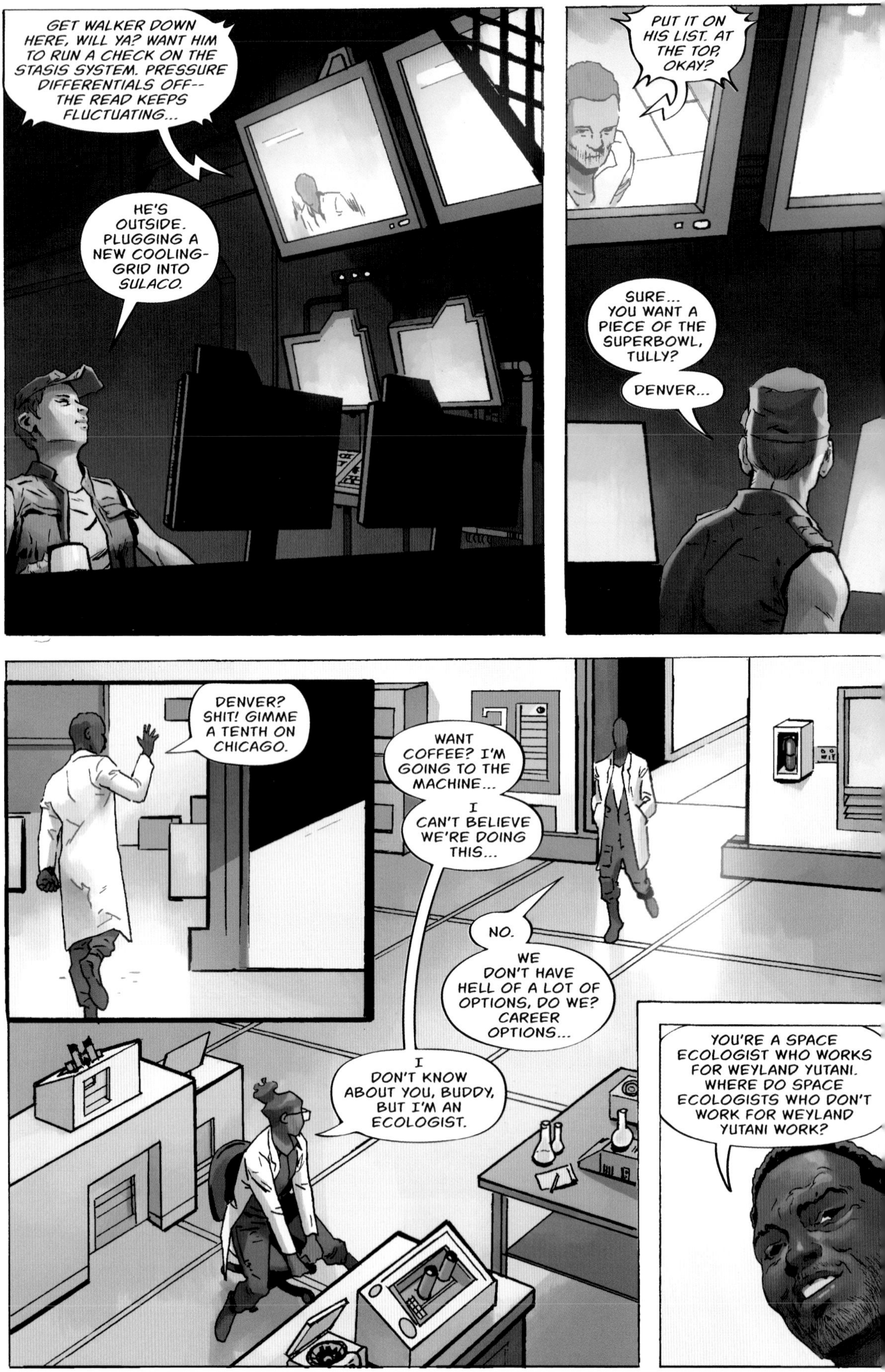
GET WALKER DOWN HERE, WILL YA? WANT HIM TO RUN A CHECK ON THE STASIS SYSTEM. PRESSURE DIFFERENTIALS OFF-- THE READ KEEPS FLUCTUATING...
HE'S OUTSIDE. PLUGGING A NEW COOLING-GRID INTO SULACO.
PUT IT ON HIS LIST. AT THE TOP, OKAY?
SURE... YOU WANT A PIECE OF THE SUPERBOWL, TULLY?
DENVER...
DENVER? SHIT! GIMME A TENTH ON CHICAGO.
WANT COFFEE? I'M GOING TO THE MACHINE...
I CAN'T BELIEVE WE'RE DOING THIS...
NO.
WE DON'T HAVE HELL OF A LOT OF OPTIONS, DO WE? CAREER OPTIONS...
I DON'T KNOW ABOUT YOU, BUDDY, BUT I'M AN ECOLOGIST.
YOU'RE A SPACE ECOLOGIST WHO WORKS FOR WEYLAND YUTANI. WHERE DO SPACE ECOLOGISTS WHO DON'T WORK FOR WEYLAND YUTANI WORK?

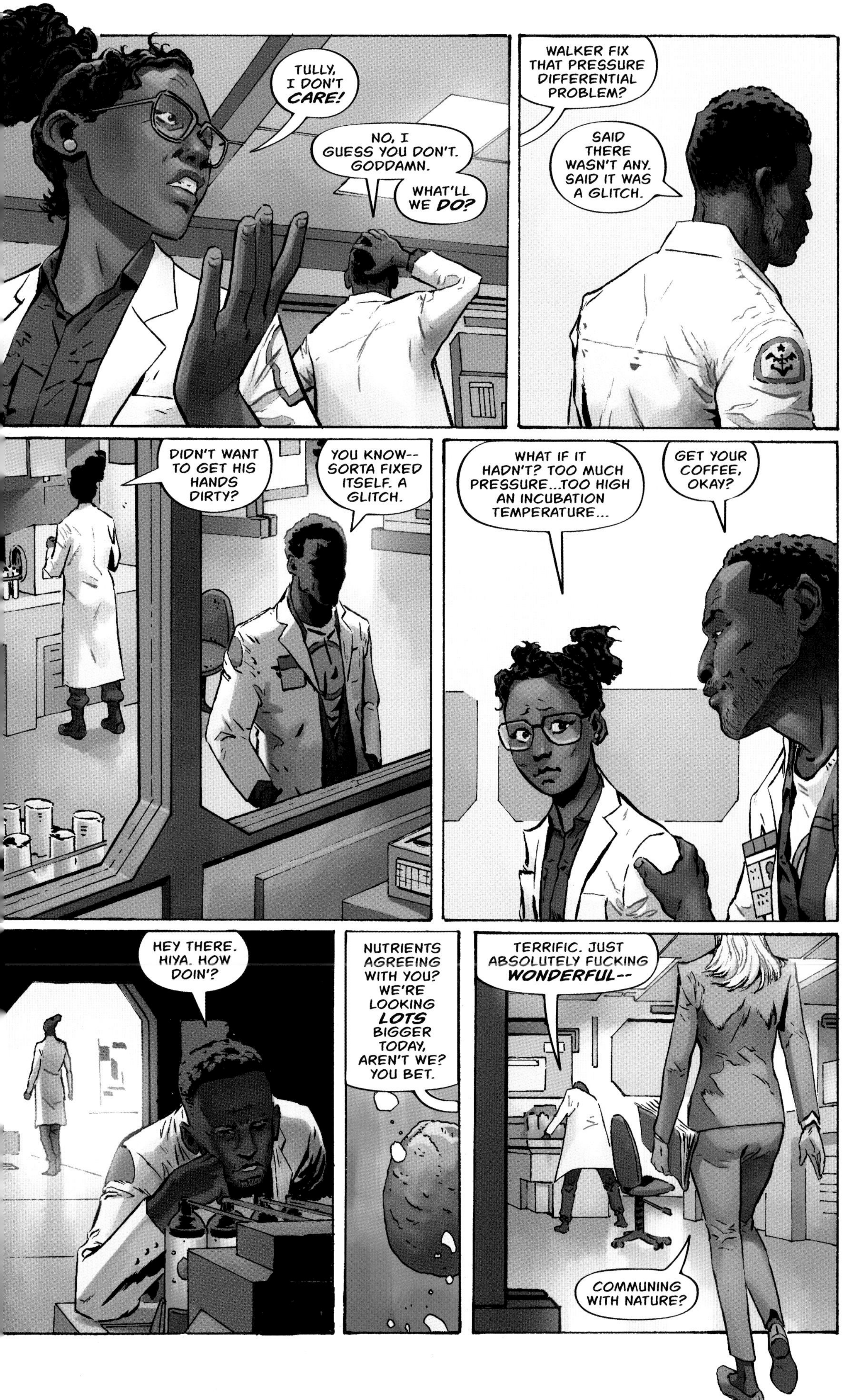
TULLY, I DON'T *CARE!*
NO, I GUESS YOU DON'T. GODDAMN.
WHAT'LL WE *DO?*
WALKER FIX THAT PRESSURE DIFFERENTIAL PROBLEM?
SAID THERE WASN'T ANY. SAID IT WAS A GLITCH.
DIDN'T WANT TO GET HIS HANDS DIRTY?
YOU KNOW-- SORTA FIXED ITSELF. A GLITCH.
WHAT IF IT HADN'T? TOO MUCH PRESSURE...TOO HIGH AN INCUBATION TEMPERATURE...
GET YOUR COFFEE, OKAY?
HEY THERE. HIYA. HOW DOIN'?
NUTRIENTS AGREEING WITH YOU? WE'RE LOOKING *LOTS* BIGGER TODAY, AREN'T WE? YOU BET.
TERRIFIC. JUST ABSOLUTELY FUCKING *WONDERFUL*--
COMMUNING WITH NATURE?

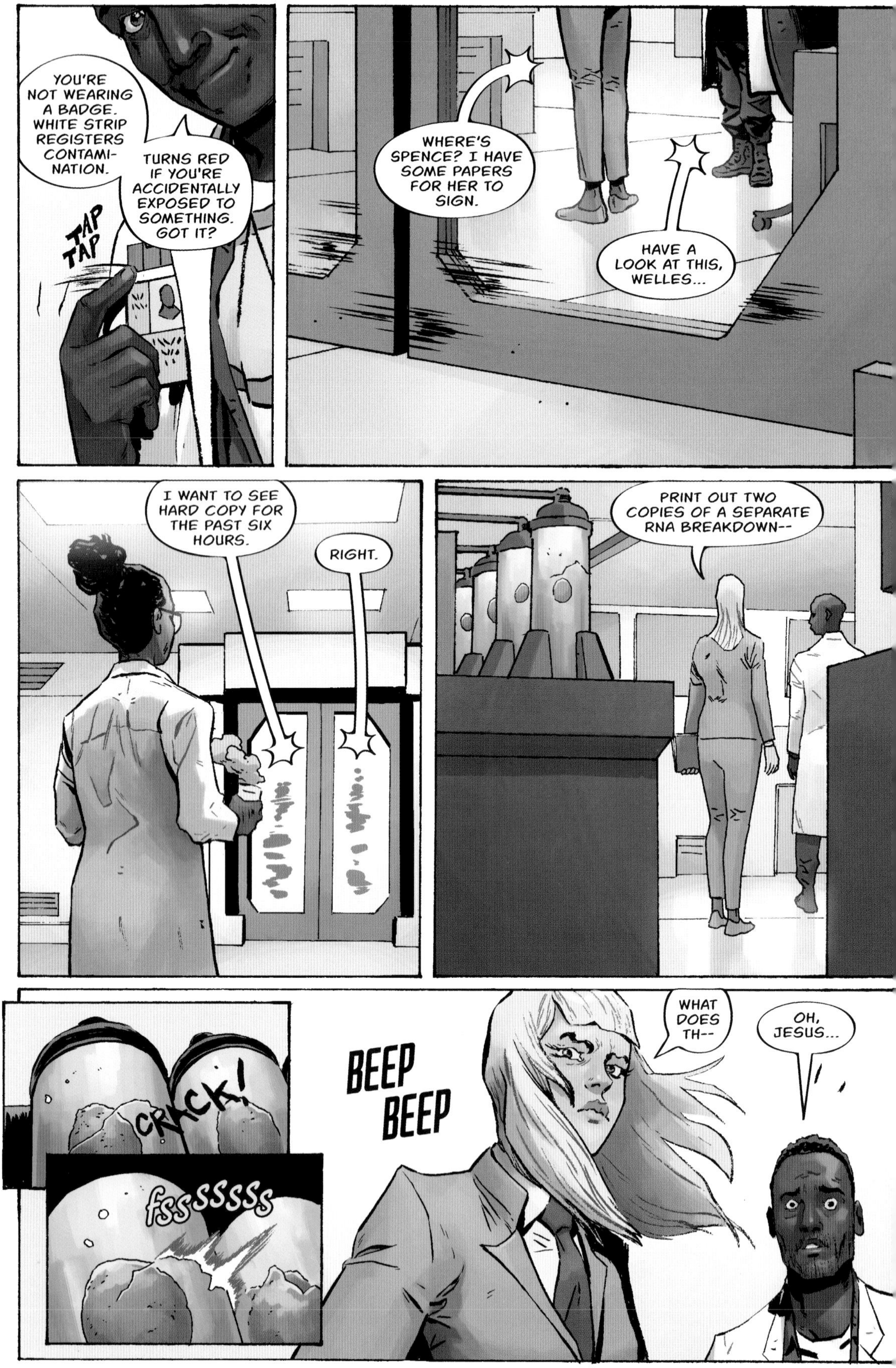
YOU'RE NOT WEARING A BADGE. WHITE STRIP REGISTERS CONTAMI-NATION.
TURNS RED IF YOU'RE ACCIDENTALLY EXPOSED TO SOMETHING. GOT IT?
TAP TAP
WHERE'S SPENCE? I HAVE SOME PAPERS FOR HER TO SIGN.
HAVE A LOOK AT THIS, WELLES...
I WANT TO SEE HARD COPY FOR THE PAST SIX HOURS.
RIGHT.
PRINT OUT TWO COPIES OF A SEPARATE RNA BREAKDOWN--
CRACK!
fssSSSSs
BEEP BEEP
WHAT DOES TH--
OH, JESUS...

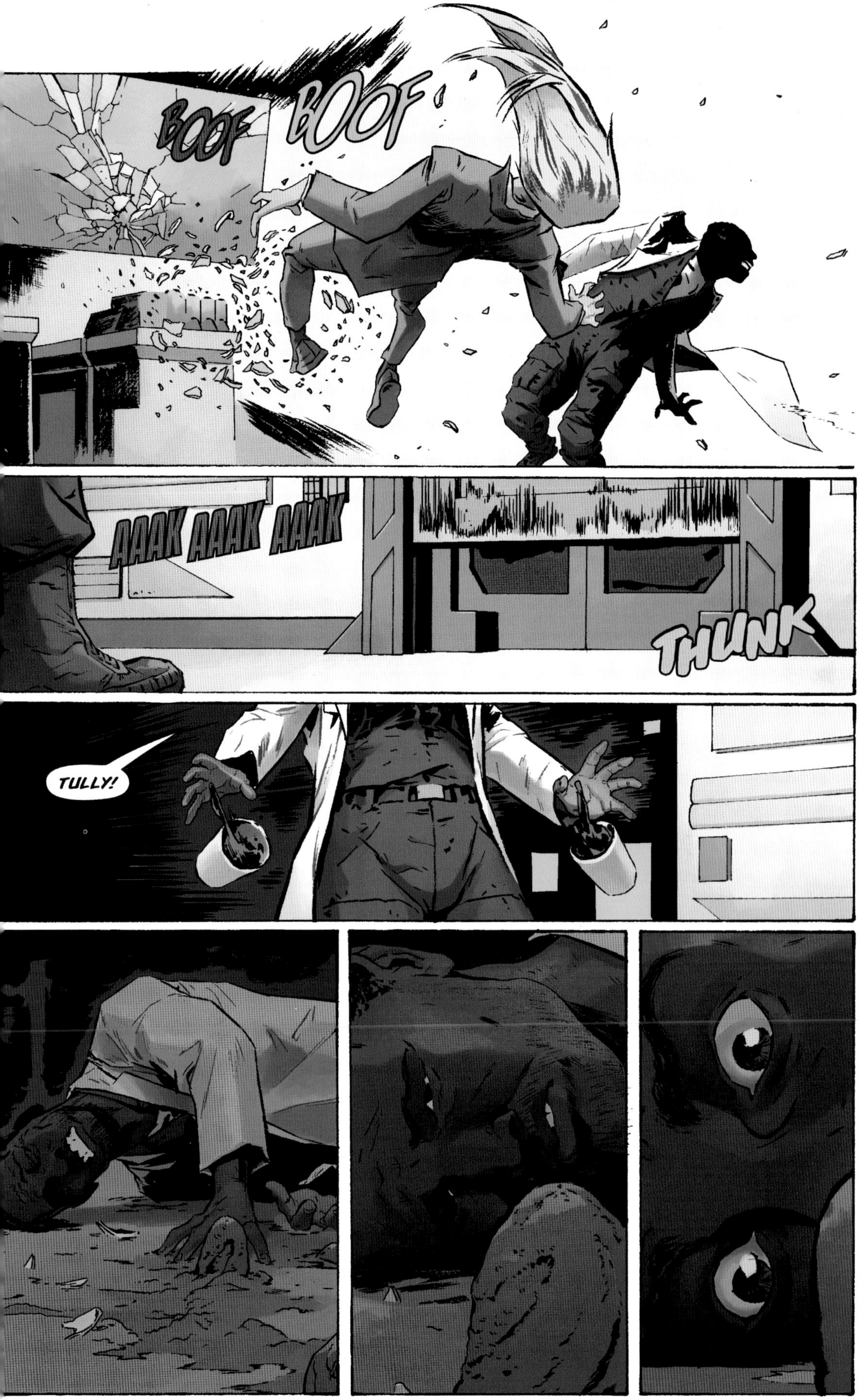
BOOF BOOF
AAAK AAAK AAAK
THUNK
TULLY!

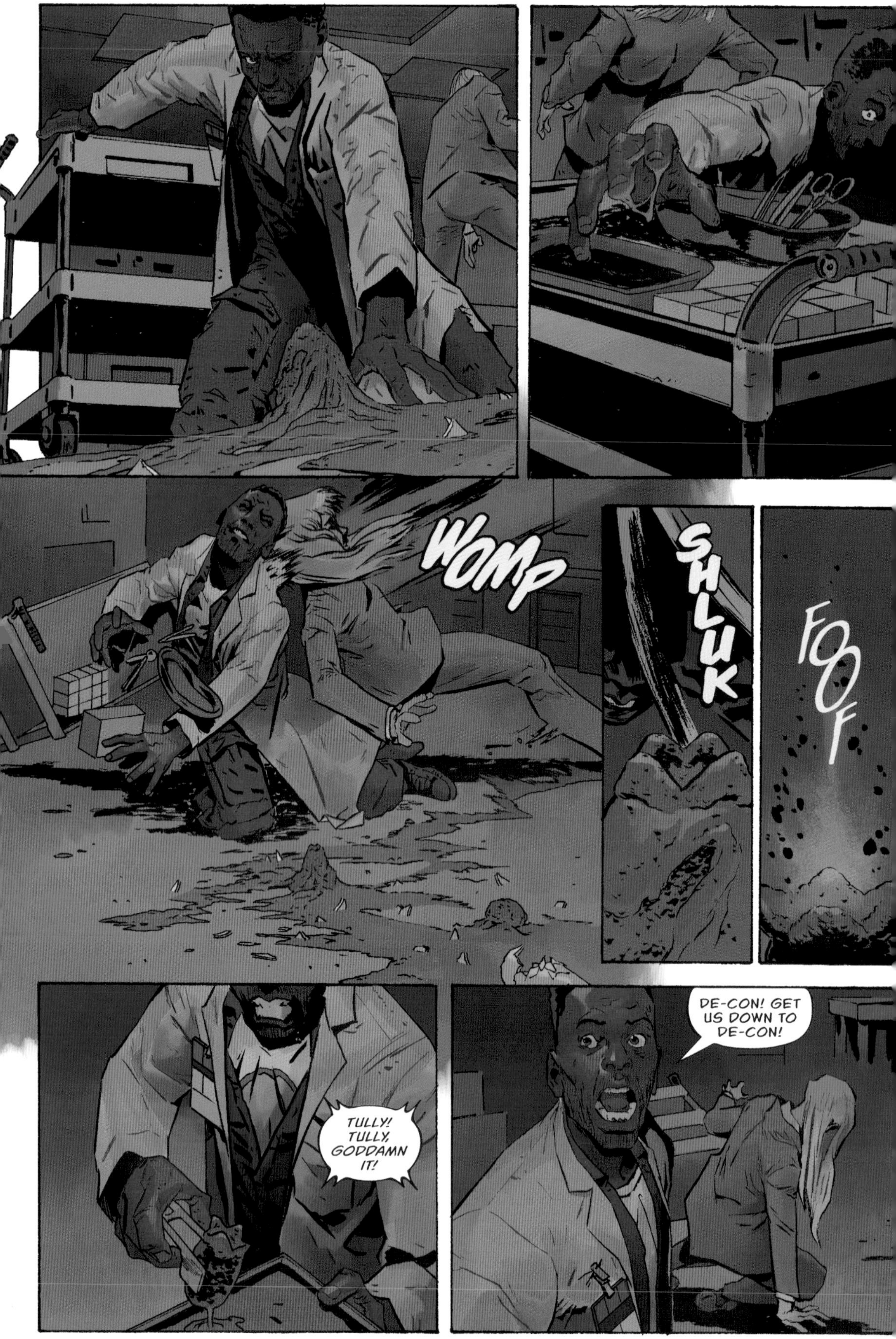
WOMP
SHLUK
FOOF
TULLY! TULLY, GODDAMN IT!
DE-CON! GET US DOWN TO DE-CON!

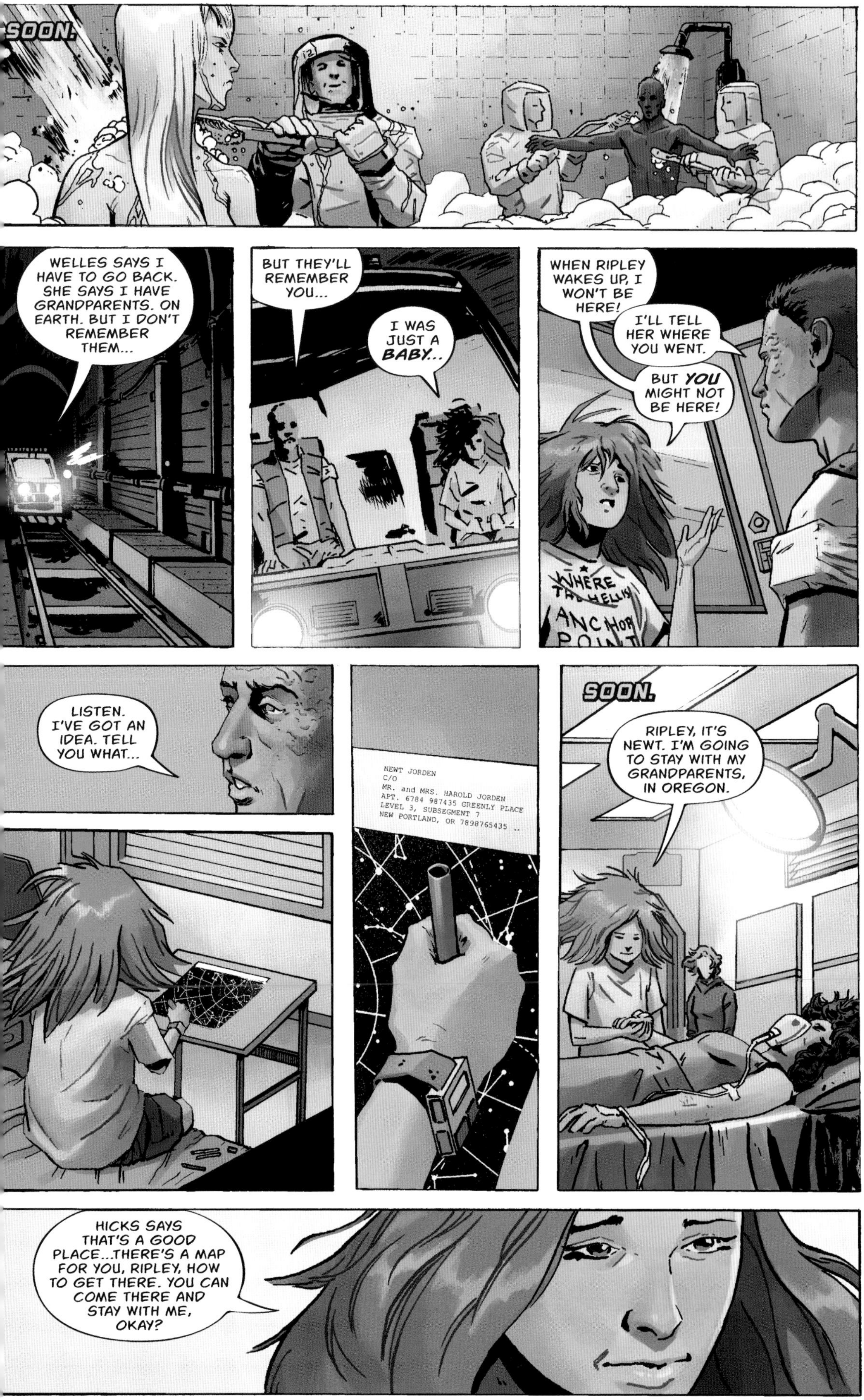
SOON.
WELLES SAYS I HAVE TO GO BACK. SHE SAYS I HAVE GRANDPARENTS. ON EARTH. BUT I DON'T REMEMBER THEM...
BUT THEY'LL REMEMBER YOU...
I WAS JUST A *BABY...*
WHEN RIPLEY WAKES UP, I WON'T BE HERE!
I'LL TELL HER WHERE YOU WENT.
BUT *YOU* MIGHT NOT BE HERE!
WHERE THE HELL IS ANCHORPOINT
LISTEN. I'VE GOT AN IDEA. TELL YOU WHAT...
NEWT JORDEN
C/O
MR. and MRS. HAROLD JORDEN
APT. 6784 987435 GREENLY PLACE
LEVEL 3, SUBSEGMENT 7
NEW PORTLAND, OR 7898765435
SOON.
RIPLEY, IT'S NEWT. I'M GOING TO STAY WITH MY GRANDPARENTS, IN OREGON.
HICKS SAYS THAT'S A GOOD PLACE...THERE'S A MAP FOR YOU, RIPLEY, HOW TO GET THERE. YOU CAN COME THERE AND STAY WITH ME, OKAY?

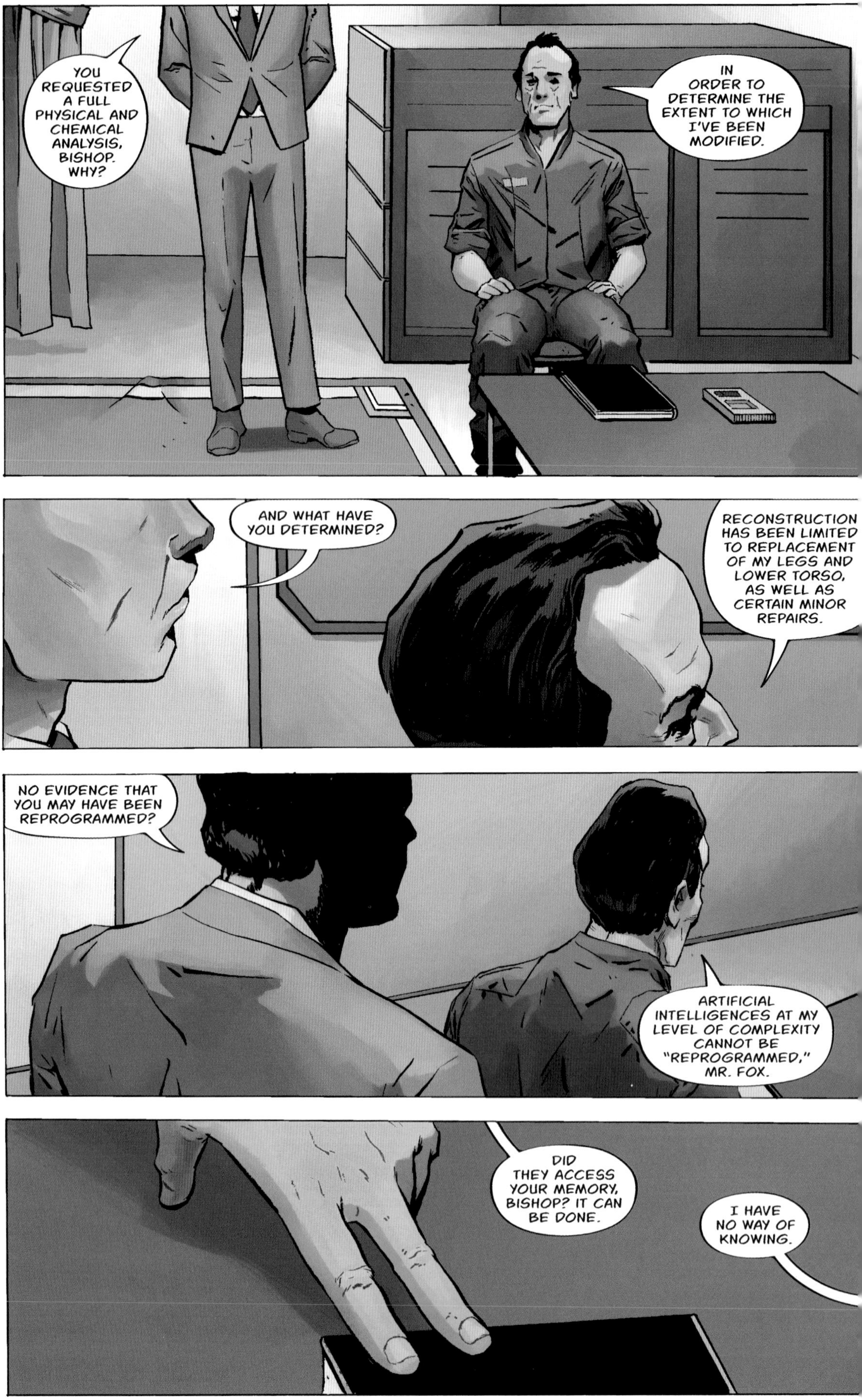
YOU REQUESTED A FULL PHYSICAL AND CHEMICAL ANALYSIS, BISHOP. WHY?
IN ORDER TO DETERMINE THE EXTENT TO WHICH I'VE BEEN MODIFIED.
AND WHAT HAVE YOU DETERMINED?
RECONSTRUCTION HAS BEEN LIMITED TO REPLACEMENT OF MY LEGS AND LOWER TORSO, AS WELL AS CERTAIN MINOR REPAIRS.
NO EVIDENCE THAT YOU MAY HAVE BEEN REPROGRAMMED?
ARTIFICIAL INTELLIGENCES AT MY LEVEL OF COMPLEXITY CANNOT BE "REPROGRAMMED," MR. FOX.
DID THEY ACCESS YOUR MEMORY, BISHOP? IT CAN BE DONE.
I HAVE NO WAY OF KNOWING.

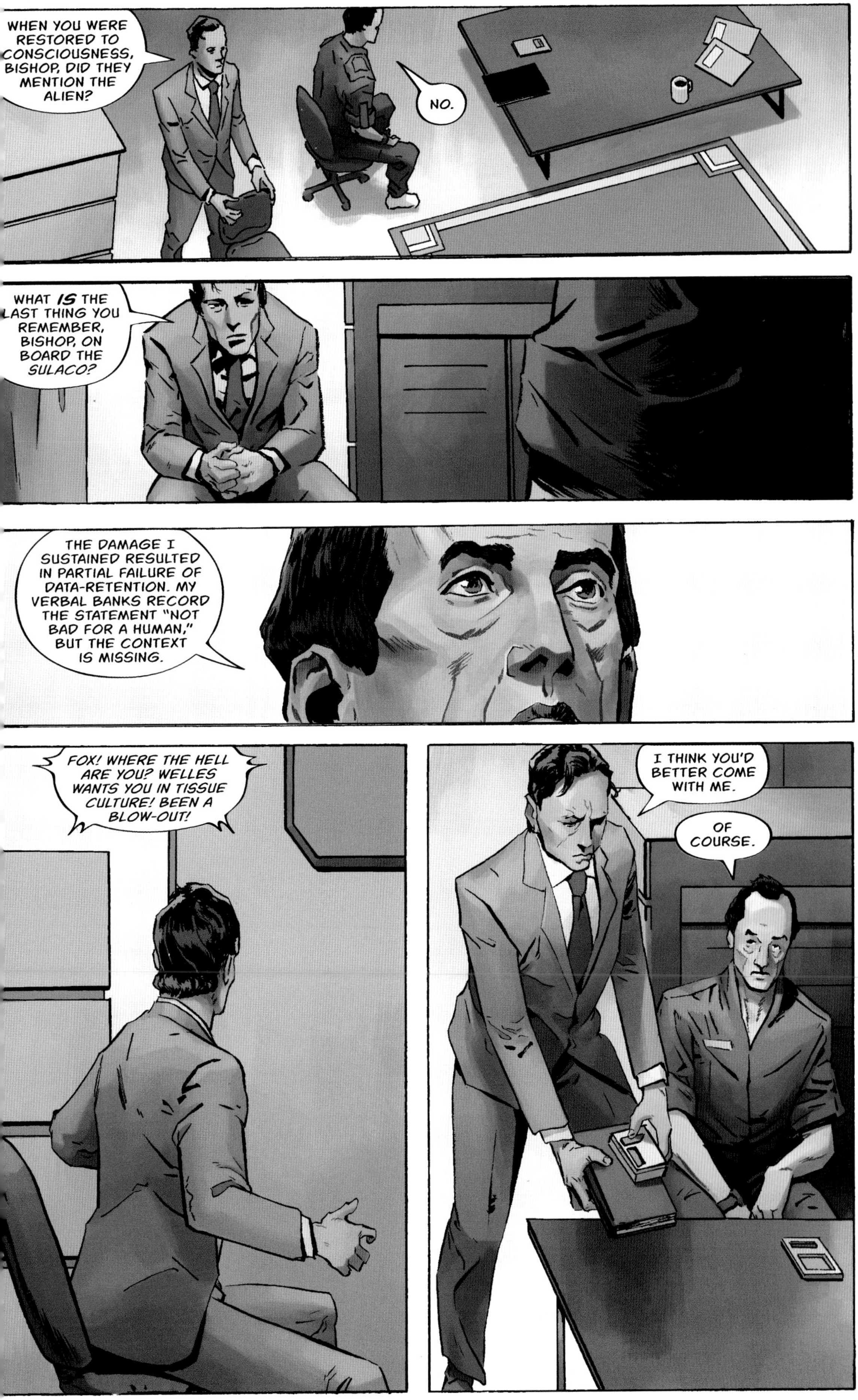
WHEN YOU WERE RESTORED TO CONSCIOUSNESS, BISHOP, DID THEY MENTION THE ALIEN?
NO.
WHAT *IS* THE LAST THING YOU REMEMBER, BISHOP, ON BOARD THE *SULACO*?
THE DAMAGE I SUSTAINED RESULTED IN PARTIAL FAILURE OF DATA-RETENTION. MY VERBAL BANKS RECORD THE STATEMENT "NOT BAD FOR A HUMAN," BUT THE CONTEXT IS MISSING.
FOX! WHERE THE HELL ARE YOU? WELLES WANTS YOU IN TISSUE CULTURE! BEEN A BLOW-OUT!
I THINK YOU'D BETTER COME WITH ME.
OF COURSE.

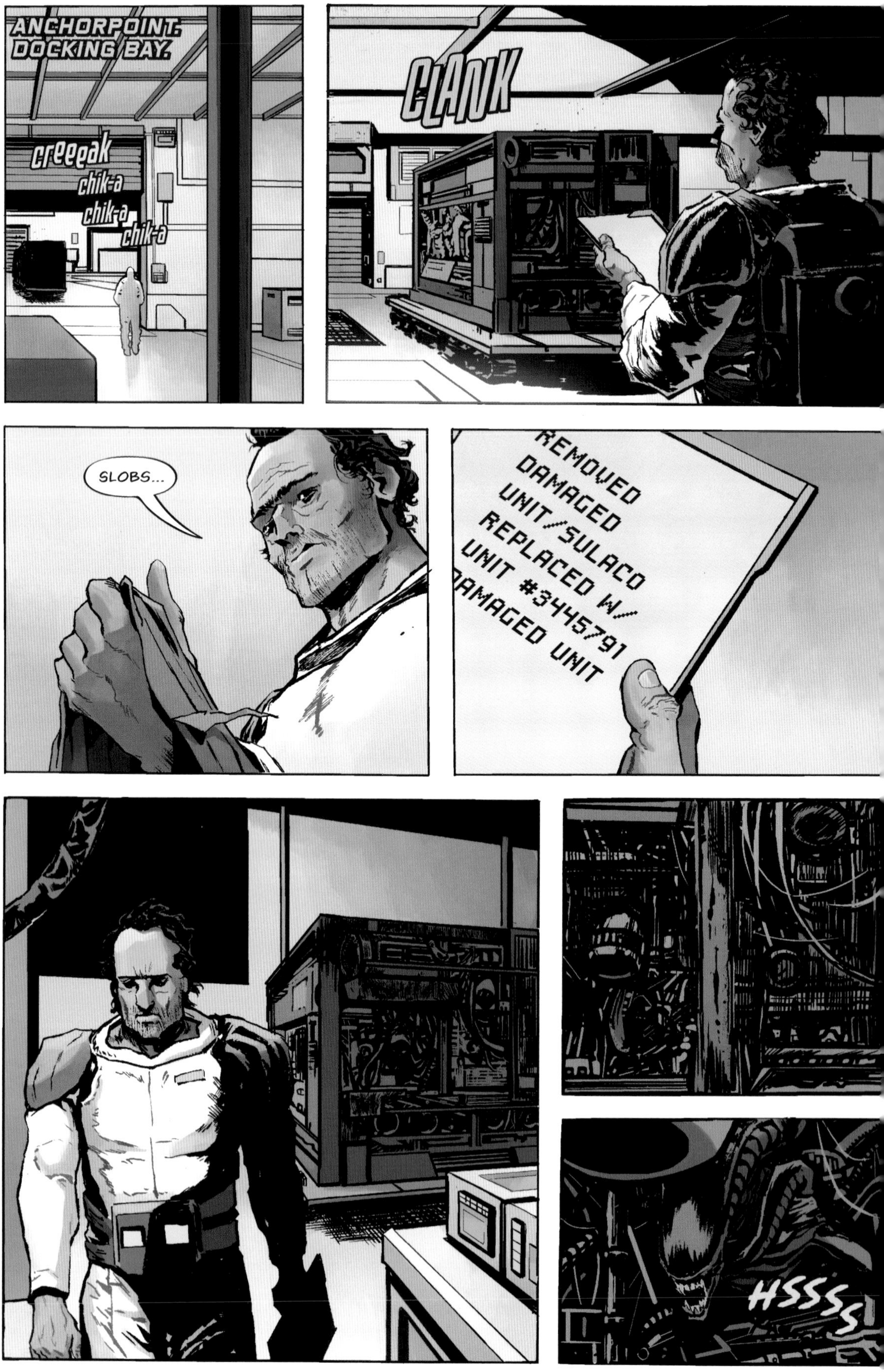
ANCHORPOINT.
DOCKING BAY.
creeeak
chik-a
chik-a
chik-a
CLANK
SLOBS...
REMOVED
DAMAGED
UNIT/SULACO
REPLACED W/
UNIT #3445791
DAMAGED UNIT
HSSSS

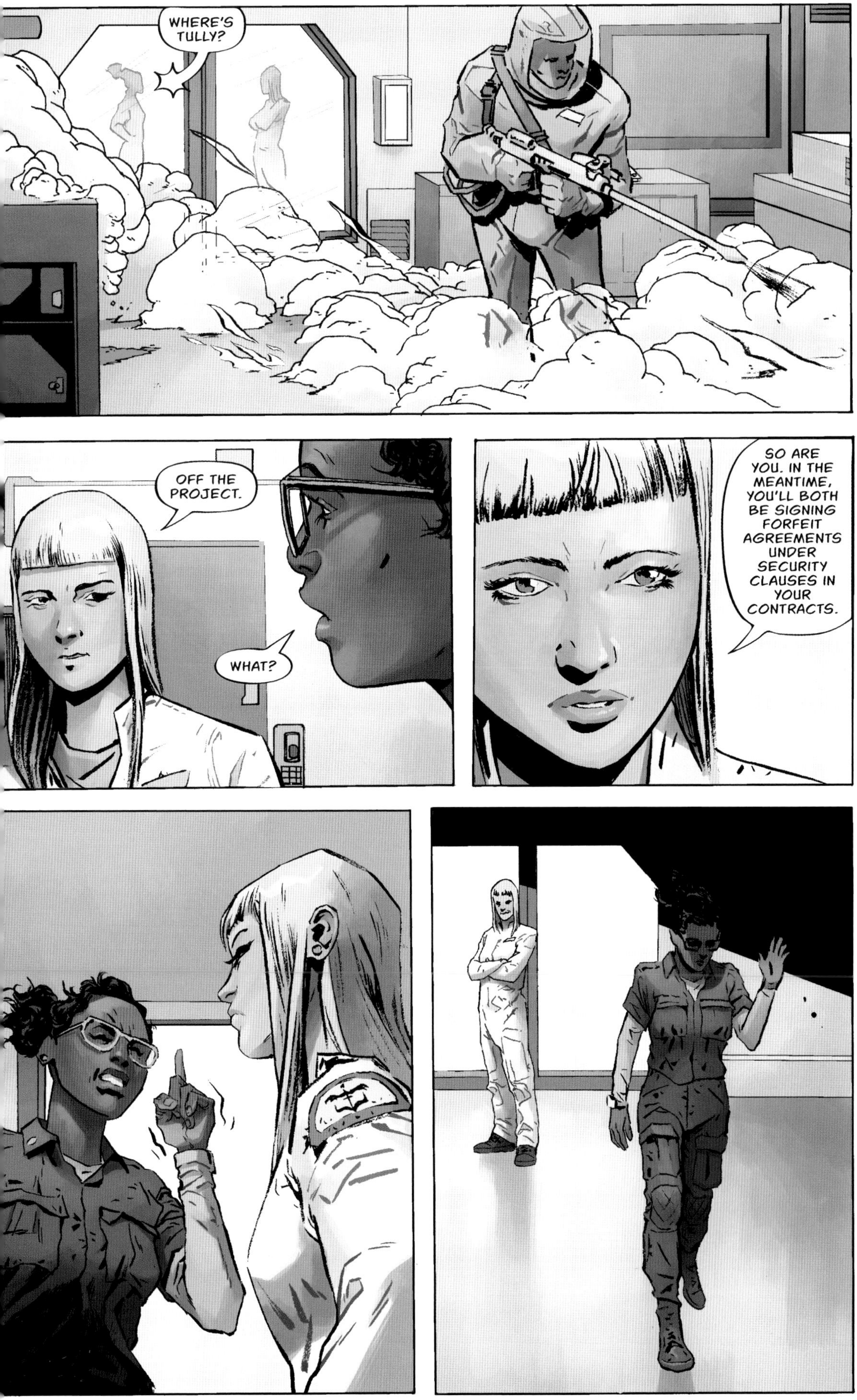
WHERE'S TULLY?
OFF THE PROJECT.
WHAT?
SO ARE YOU. IN THE MEANTIME, YOU'LL BOTH BE SIGNING FORFEIT AGREEMENTS UNDER SECURITY CLAUSES IN YOUR CONTRACTS.

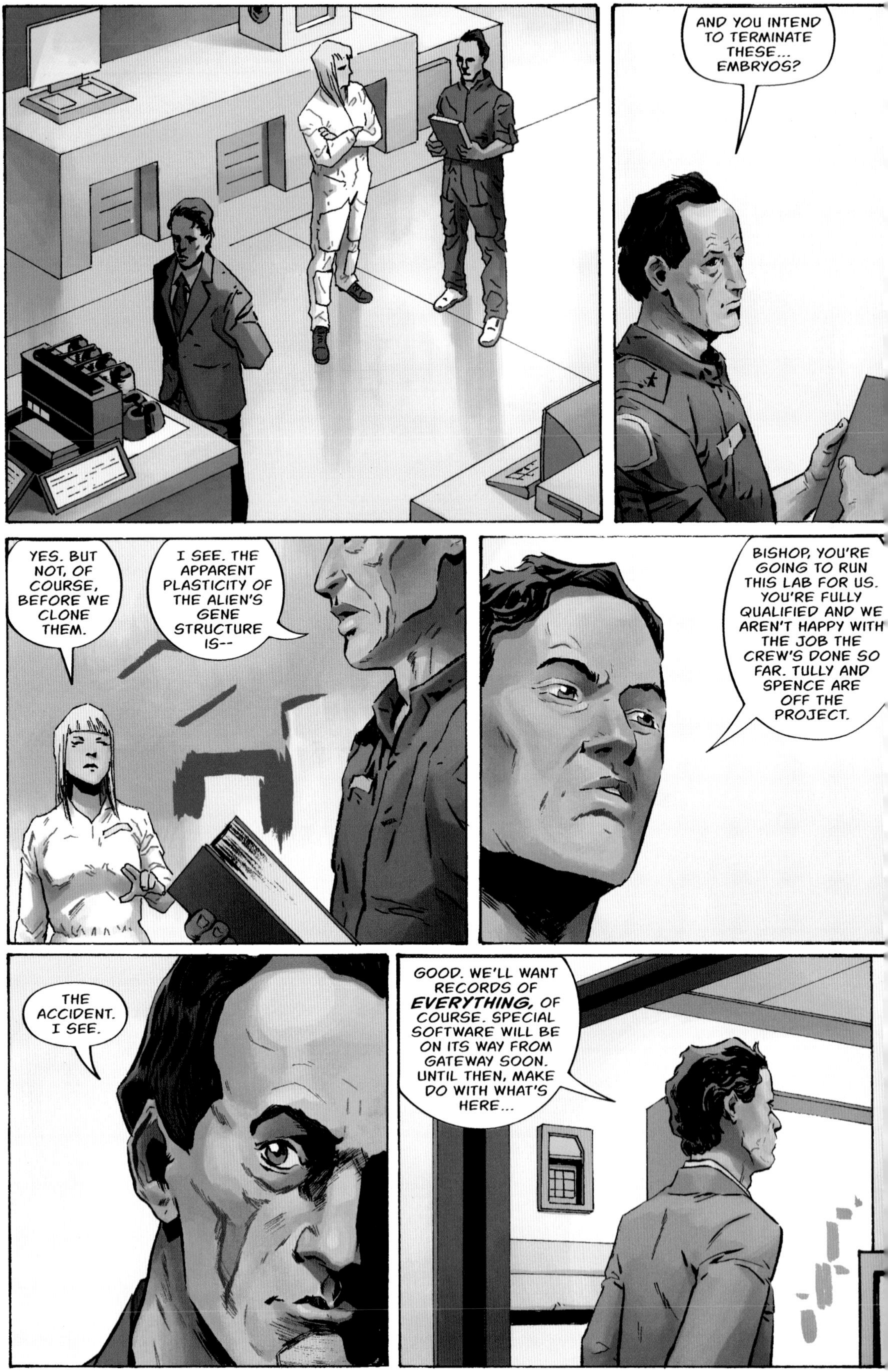
AND YOU INTEND TO TERMINATE THESE... EMBRYOS?
YES. BUT NOT, OF COURSE, BEFORE WE CLONE THEM.
I SEE. THE APPARENT PLASTICITY OF THE ALIEN'S GENE STRUCTURE IS--
BISHOP, YOU'RE GOING TO RUN THIS LAB FOR US. YOU'RE FULLY QUALIFIED AND WE AREN'T HAPPY WITH THE JOB THE CREW'S DONE SO FAR. TULLY AND SPENCE ARE OFF THE PROJECT.
THE ACCIDENT. I SEE.
GOOD. WE'LL WANT RECORDS OF *EVERYTHING,* OF COURSE. SPECIAL SOFTWARE WILL BE ON ITS WAY FROM GATEWAY SOON. UNTIL THEN, MAKE DO WITH WHAT'S HERE...

HICKS? SHE READY? SULACO'S REVISED ETD GIVES HER TWENTY MINUTES TO BOARD AND ICE DOWN.

SULACO/AUTOPILOT
DEPART.
BIOHAZARD SWEEP:
NEGATIVE
REPAIR STATUS:
POSITIVE
DESTINATION:
GATEWAY

HALLIDAY'LL GET YOU ON BOARD AND INTO YOUR HYPERSLEEP CHAMBER.

GOOD LUCK IN OREGON.

I KNOW.

WHERE THE HELL IS INCORPOINT?

HICKS...

YEAH?

AFFIRMATIVE.

AFFIRMATIVE.

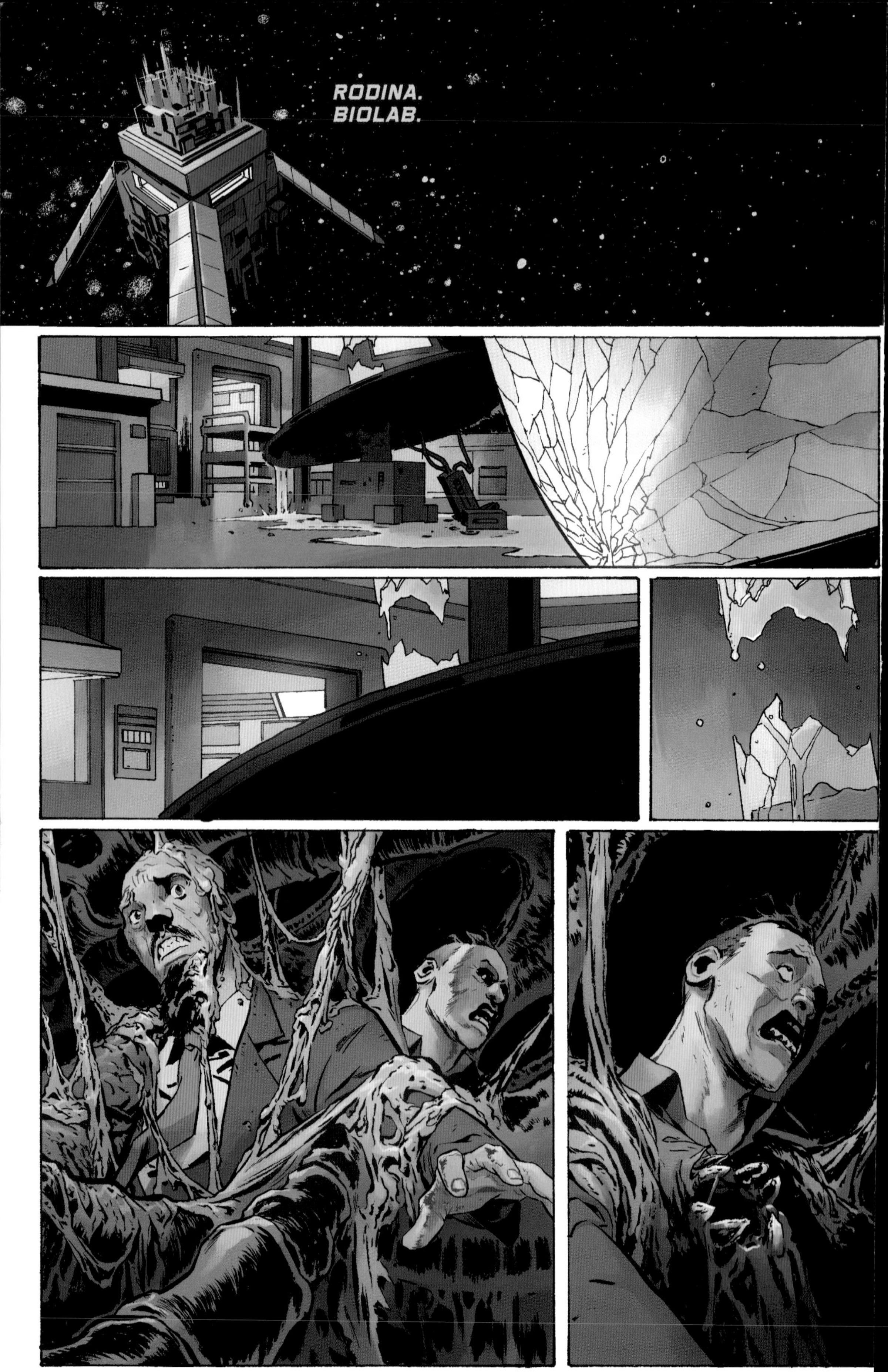
RODINA.
BIOLAB.

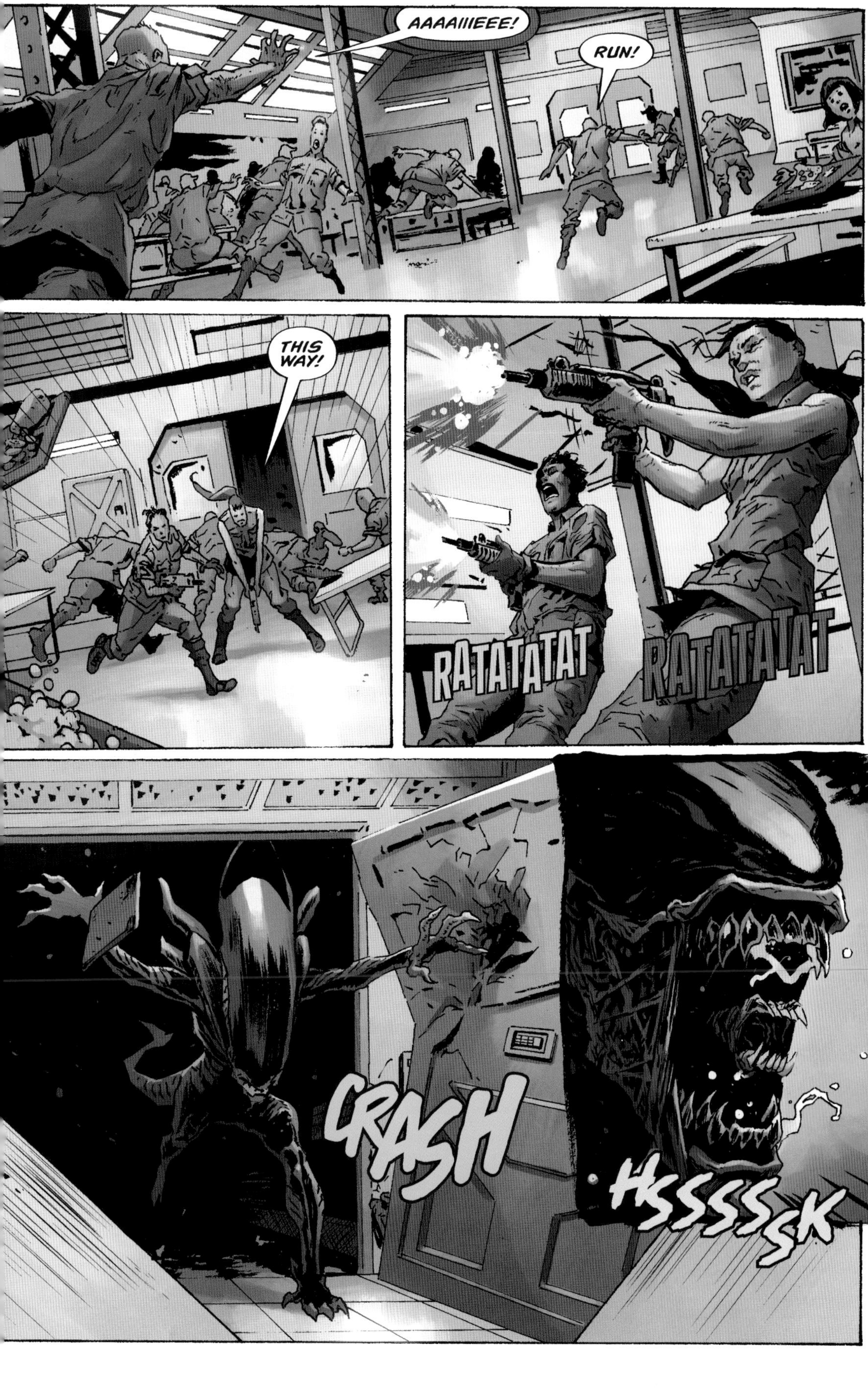
AAAAIIIEEE!
RUN!
THIS WAY!
RATATATAT
RATATATAT
CRASH
HSSSSSK

IT'S COMING!

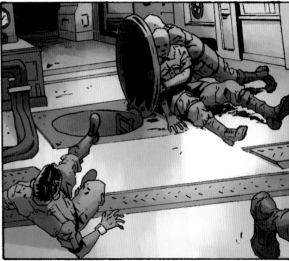

HSSSS

SLAM click

WHAM WHAM WHAM WHAM

SKREE

WHAM WHAM WHAM WHAM

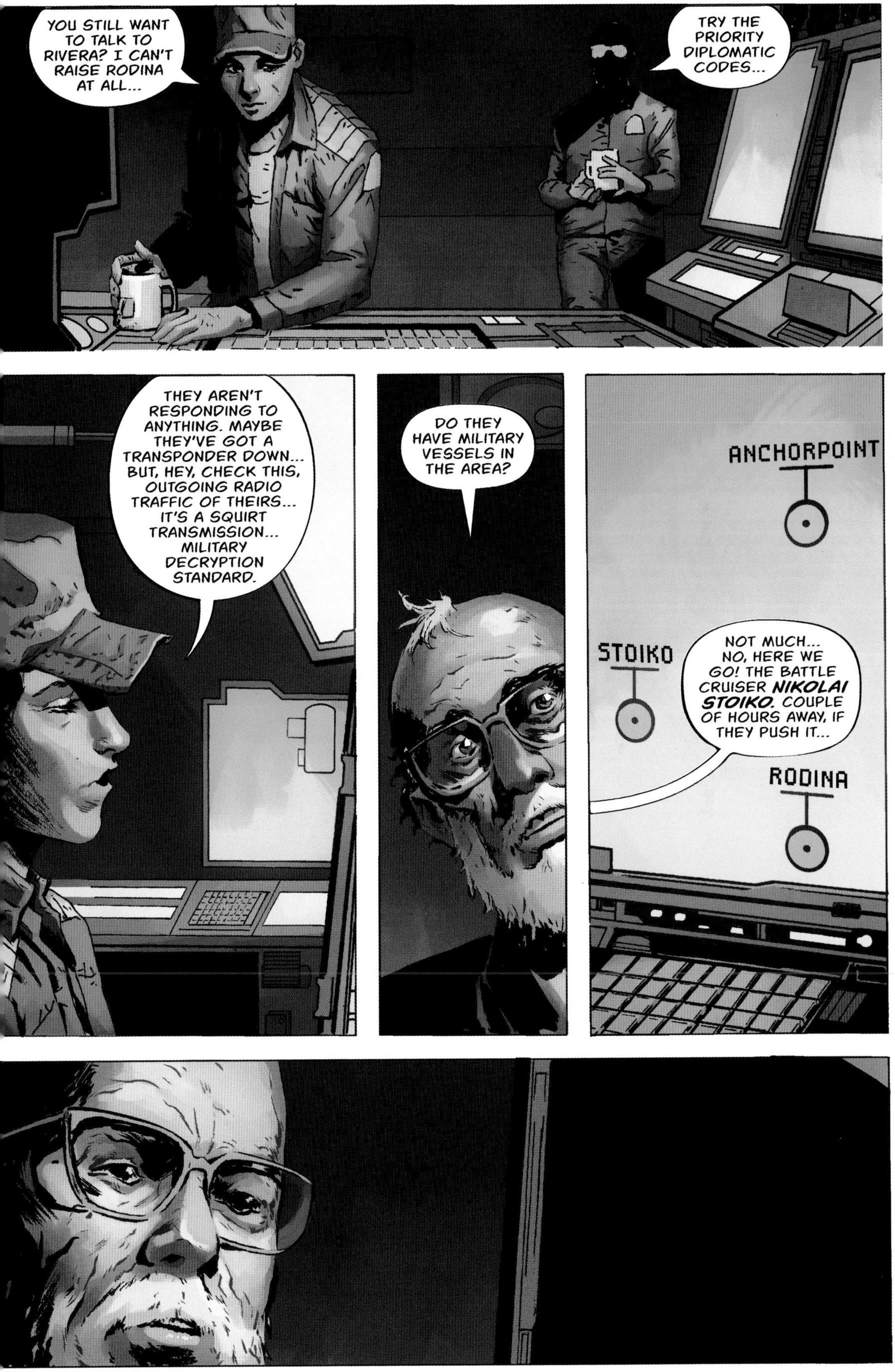
YOU STILL WANT TO TALK TO RIVERA? I CAN'T RAISE RODINA AT ALL...
TRY THE PRIORITY DIPLOMATIC CODES...
THEY AREN'T RESPONDING TO ANYTHING. MAYBE THEY'VE GOT A TRANSPONDER DOWN... BUT, HEY, CHECK THIS, OUTGOING RADIO TRAFFIC OF THEIRS... IT'S A SQUIRT TRANSMISSION... MILITARY DECRYPTION STANDARD.
DO THEY HAVE MILITARY VESSELS IN THE AREA?
ANCHORPOINT
STOIKO
NOT MUCH... NO, HERE WE GO! THE BATTLE CRUISER ***NIKOLAI STOIKO.*** COUPLE OF HOURS AWAY, IF THEY PUSH IT...
RODINA

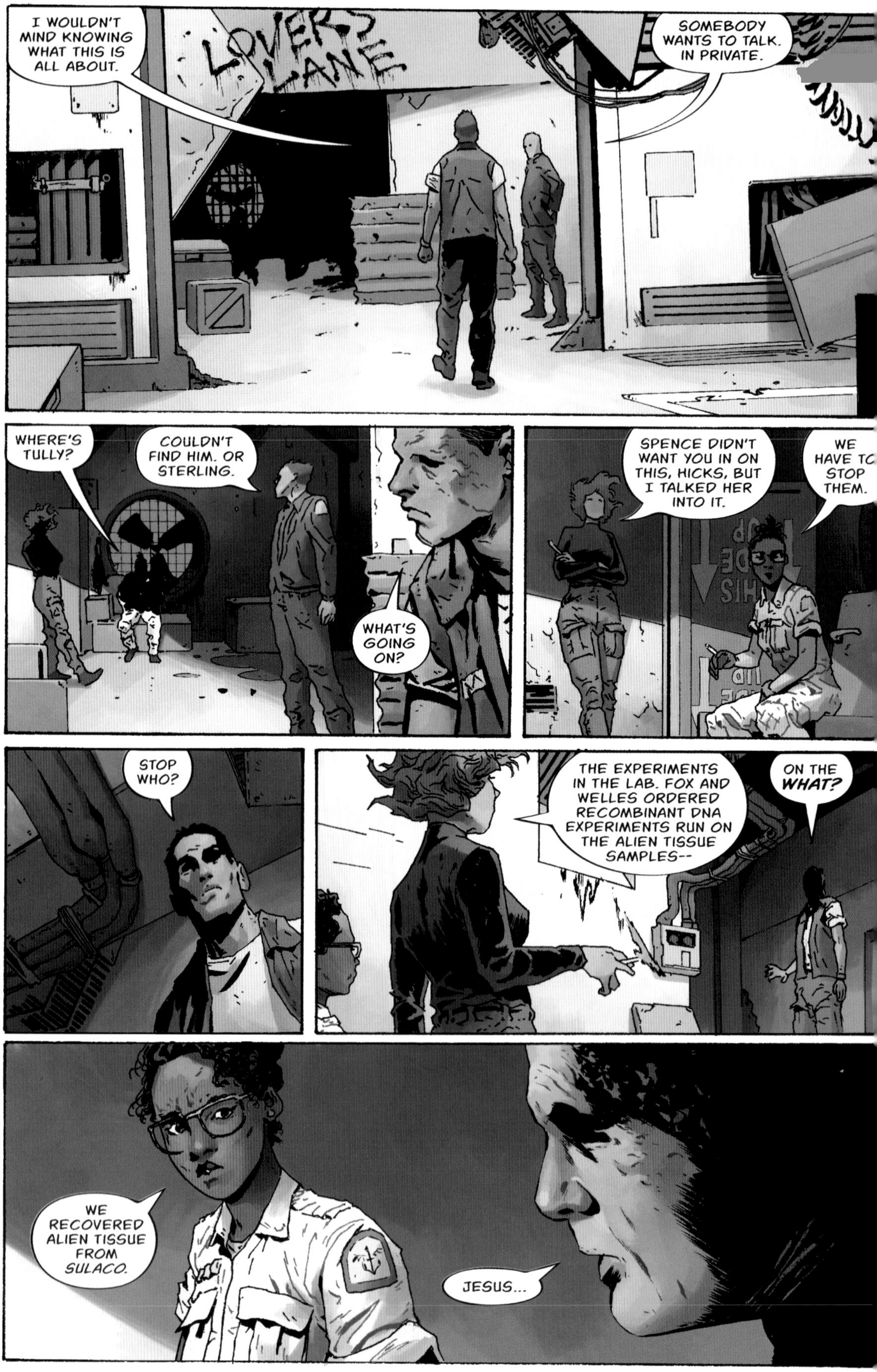
LOVERS LANE
I WOULDN'T MIND KNOWING WHAT THIS IS ALL ABOUT.
SOMEBODY WANTS TO TALK. IN PRIVATE.
WHERE'S TULLY?
COULDN'T FIND HIM. OR STERLING.
WHAT'S GOING ON?
SPENCE DIDN'T WANT YOU IN ON THIS, HICKS, BUT I TALKED HER INTO IT.
WE HAVE TO STOP THEM.
STOP WHO?
THE EXPERIMENTS IN THE LAB. FOX AND WELLES ORDERED RECOMBINANT DNA EXPERIMENTS RUN ON THE ALIEN TISSUE SAMPLES--
ON THE *WHAT?*
WE RECOVERED ALIEN TISSUE FROM *SULACO.*
JESUS...

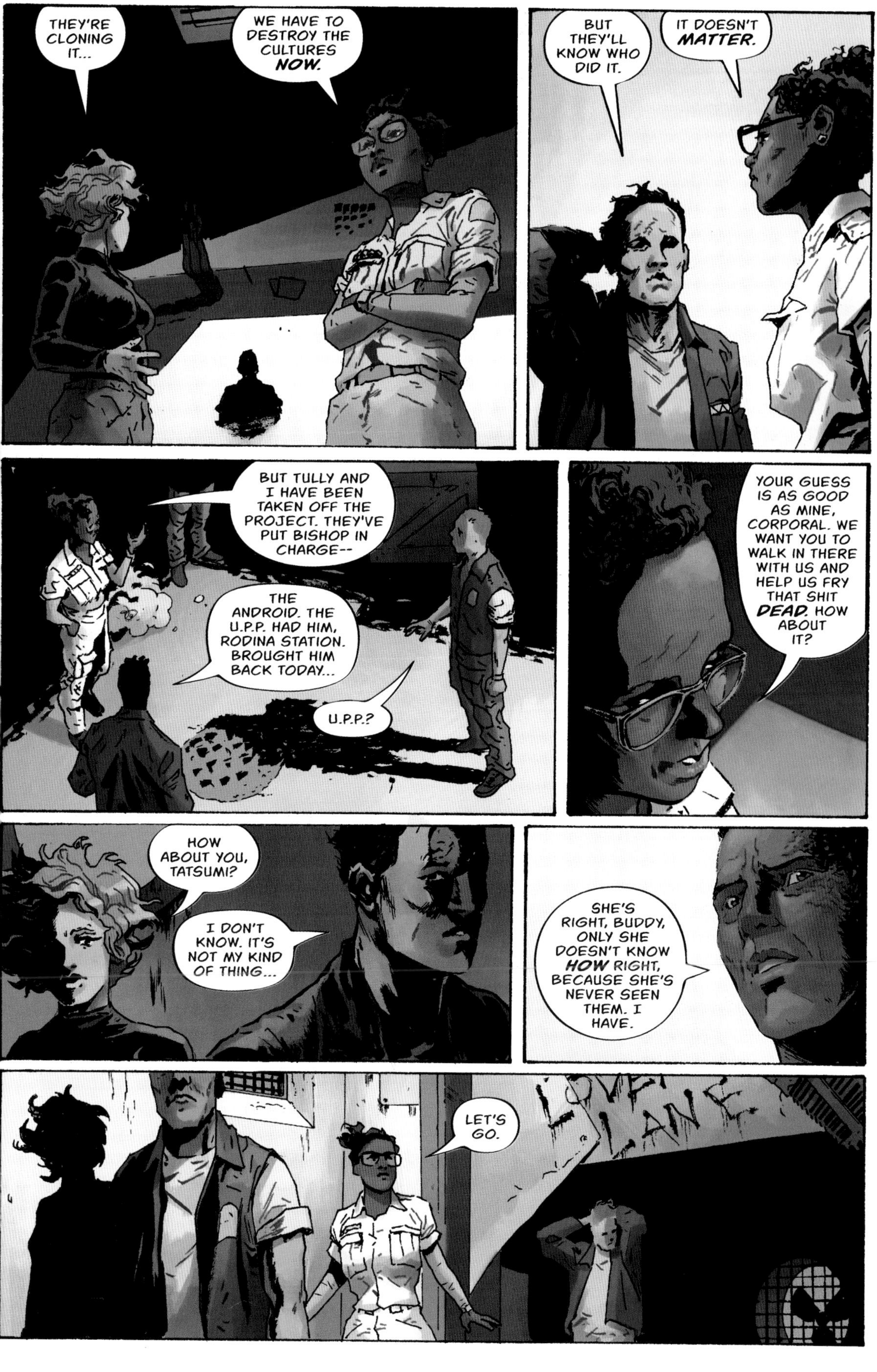
THEY'RE CLONING IT...
WE HAVE TO DESTROY THE CULTURES NOW.
BUT THEY'LL KNOW WHO DID IT.
IT DOESN'T MATTER.
BUT TULLY AND I HAVE BEEN TAKEN OFF THE PROJECT. THEY'VE PUT BISHOP IN CHARGE--
THE ANDROID. THE U.P.P. HAD HIM, RODINA STATION. BROUGHT HIM BACK TODAY...
U.P.P.?
YOUR GUESS IS AS GOOD AS MINE, CORPORAL. WE WANT YOU TO WALK IN THERE WITH US AND HELP US FRY THAT SHIT DEAD. HOW ABOUT IT?
HOW ABOUT YOU, TATSUMI?
I DON'T KNOW. IT'S NOT MY KIND OF THING...
SHE'S RIGHT, BUDDY, ONLY SHE DOESN'T KNOW HOW RIGHT, BECAUSE SHE'S NEVER SEEN THEM. I HAVE.
LET'S GO.

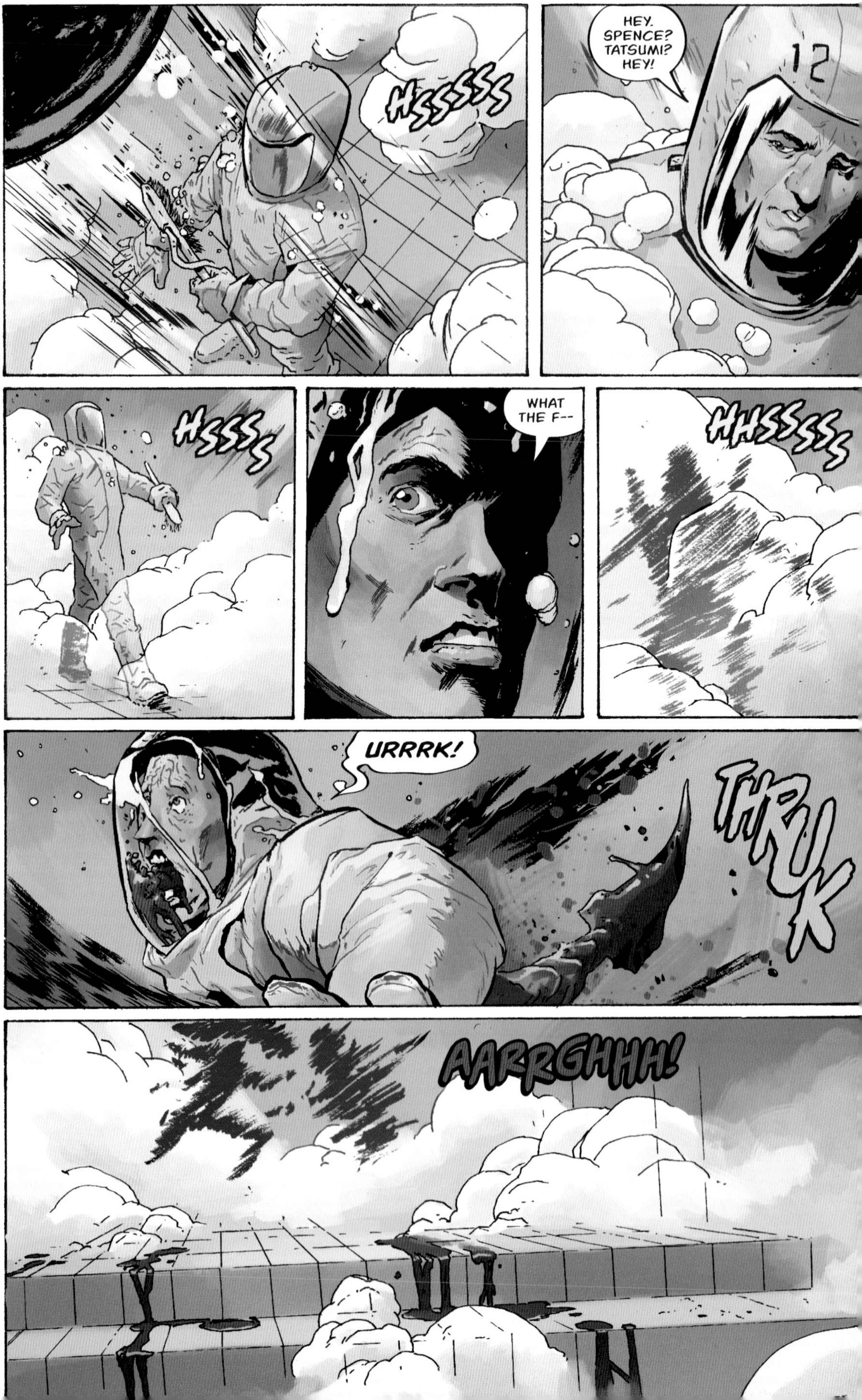
HSSSSS
HEY. SPENCE? TATSUMI? HEY!
12
HSSSS
WHAT THE F--
HHSSSSS
URRRK!
THRUK
AARRGHHH!

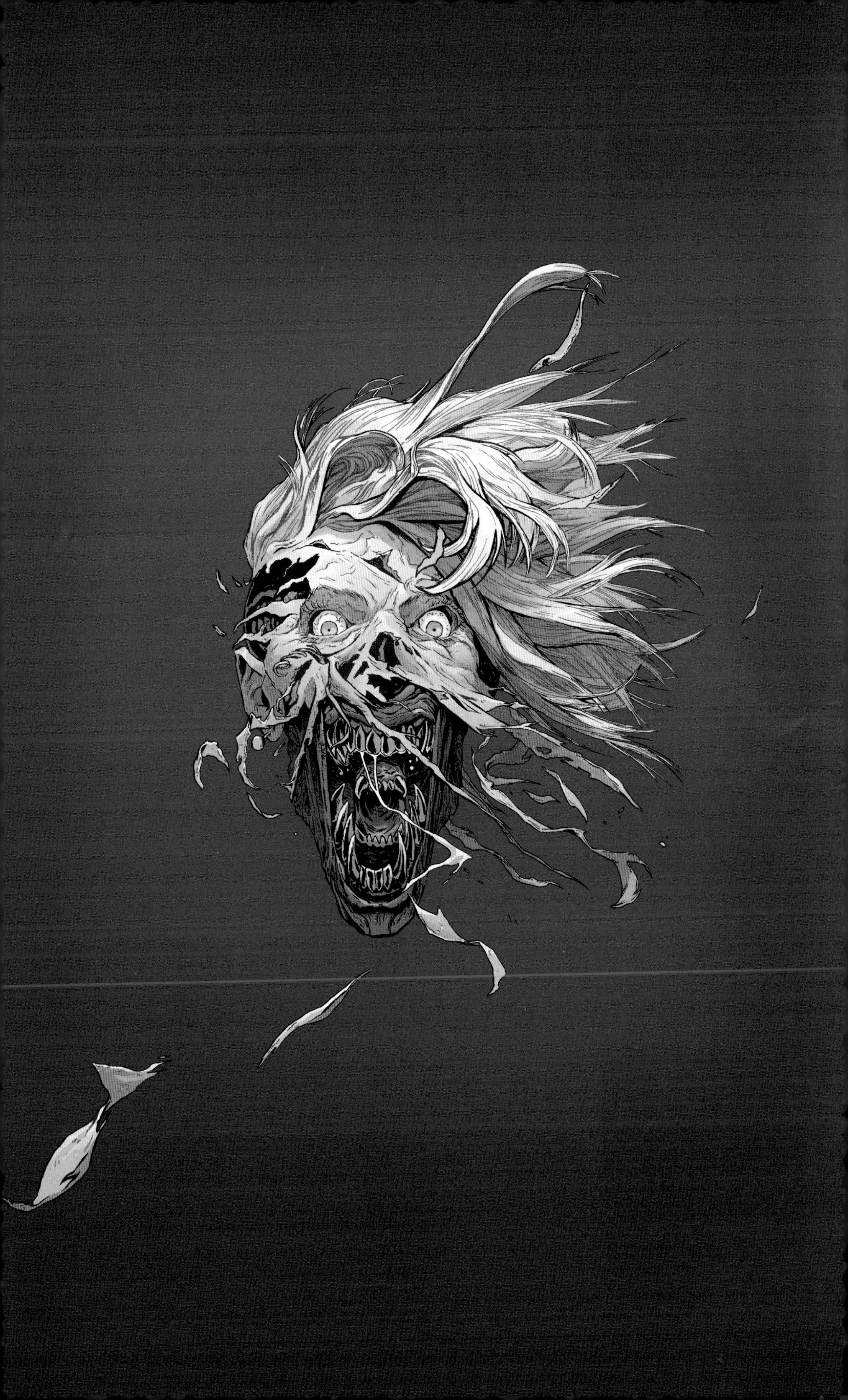

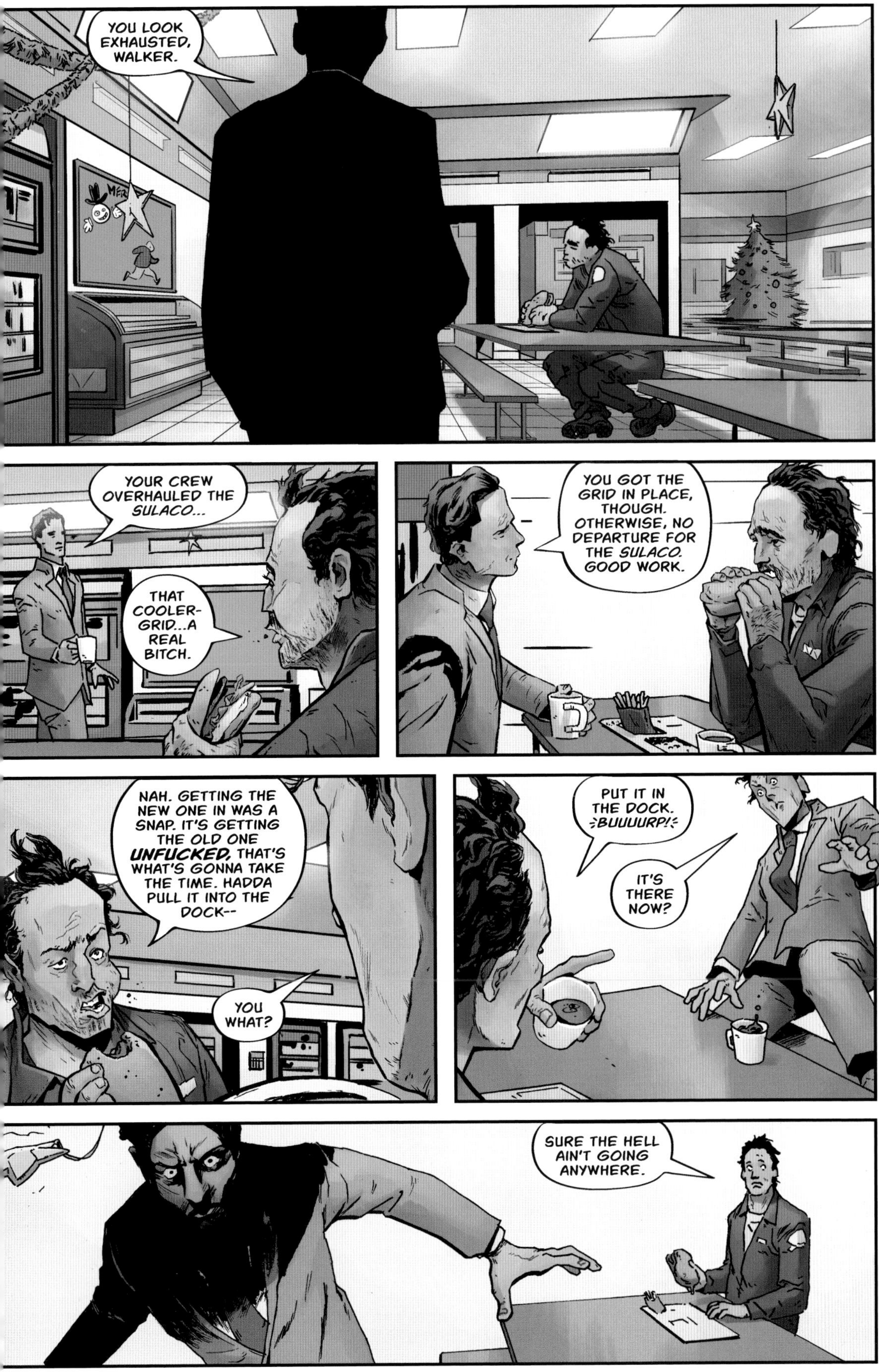
YOU LOOK EXHAUSTED, WALKER.
YOUR CREW OVERHAULED THE *SULACO*...
THAT COOLER-GRID...A REAL BITCH.
YOU GOT THE GRID IN PLACE, THOUGH. OTHERWISE, NO DEPARTURE FOR THE *SULACO*. GOOD WORK.
NAH. GETTING THE NEW ONE IN WAS A SNAP. IT'S GETTING THE OLD ONE ***UNFUCKED,*** THAT'S WHAT'S GONNA TAKE THE TIME. HADDA PULL IT INTO THE DOCK--
YOU WHAT?
PUT IT IN THE DOCK. *BUUUURP!*
IT'S THERE NOW?
SURE THE HELL AIN'T GOING ANYWHERE.

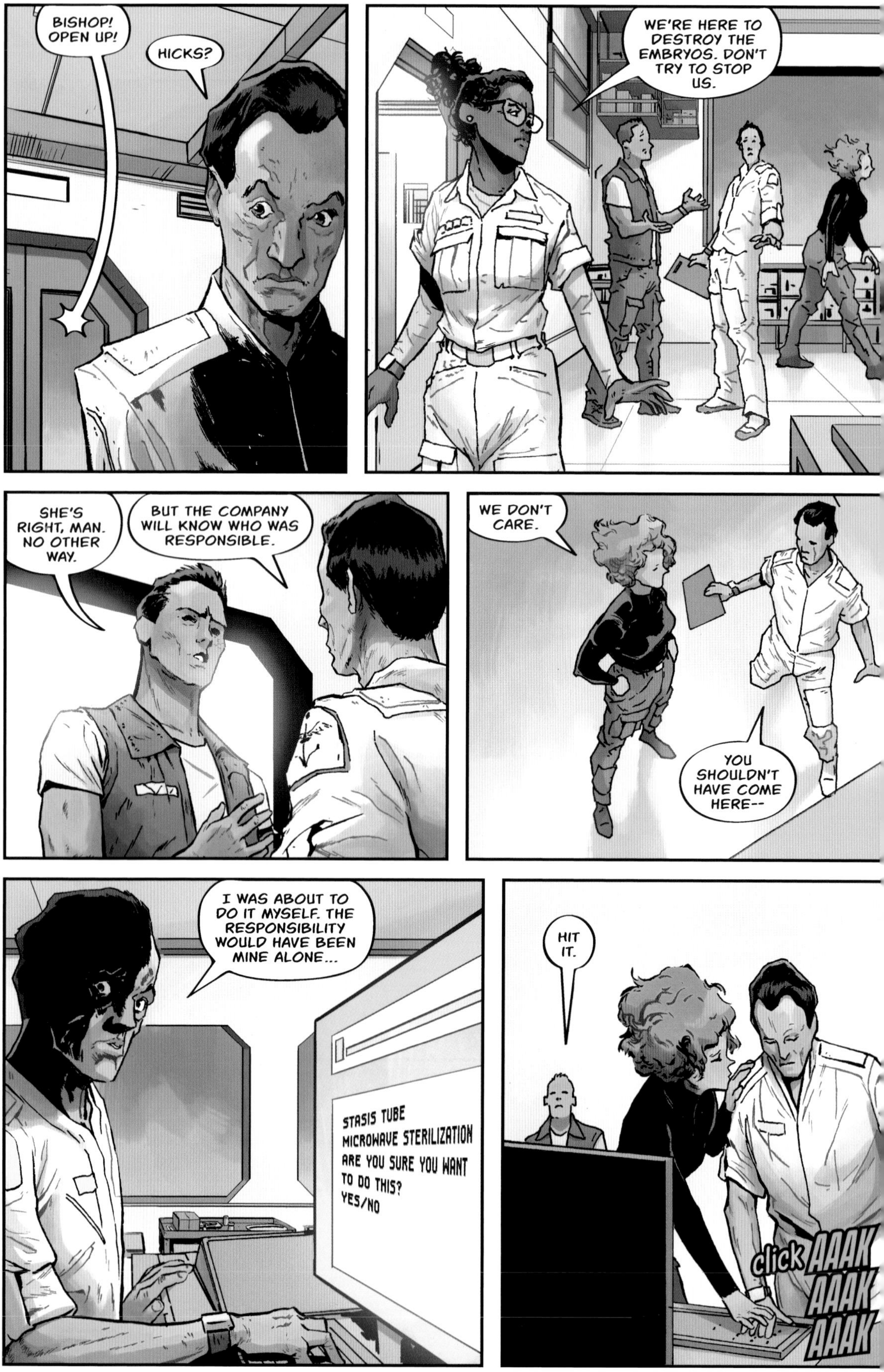
BISHOP! OPEN UP!
HICKS?
WE'RE HERE TO DESTROY THE EMBRYOS. DON'T TRY TO STOP US.
SHE'S RIGHT, MAN. NO OTHER WAY.
BUT THE COMPANY WILL KNOW WHO WAS RESPONSIBLE.
WE DON'T CARE.
YOU SHOULDN'T HAVE COME HERE--
I WAS ABOUT TO DO IT MYSELF. THE RESPONSIBILITY WOULD HAVE BEEN MINE ALONE...
STASIS TUBE
MICROWAVE STERILIZATION
ARE YOU SURE YOU WANT
TO DO THIS?
YES/NO
HIT IT.
click AAAK AAAK AAAK

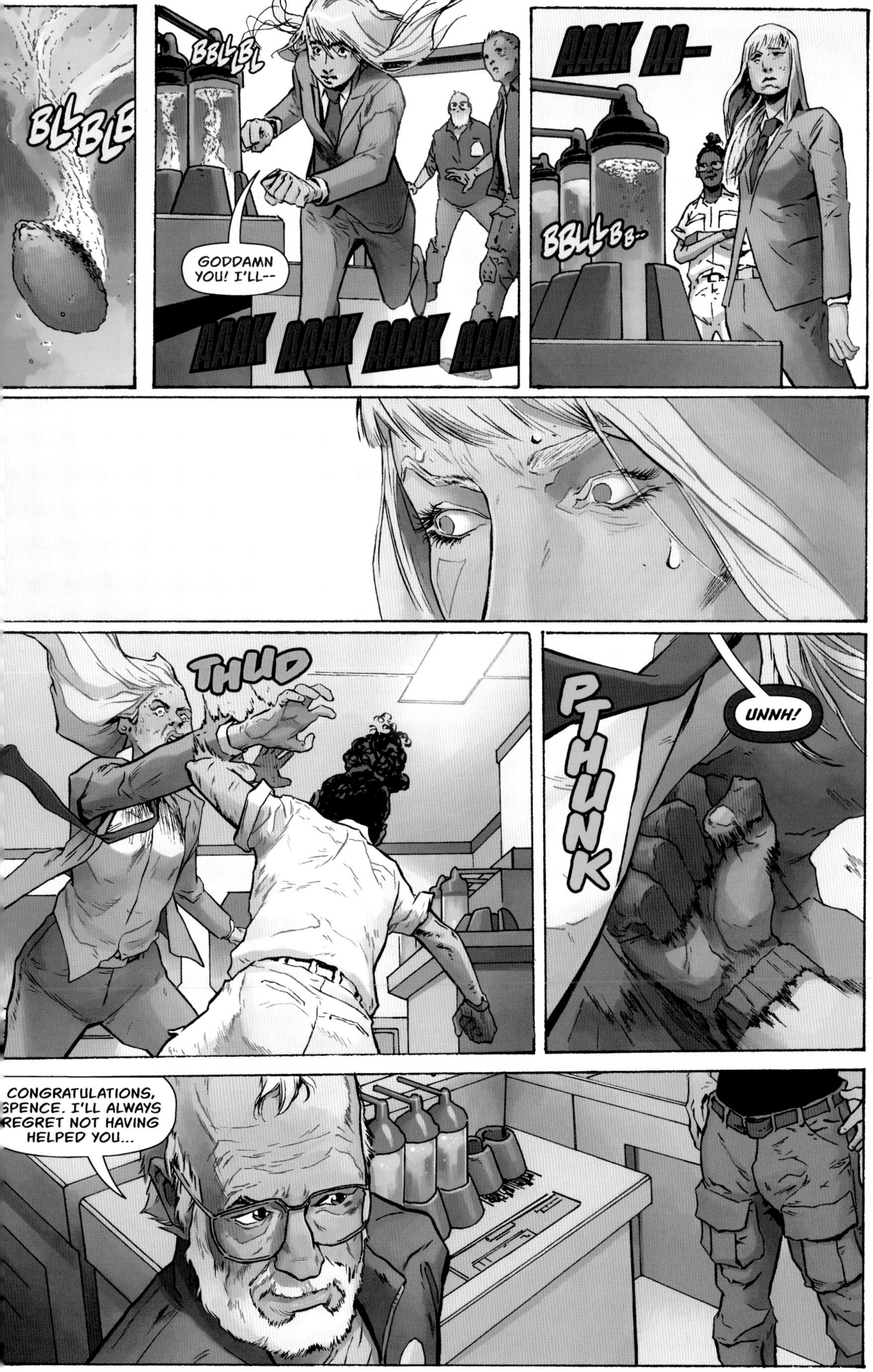
BLLBLE
BBLLBL
GODDAMN YOU! I'LL--
AAAK AAAK AAAK AAA
AAAK AA--
BBLLLBB--
THUD
PTHUNK
UNNH!
CONGRATULATIONS, SPENCE. I'LL ALWAYS REGRET NOT HAVING HELPED YOU...

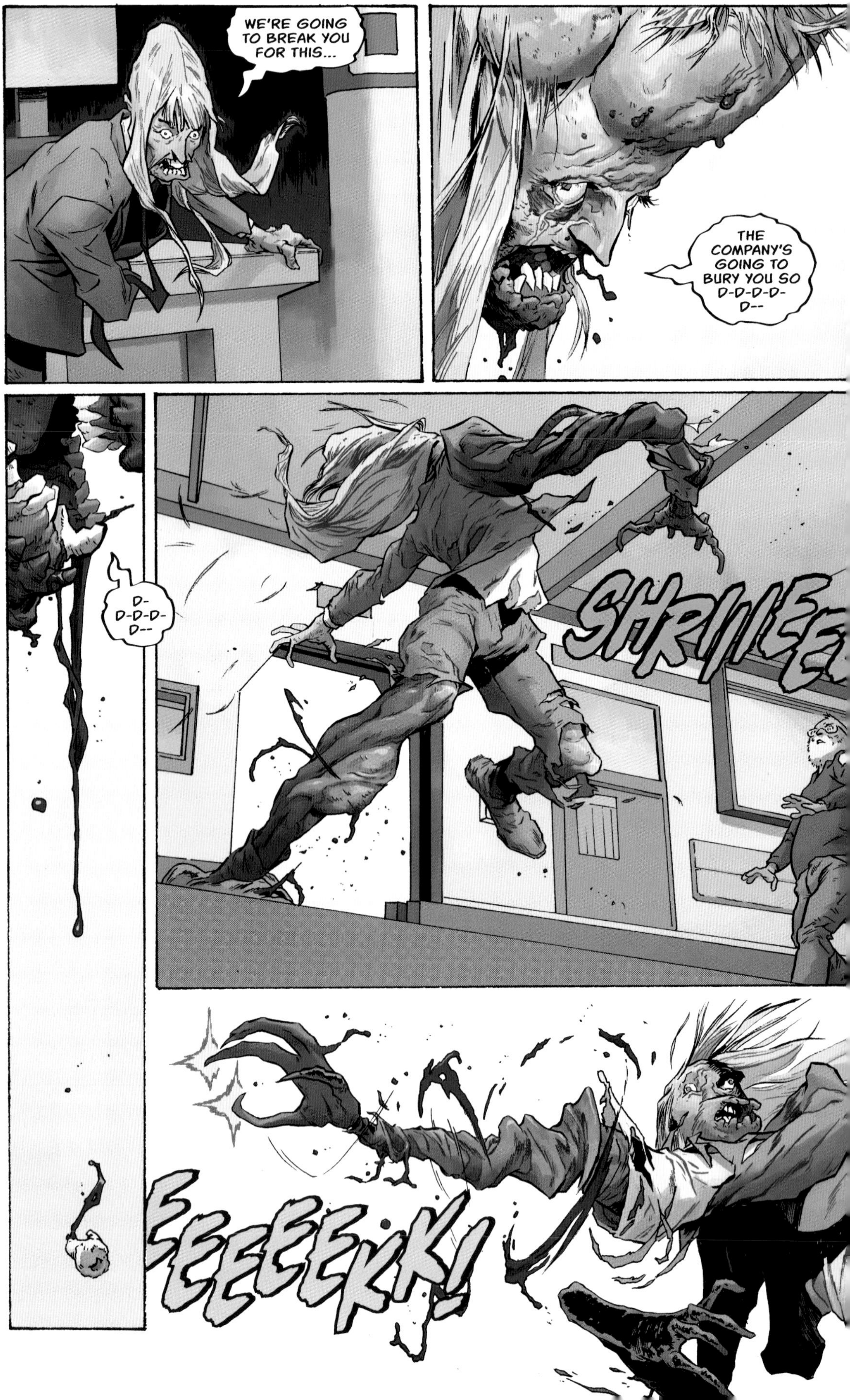
WE'RE GOING TO BREAK YOU FOR THIS...
THE COMPANY'S GOING TO BURY YOU SO D-D-D-D-D--
D- D-D-D-D--
SHRIIIEEEEEEEEKK!

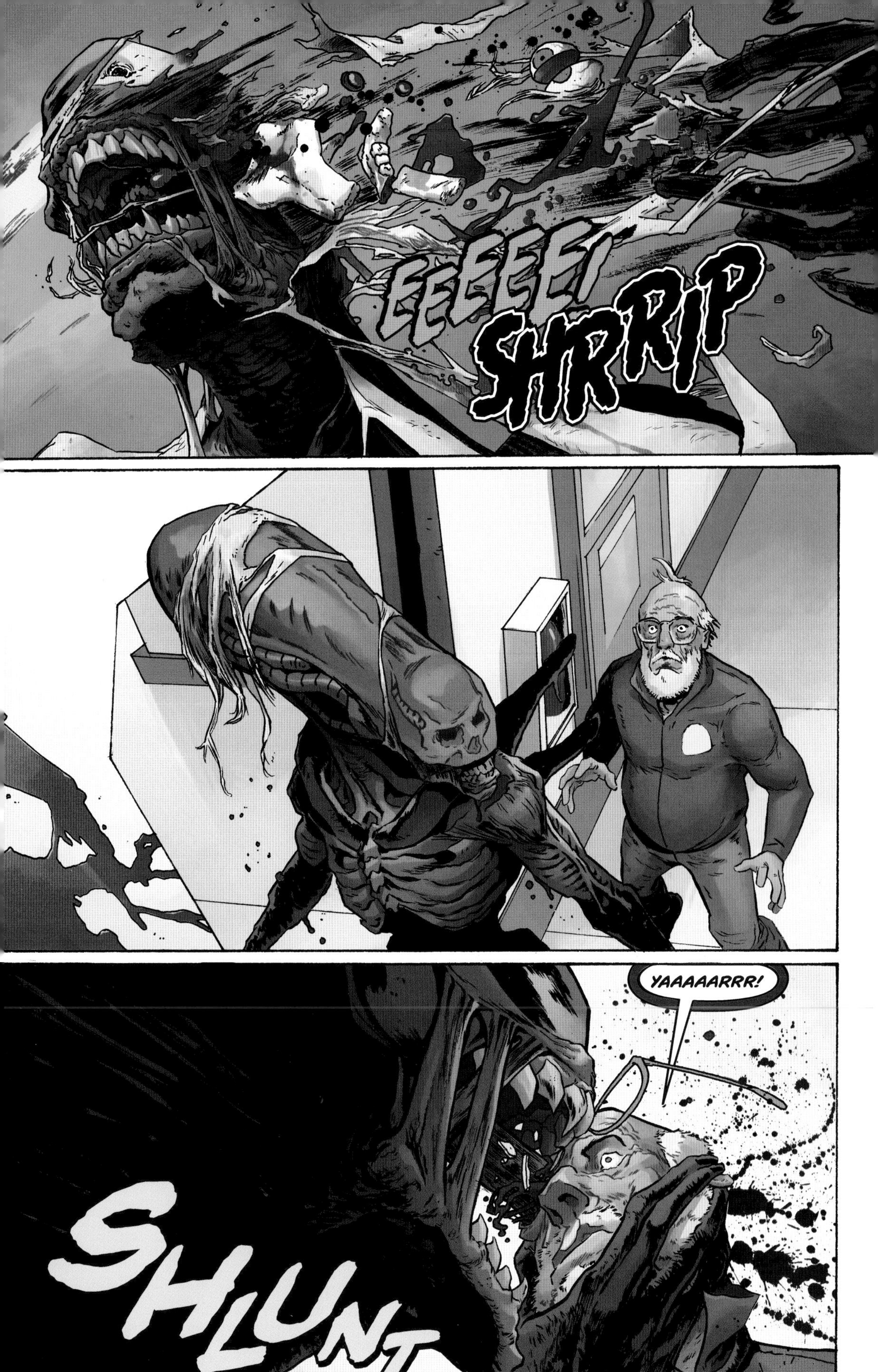
EEEEEI
SHRRIP
YAAAAARRR!
SHLUNT

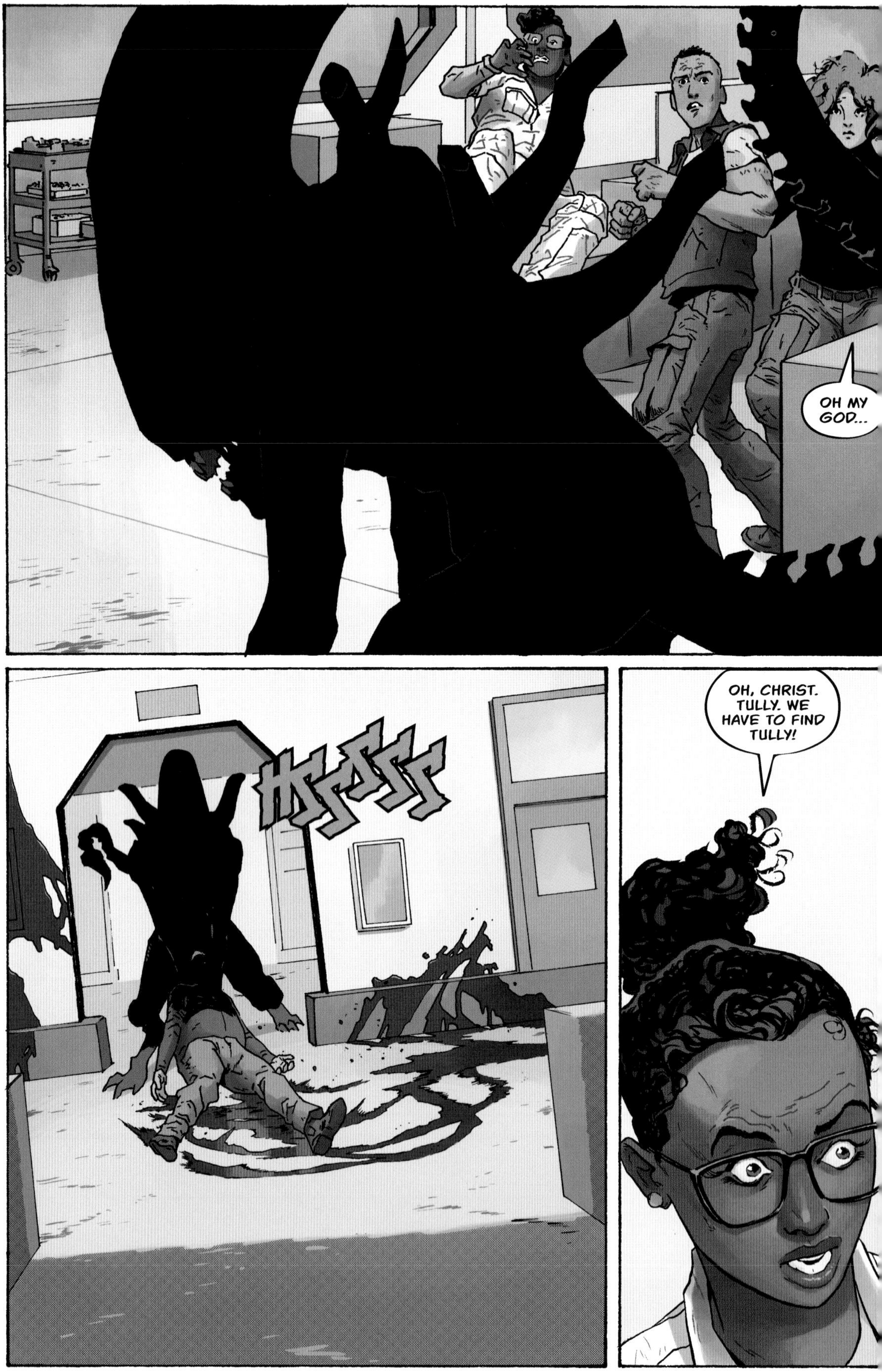
OH MY GOD...
HSSSS
OH, CHRIST. TULLY. WE HAVE TO FIND TULLY!

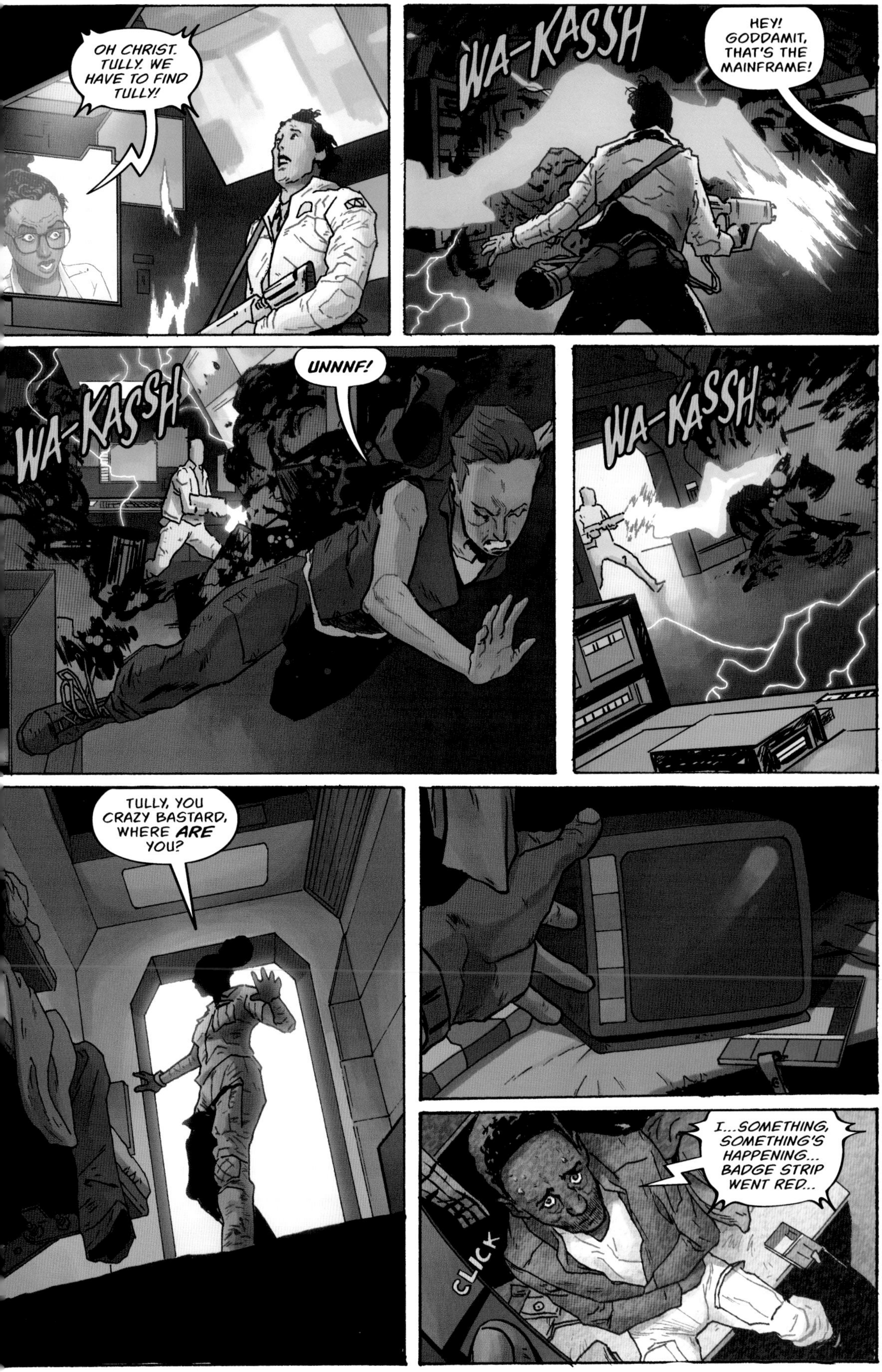
OH CHRIST. TULLY. WE HAVE TO FIND TULLY!
WA-KASSH
HEY! GODDAMIT, THAT'S THE MAINFRAME!
WA-KASSH
UNNNF!
WA-KASSH
TULLY, YOU CRAZY BASTARD, WHERE ARE YOU?
CLICK
I...SOMETHING, SOMETHING'S HAPPENING... BADGE STRIP WENT RED...

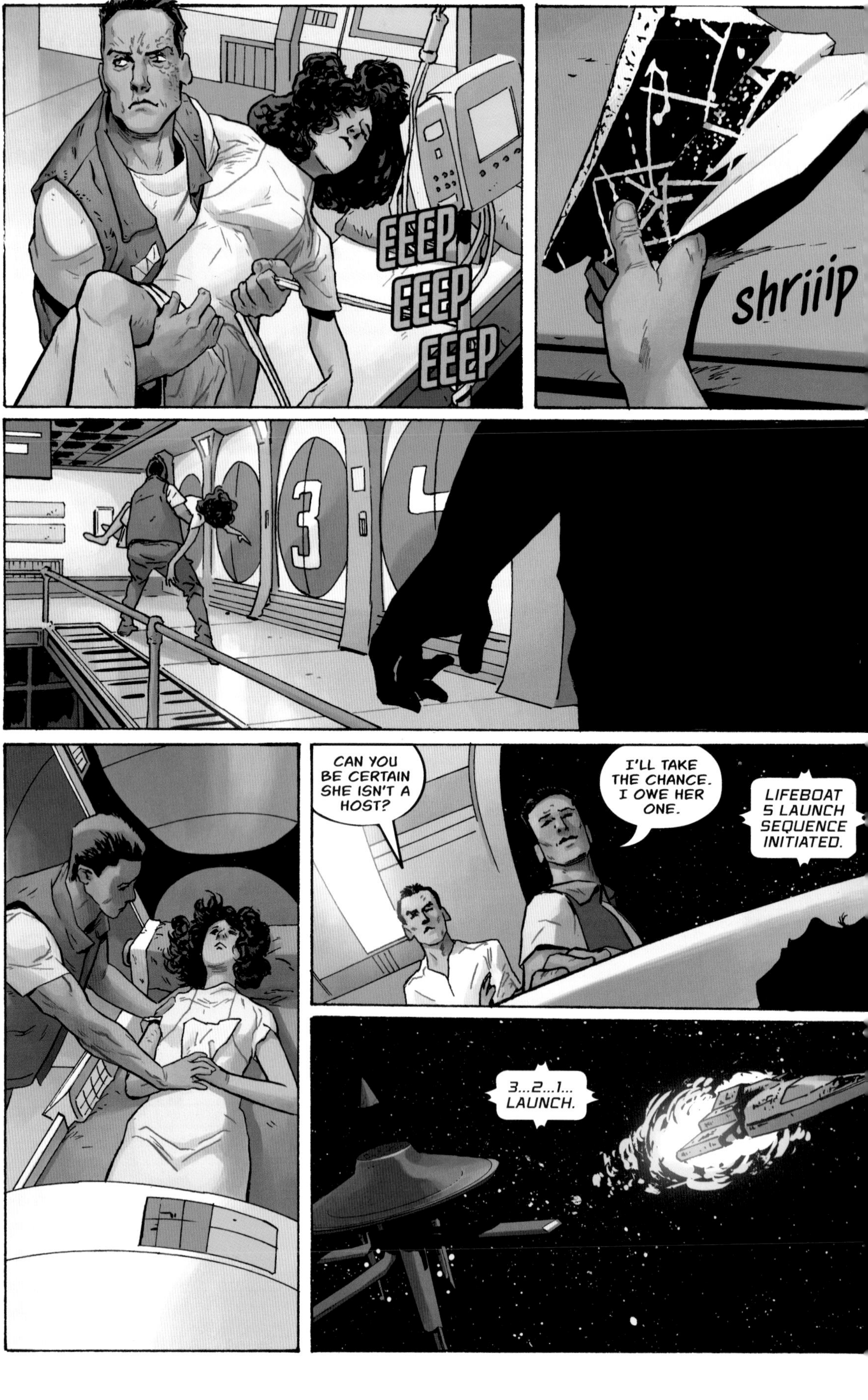
EEEP
EEEP
EEEP
shriiip
CAN YOU BE CERTAIN SHE ISN'T A HOST?
I'LL TAKE THE CHANCE. I OWE HER ONE.
LIFEBOAT 5 LAUNCH SEQUENCE INITIATED.
3...2...1... LAUNCH.

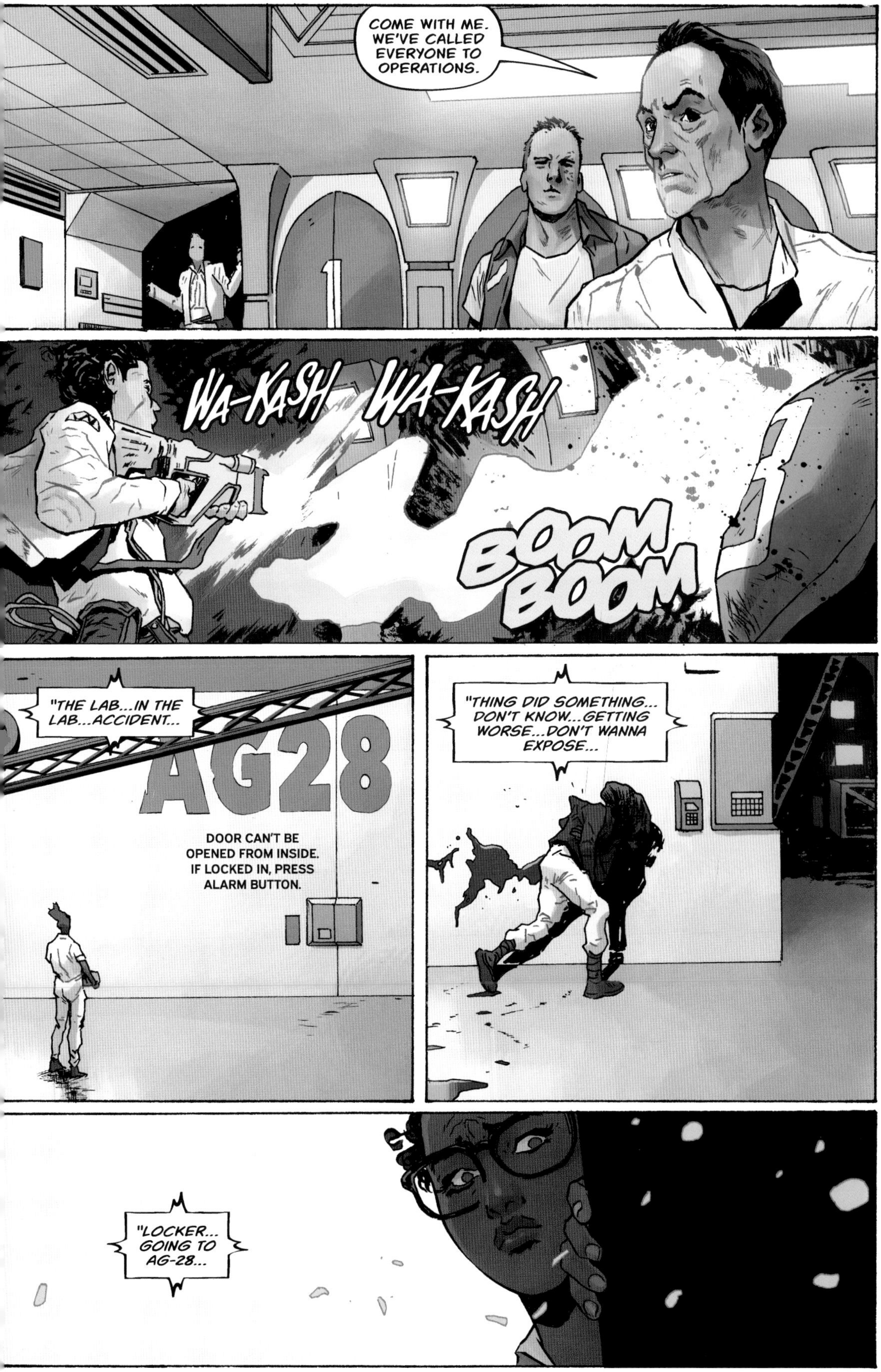
COME WITH ME. WE'VE CALLED EVERYONE TO OPERATIONS.
WA-KASH WA-KASH
BOOM BOOM
"THE LAB...IN THE LAB...ACCIDENT...
AG28
DOOR CAN'T BE OPENED FROM INSIDE. IF LOCKED IN, PRESS ALARM BUTTON.
"THING DID SOMETHING... DON'T KNOW...GETTING WORSE...DON'T WANNA EXPOSE...
"LOCKER... GOING TO AG-28...

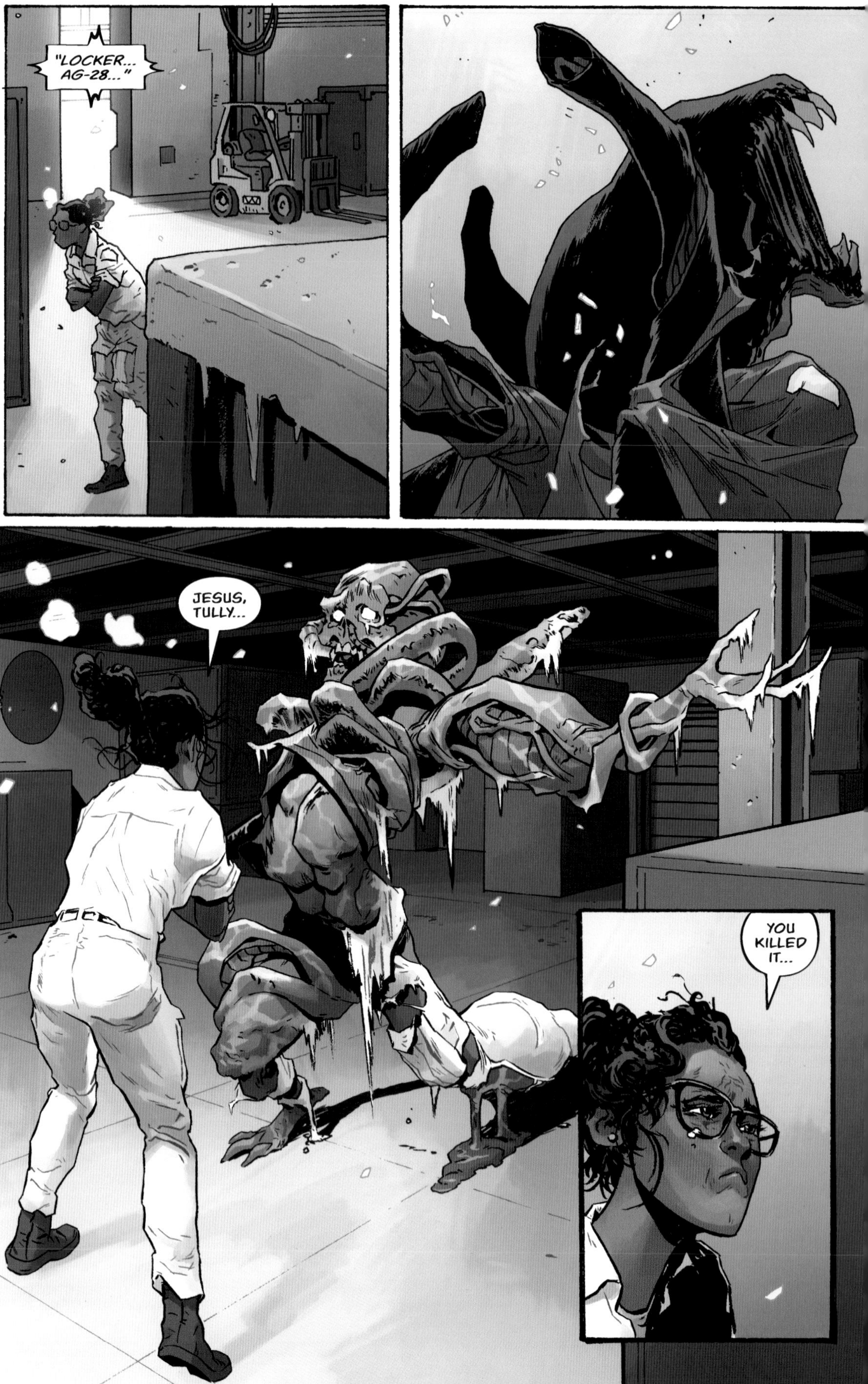
"LOCKER... AG-28..."
JESUS, TULLY...
YOU KILLED IT...

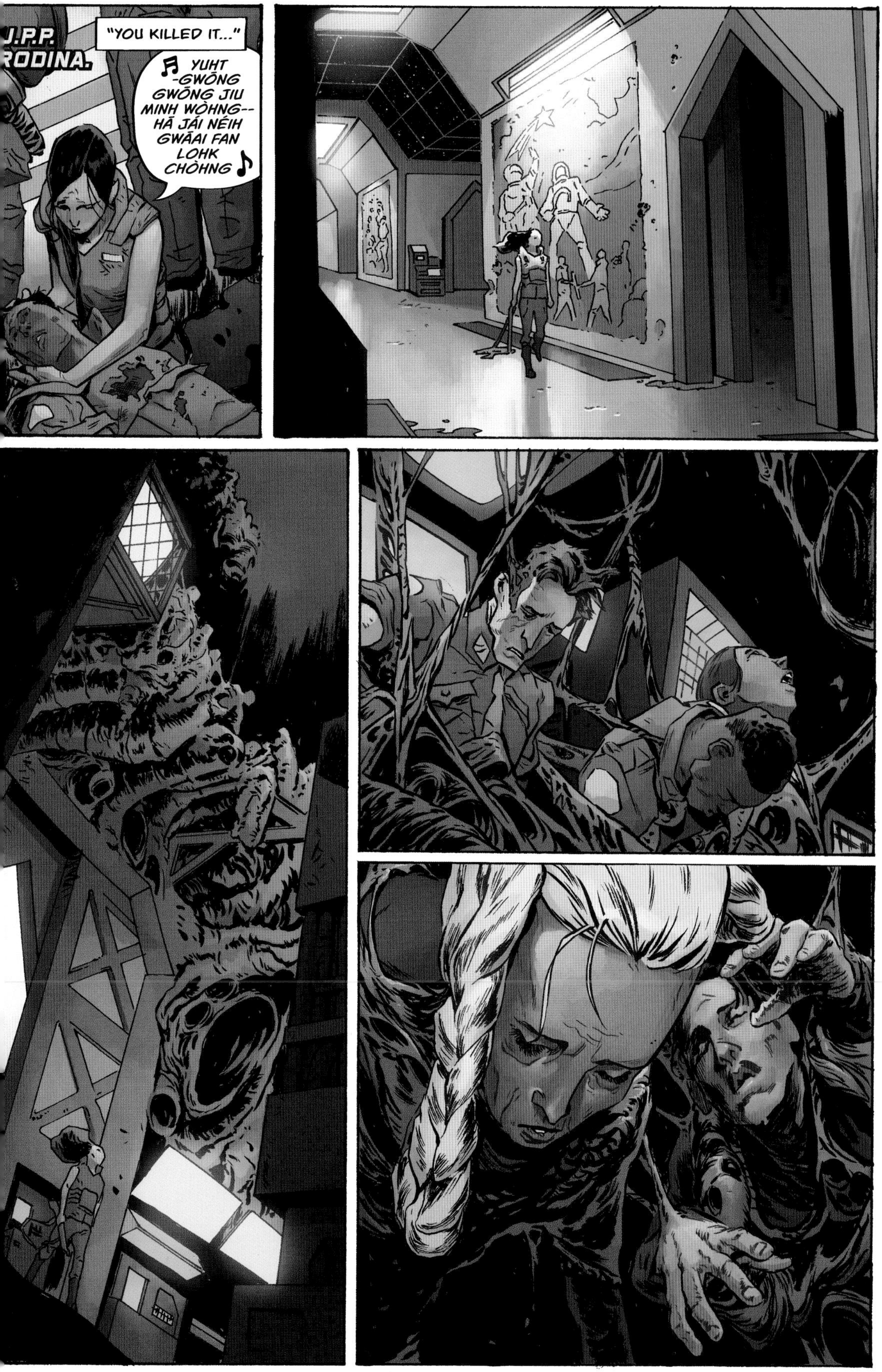
J.P.P.
RODINA.
"YOU KILLED IT..."
♬ YUHT -GWŌNG GWŌNG JIU MINH WÒHNG-- HĀ JÁI NÉIH GWĀAI FAN LOHK CHÒHNG ♪

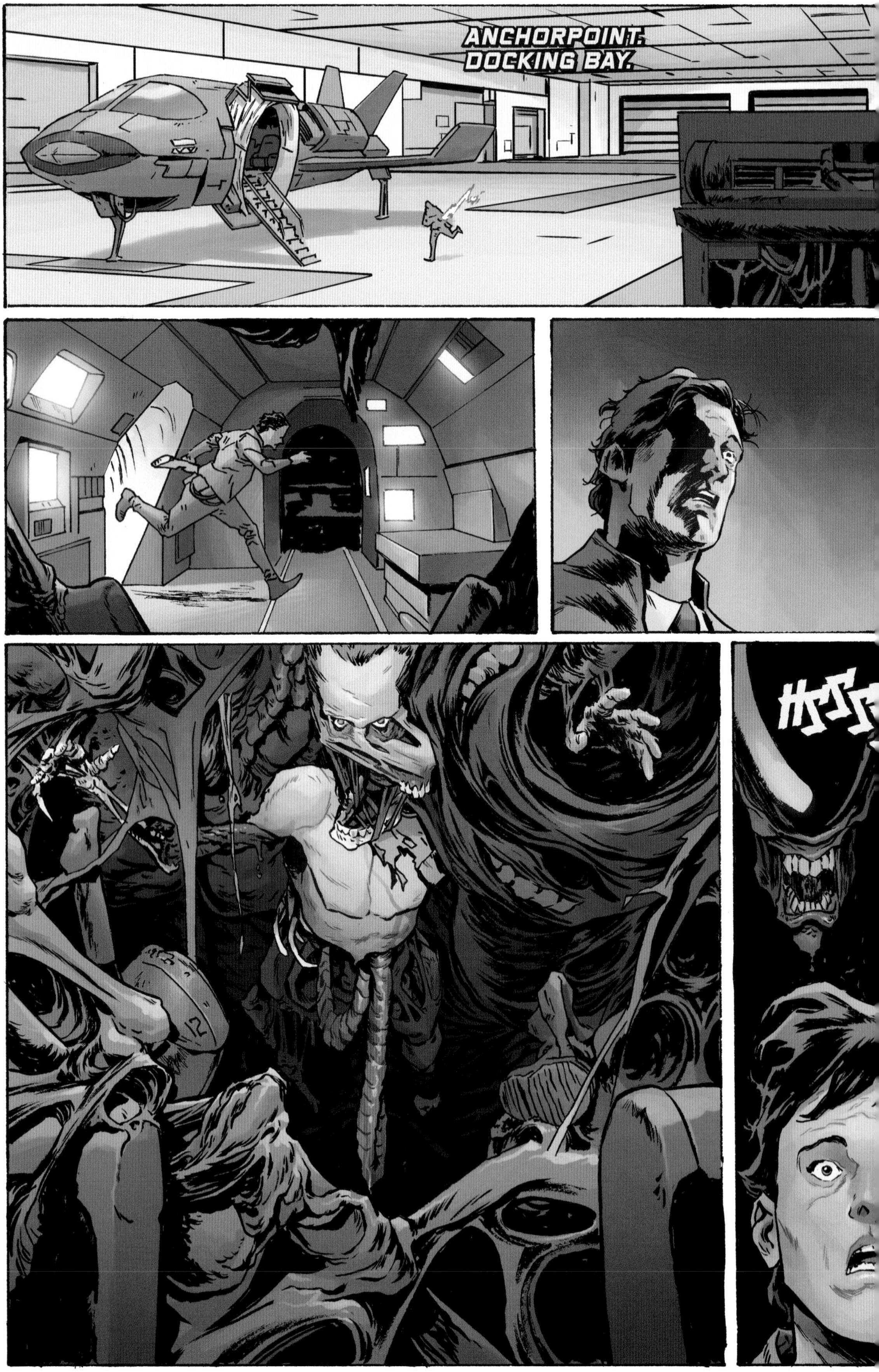
ANCHORPOINT.
DOCKING BAY.

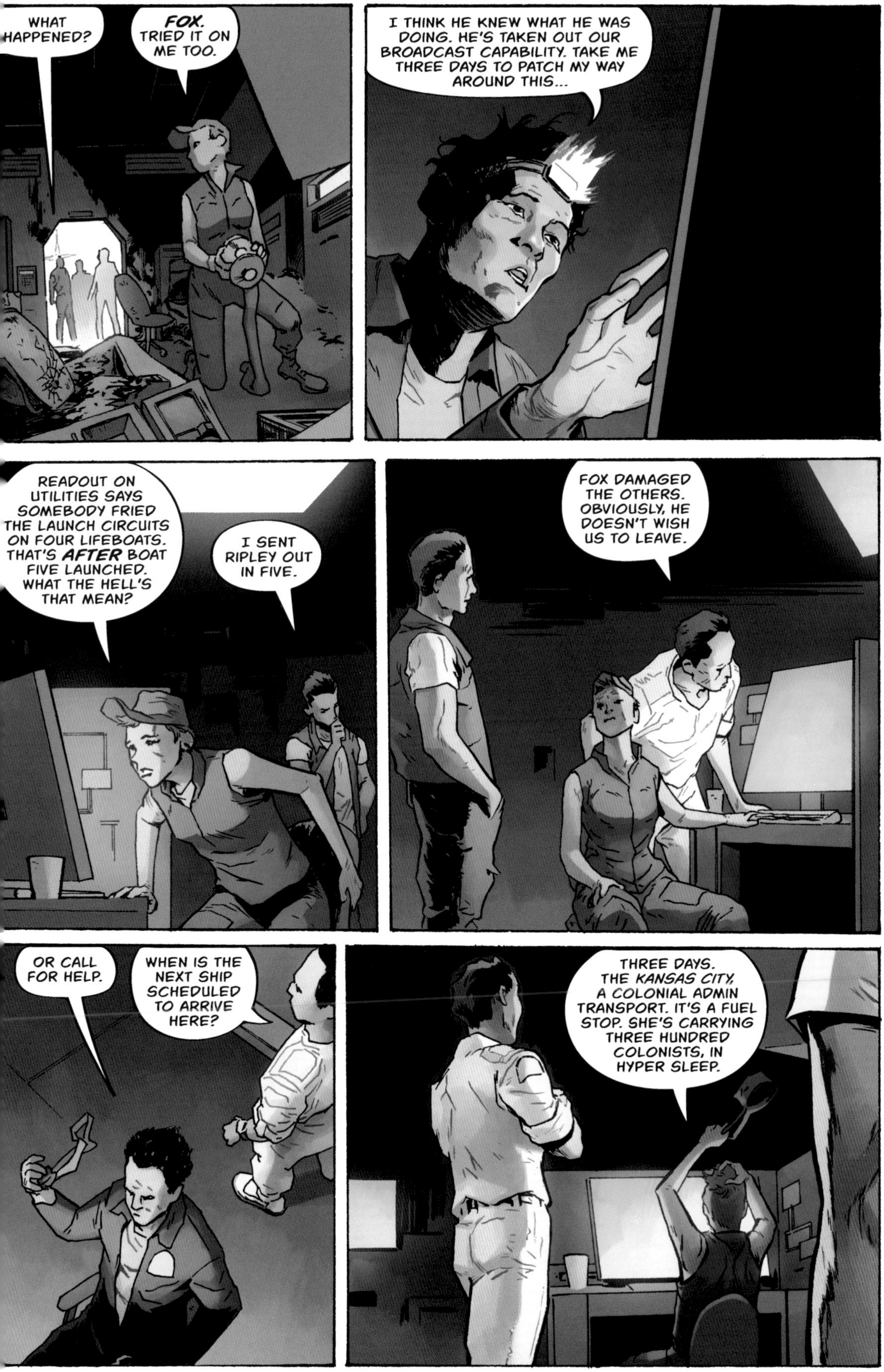
WHAT HAPPENED?
FOX. TRIED IT ON ME TOO.
I THINK HE KNEW WHAT HE WAS DOING. HE'S TAKEN OUT OUR BROADCAST CAPABILITY. TAKE ME THREE DAYS TO PATCH MY WAY AROUND THIS...
READOUT ON UTILITIES SAYS SOMEBODY FRIED THE LAUNCH CIRCUITS ON FOUR LIFEBOATS. THAT'S AFTER BOAT FIVE LAUNCHED. WHAT THE HELL'S THAT MEAN?
I SENT RIPLEY OUT IN FIVE.
FOX DAMAGED THE OTHERS. OBVIOUSLY, HE DOESN'T WISH US TO LEAVE.
OR CALL FOR HELP.
WHEN IS THE NEXT SHIP SCHEDULED TO ARRIVE HERE?
THREE DAYS. THE KANSAS CITY, A COLONIAL ADMIN TRANSPORT. IT'S A FUEL STOP. SHE'S CARRYING THREE HUNDRED COLONISTS, IN HYPER SLEEP.

HEY! I'M GETTING SOMETHING! THE SOCIALIST SPACE BROTHERS ARE BACK ON LINE...

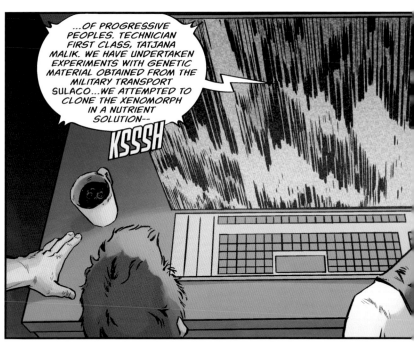

...OF PROGRESSIVE PEOPLES. TECHNICIAN FIRST CLASS, TATJANA MALIK. WE HAVE UNDERTAKEN EXPERIMENTS WITH GENETIC MATERIAL OBTAINED FROM THE MILITARY TRANSPORT SULACO...WE ATTEMPTED TO CLONE THE XENOMORPH IN A NUTRIENT SOLUTION--

KSSSH

...OCCURRED IN THE FIFTEENTH HOUR...ATTEMPTED MODIFICATION OF THE GENETIC STRUCTURE HAS RESULTED IN A VARIANT--

KKSHH

...TO WARN YOU: YOU MUST TERMINATE ANY EXPERIMENT WITH THE MATERIAL NOW. IT CANNOT BE CONTAINED. THERE IS NO--

KSHHH

RODINA'S GOT COMPANY...THE *STOIKO.* RODINA SENT A SQUIRT TRANSMISSION IN MILITARY CODE...

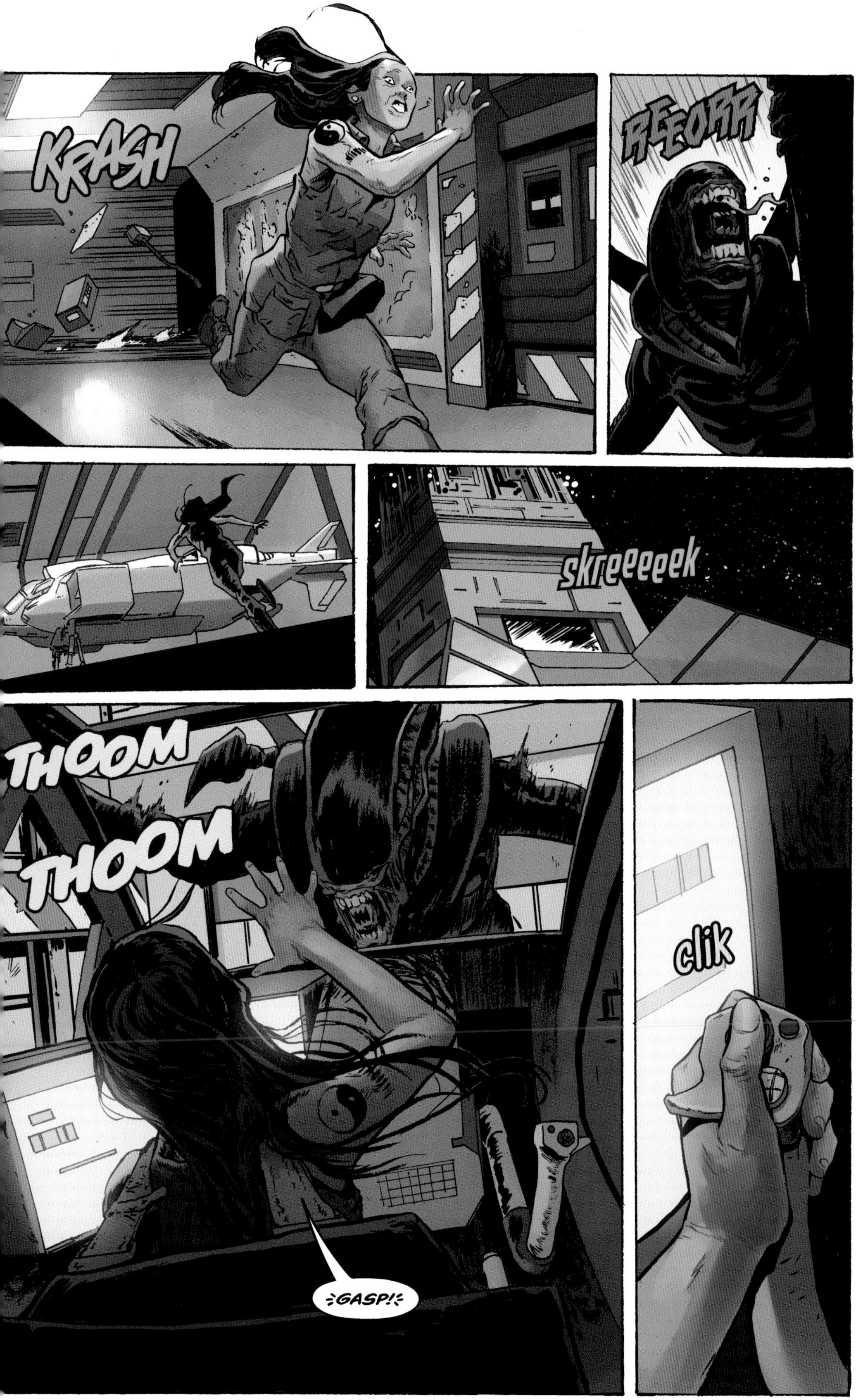
KRASH
REEORR
skreeeeek
THOOM
THOOM
GASP!
clik

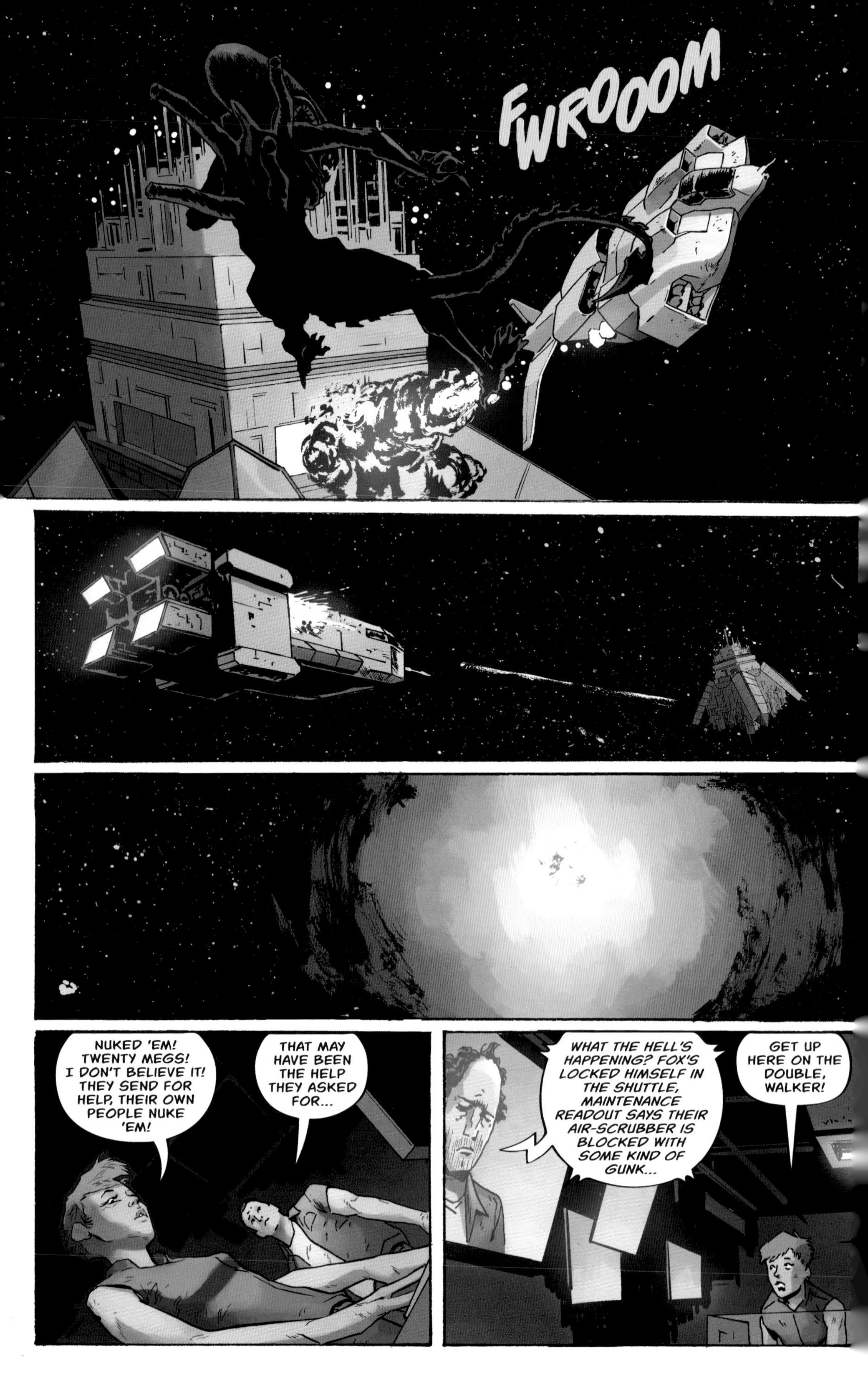
FWROOOM
NUKED 'EM! TWENTY MEGS! I DON'T BELIEVE IT! THEY SEND FOR HELP, THEIR OWN PEOPLE NUKE 'EM!
THAT MAY HAVE BEEN THE HELP THEY ASKED FOR...
WHAT THE HELL'S HAPPENING? FOX'S LOCKED HIMSELF IN THE SHUTTLE, MAINTENANCE READOUT SAYS THEIR AIR-SCRUBBER IS BLOCKED WITH SOME KIND OF GUNK...
GET UP HERE ON THE DOUBLE, WALKER!

SHE FOUND TULLY...

HE'S DEAD. TULLY'S DEAD. HE STARTED TO...LIKE WELLES. BUT HE KNEW...HE DRAGGED HIMSELF TO DEEPFREEZE, LOCKED HIMSELF IN. HE...KILLED IT...

WHERE'S THE ARMAMENT LOCKER?

THERE ISN'T ANY. THIS IS A NONMILITARY PROJECT. WE WANTED TO SET AN EXAMPLE...

ANYTHING! A GUN...

COME WITH ME.

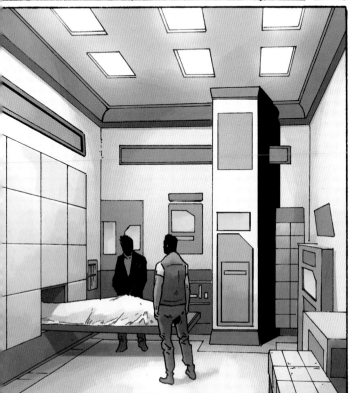

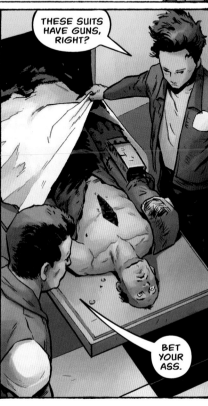

THESE SUITS HAVE GUNS, RIGHT?

BET YOUR ASS.

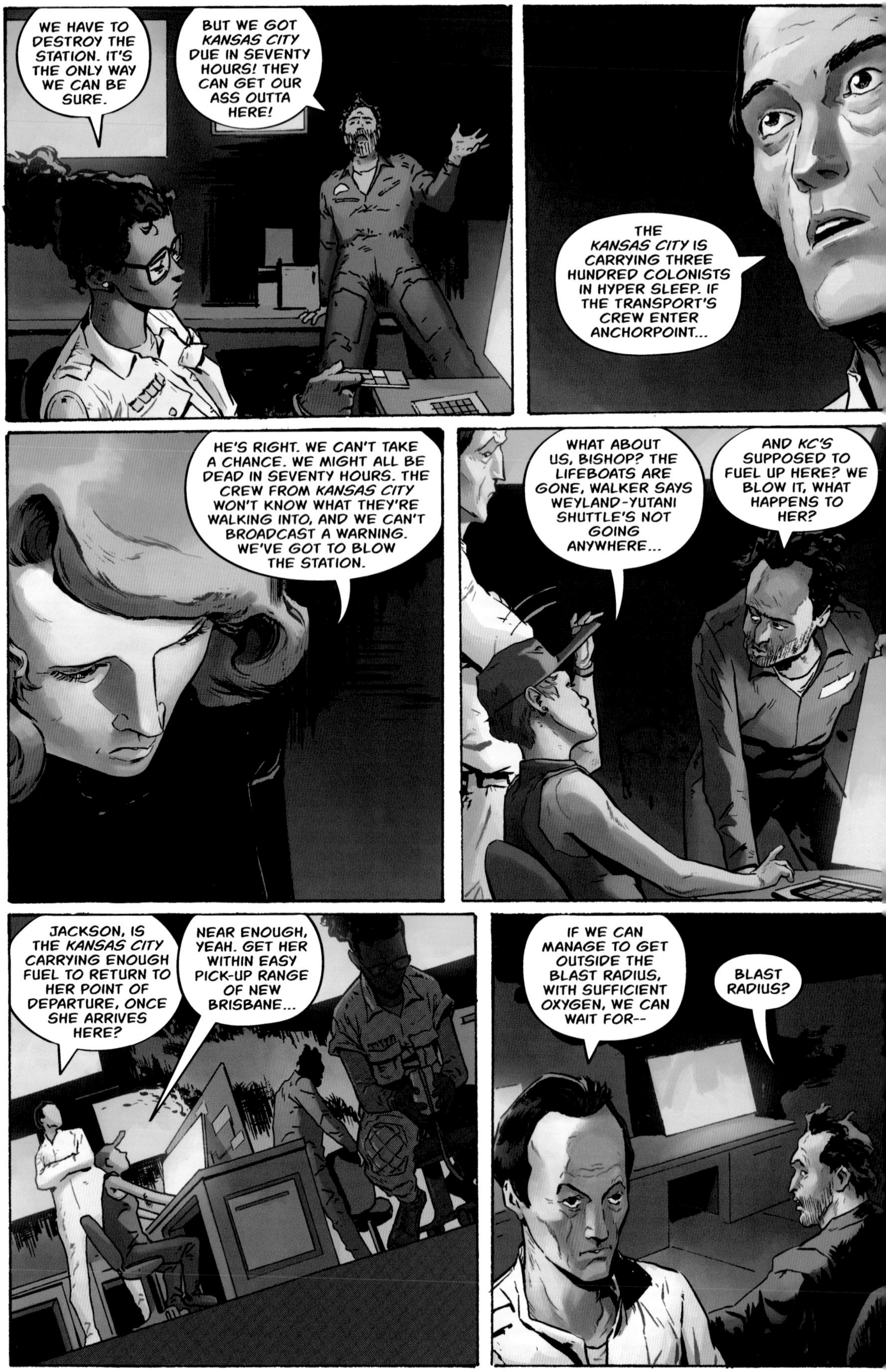
WE HAVE TO DESTROY THE STATION. IT'S THE ONLY WAY WE CAN BE SURE.
BUT WE GOT *KANSAS CITY* DUE IN SEVENTY HOURS! THEY CAN GET OUR ASS OUTTA HERE!
THE *KANSAS CITY* IS CARRYING THREE HUNDRED COLONISTS IN HYPER SLEEP. IF THE TRANSPORT'S CREW ENTER ANCHORPOINT...
HE'S RIGHT. WE CAN'T TAKE A CHANCE. WE MIGHT ALL BE DEAD IN SEVENTY HOURS. THE CREW FROM *KANSAS CITY* WON'T KNOW WHAT THEY'RE WALKING INTO, AND WE CAN'T BROADCAST A WARNING. WE'VE GOT TO BLOW THE STATION.
WHAT ABOUT US, BISHOP? THE LIFEBOATS ARE GONE, WALKER SAYS WEYLAND-YUTANI SHUTTLE'S NOT GOING ANYWHERE...
AND KC'S SUPPOSED TO FUEL UP HERE? WE BLOW IT, WHAT HAPPENS TO HER?
JACKSON, IS THE *KANSAS CITY* CARRYING ENOUGH FUEL TO RETURN TO HER POINT OF DEPARTURE, ONCE SHE ARRIVES HERE?
NEAR ENOUGH, YEAH. GET HER WITHIN EASY PICK-UP RANGE OF NEW BRISBANE...
IF WE CAN MANAGE TO GET OUTSIDE THE BLAST RADIUS, WITH SUFFICIENT OXYGEN, WE CAN WAIT FOR--
BLAST RADIUS?

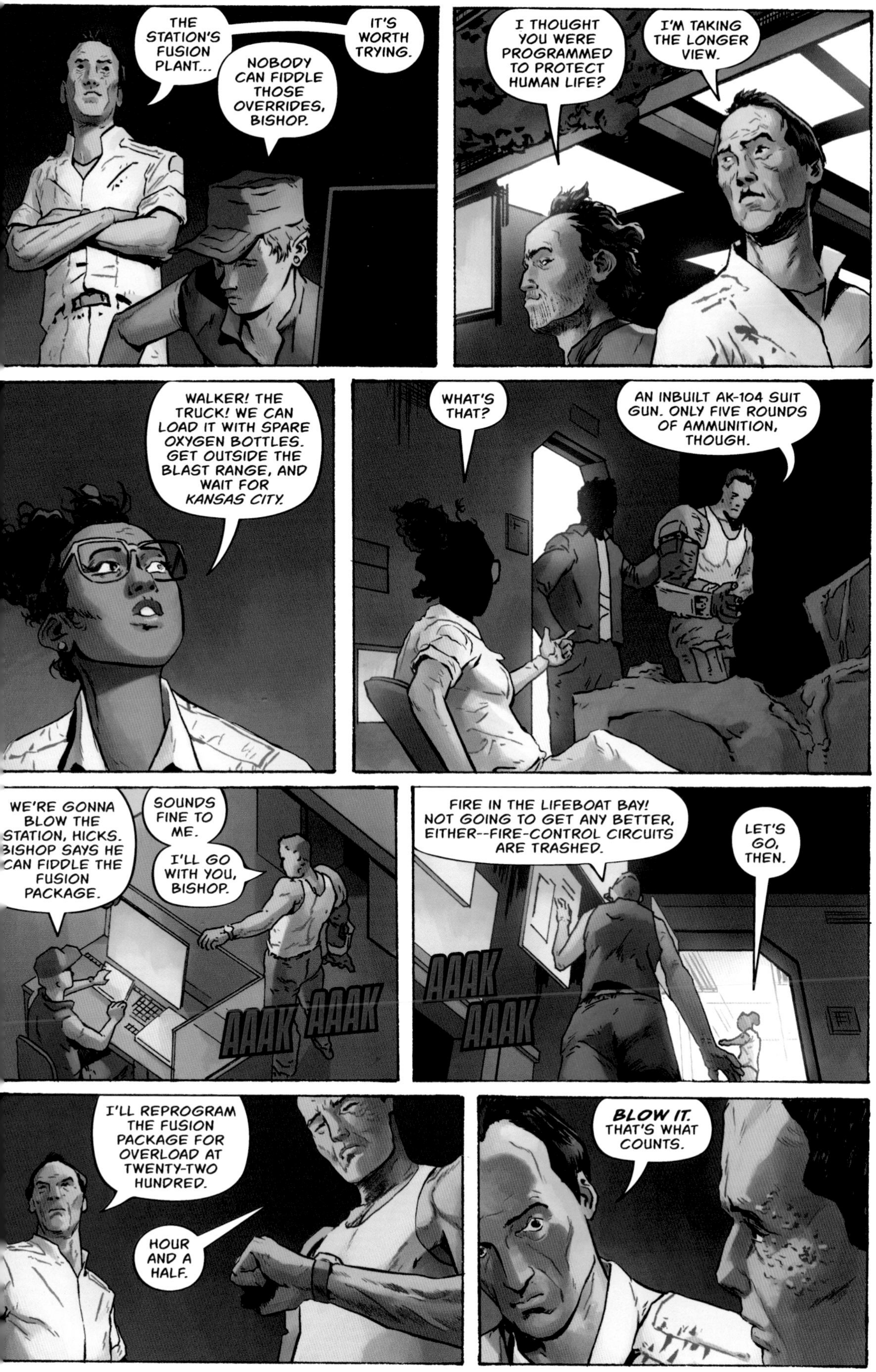
THE STATION'S FUSION PLANT...
IT'S WORTH TRYING.
NOBODY CAN FIDDLE THOSE OVERRIDES, BISHOP.
I THOUGHT YOU WERE PROGRAMMED TO PROTECT HUMAN LIFE?
I'M TAKING THE LONGER VIEW.
WALKER! THE TRUCK! WE CAN LOAD IT WITH SPARE OXYGEN BOTTLES. GET OUTSIDE THE BLAST RANGE, AND WAIT FOR *KANSAS CITY.*
WHAT'S THAT?
AN INBUILT AK-104 SUIT GUN. ONLY FIVE ROUNDS OF AMMUNITION, THOUGH.
WE'RE GONNA BLOW THE STATION, HICKS. BISHOP SAYS HE CAN FIDDLE THE FUSION PACKAGE.
SOUNDS FINE TO ME.
I'LL GO WITH YOU, BISHOP.
AAAK AAAK
FIRE IN THE LIFEBOAT BAY! NOT GOING TO GET ANY BETTER, EITHER--FIRE-CONTROL CIRCUITS ARE TRASHED.
LET'S GO, THEN.
AAAK AAAK
I'LL REPROGRAM THE FUSION PACKAGE FOR OVERLOAD AT TWENTY-TWO HUNDRED.
HOUR AND A HALF.
BLOW IT. THAT'S WHAT COUNTS.

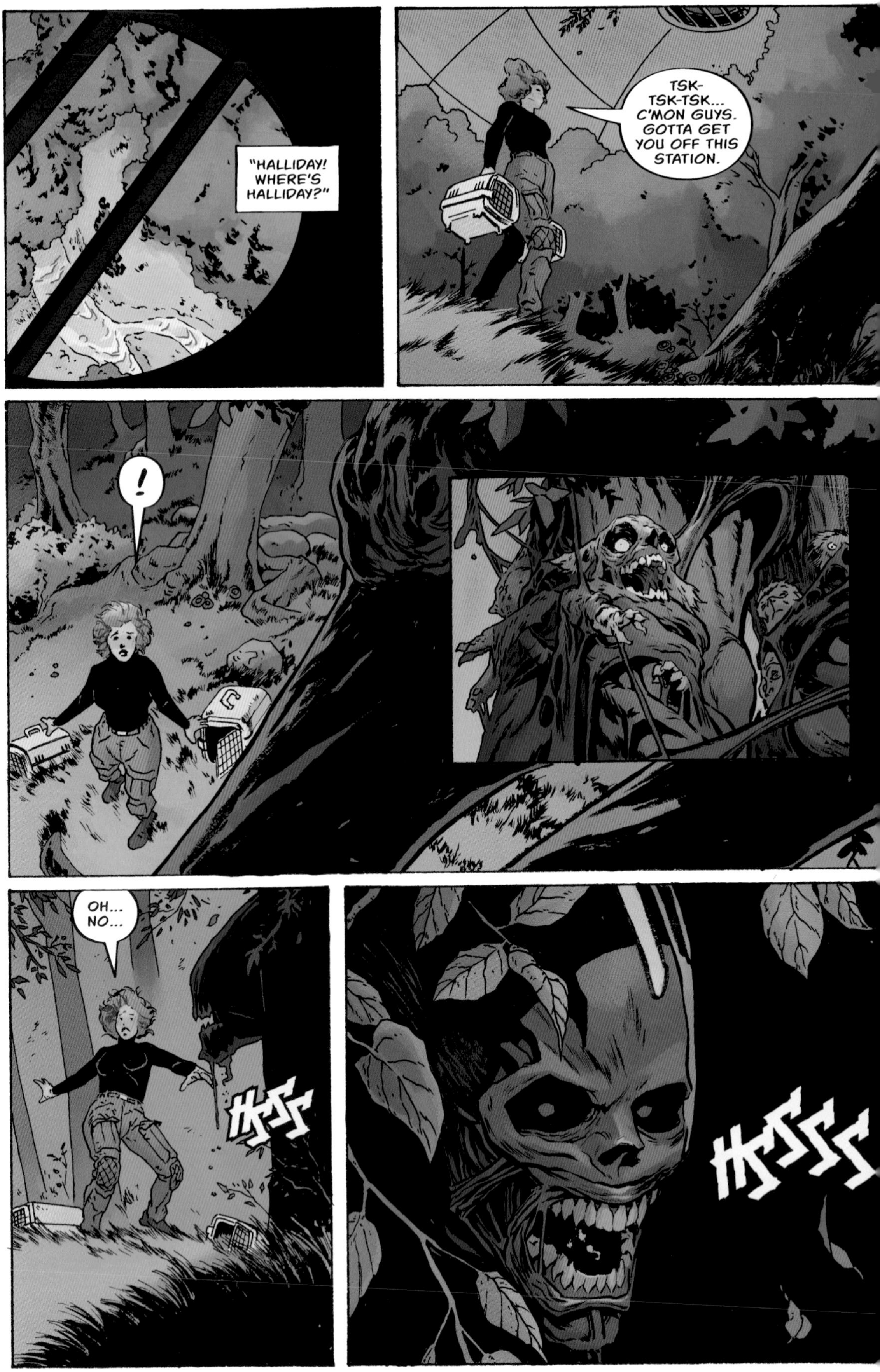
"HALLIDAY! WHERE'S HALLIDAY?"
TSK-TSK-TSK... C'MON GUYS. GOTTA GET YOU OFF THIS STATION.
!
OH... NO...
HSSS
HSSSS

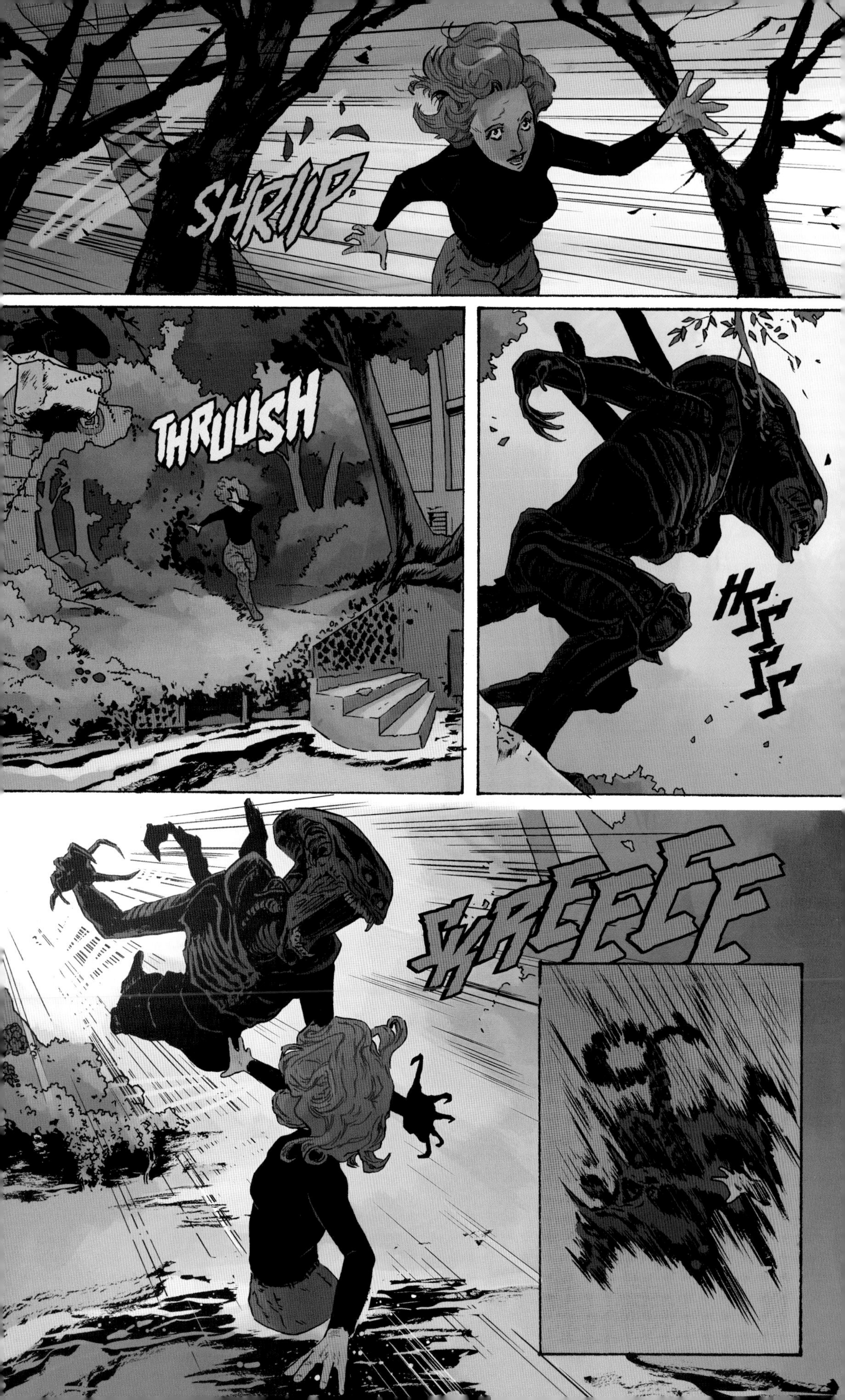
SHRIIP
THRUUSH
HSSS
SKREEEE

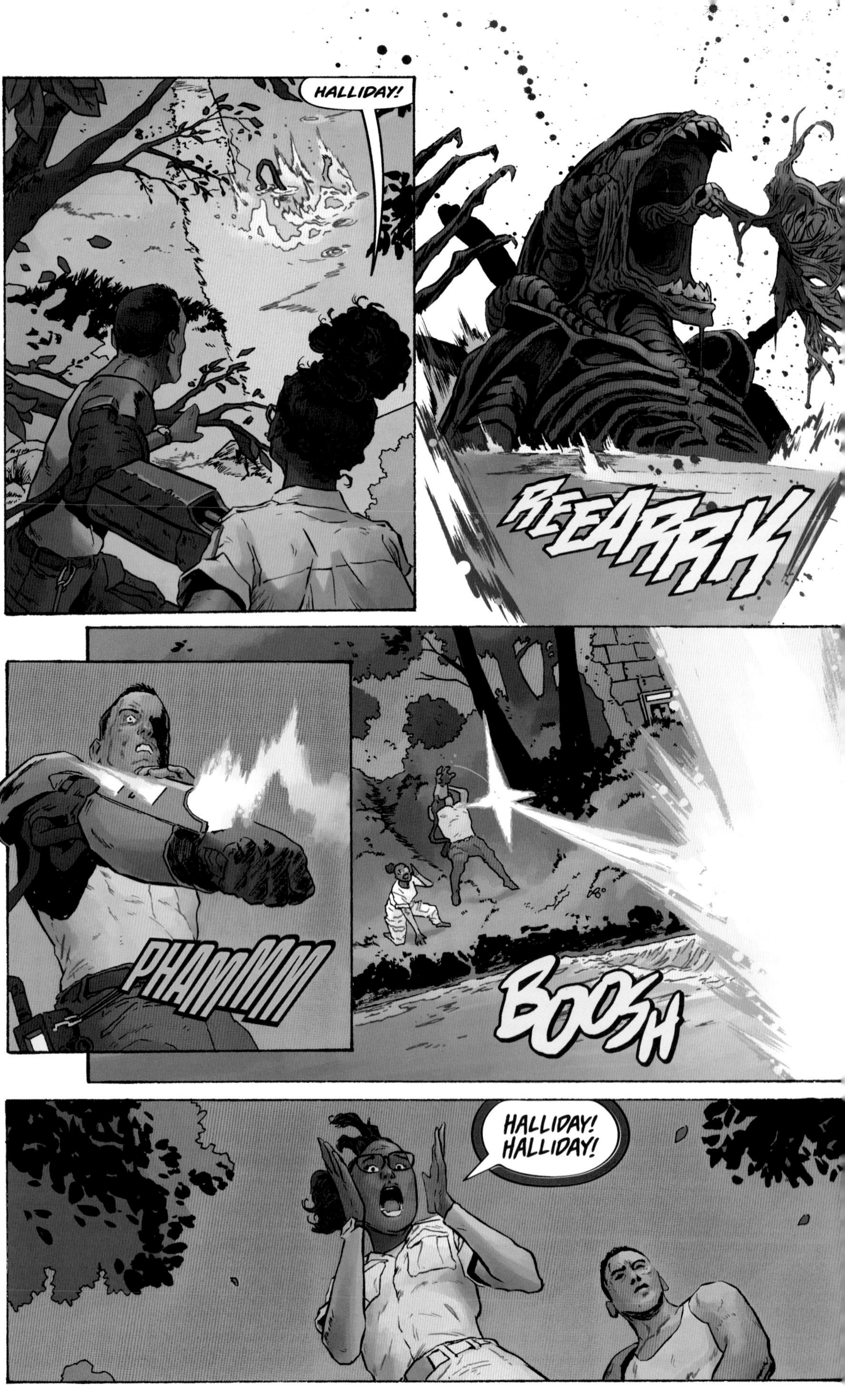
HALLIDAY!
REEARRRK
PHAMMM
BOOSH
HALLIDAY! HALLIDAY!

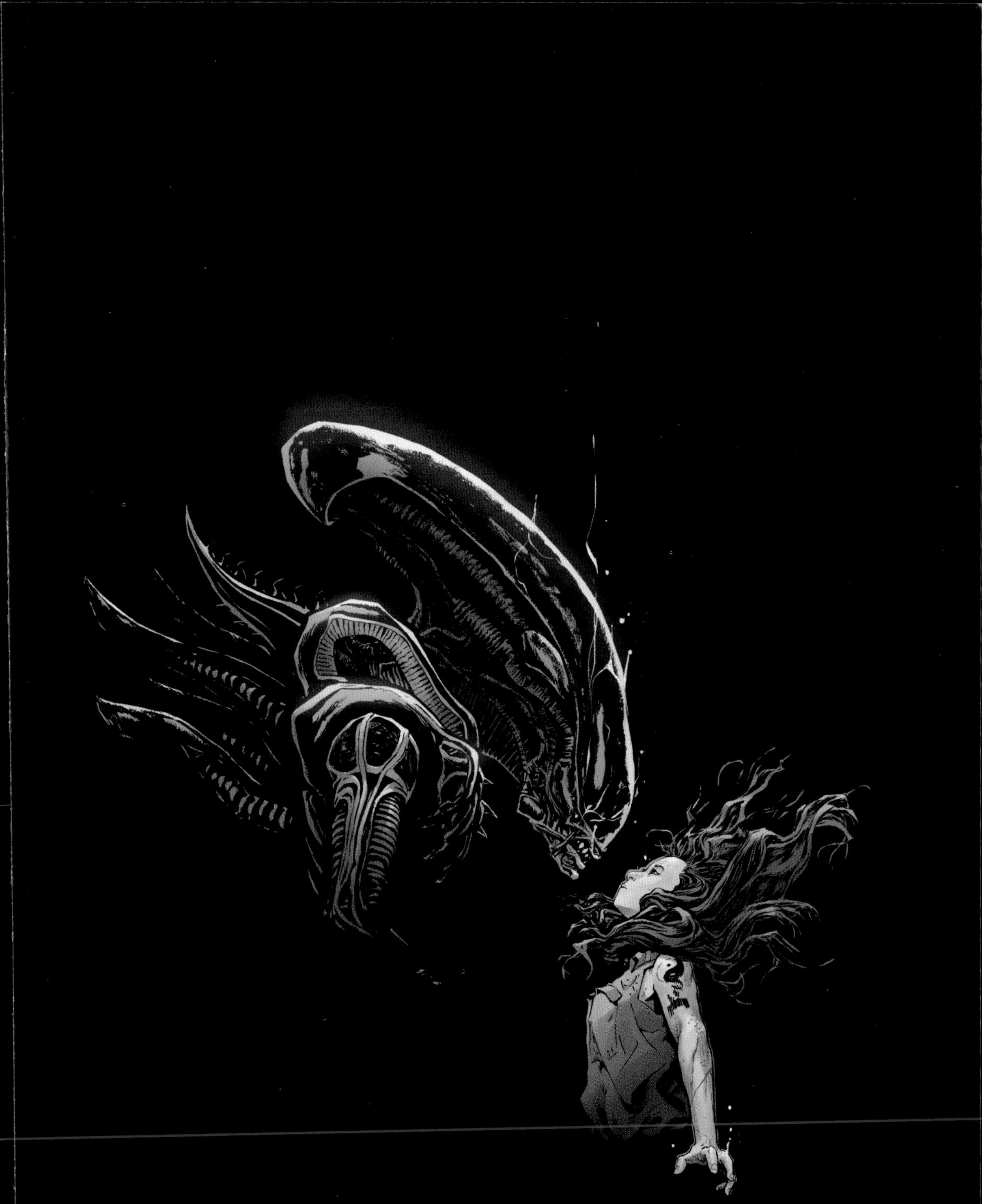

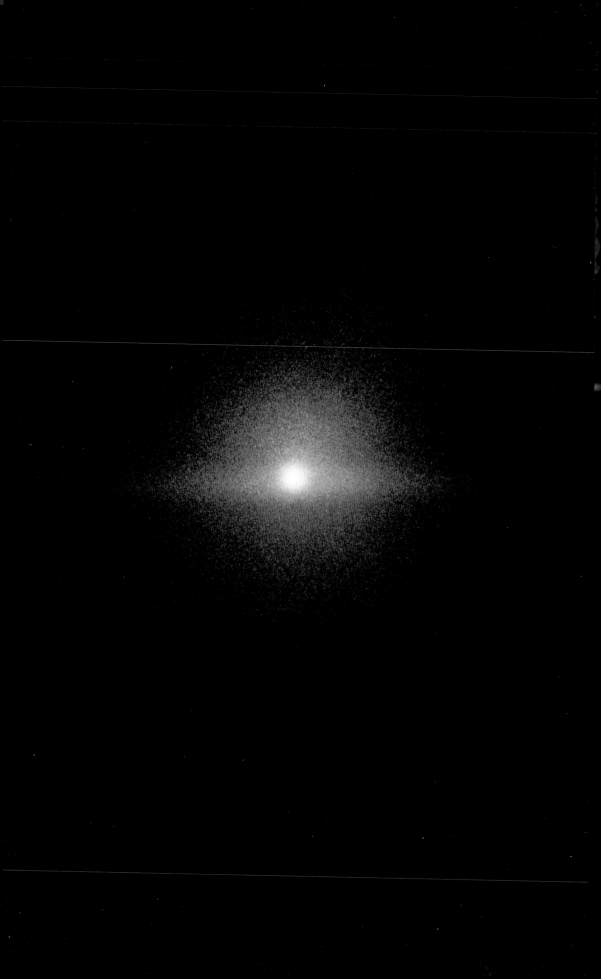

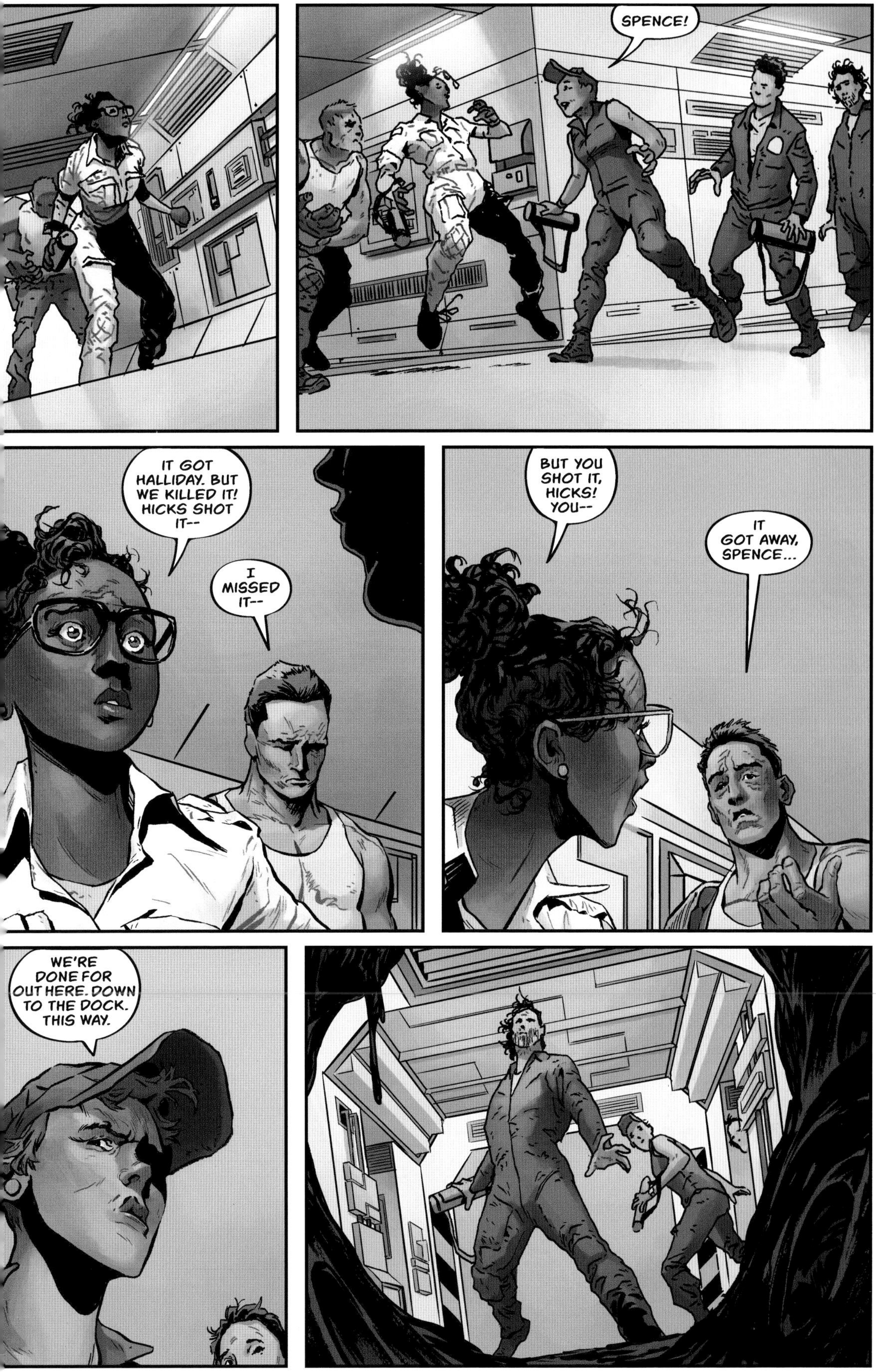

SPENCE!
IT GOT HALLIDAY. BUT WE KILLED IT! HICKS SHOT IT--
I MISSED IT--
BUT YOU SHOT IT, HICKS! YOU--
IT GOT AWAY, SPENCE...
WE'RE DONE FOR OUT HERE. DOWN TO THE DOCK. THIS WAY.

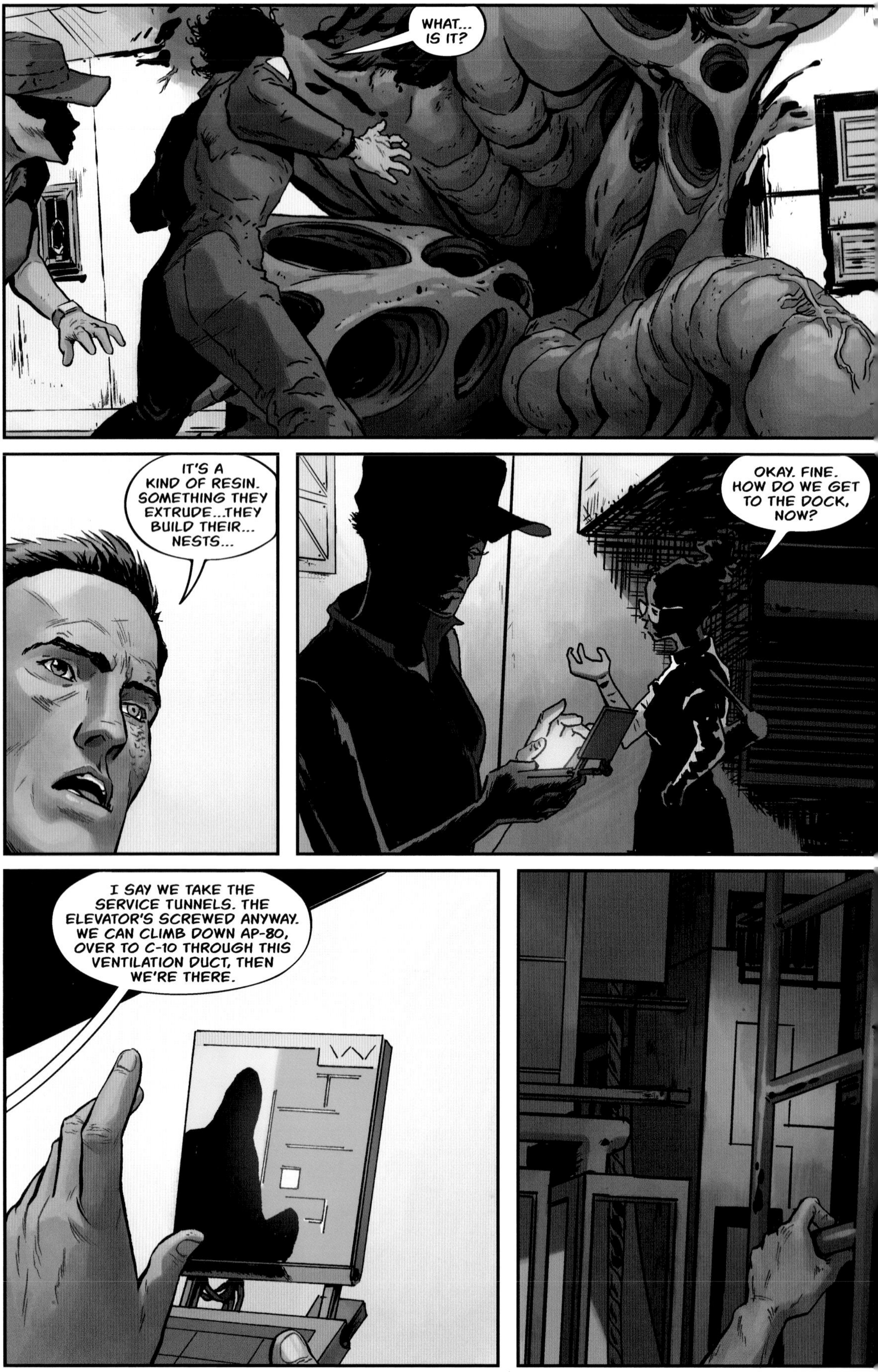
WHAT... IS IT?
IT'S A KIND OF RESIN. SOMETHING THEY EXTRUDE...THEY BUILD THEIR... NESTS...
OKAY. FINE. HOW DO WE GET TO THE DOCK, NOW?
I SAY WE TAKE THE SERVICE TUNNELS. THE ELEVATOR'S SCREWED ANYWAY. WE CAN CLIMB DOWN AP-80, OVER TO C-10 THROUGH THIS VENTILATION DUCT, THEN WE'RE THERE.

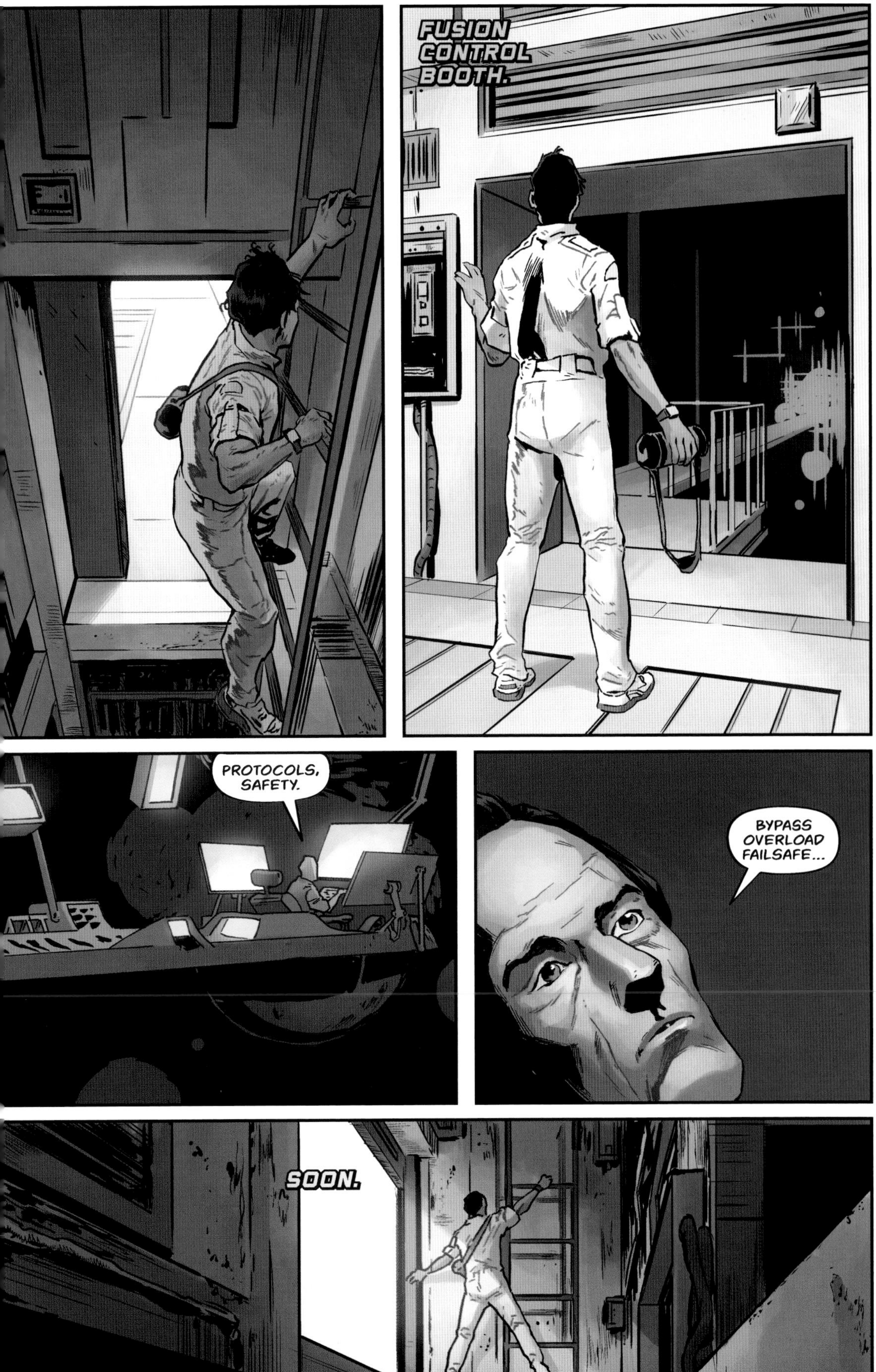
FUSION CONTROL BOOTH.
PROTOCOLS, SAFETY.
BYPASS OVERLOAD FAILSAFE...
SOON.

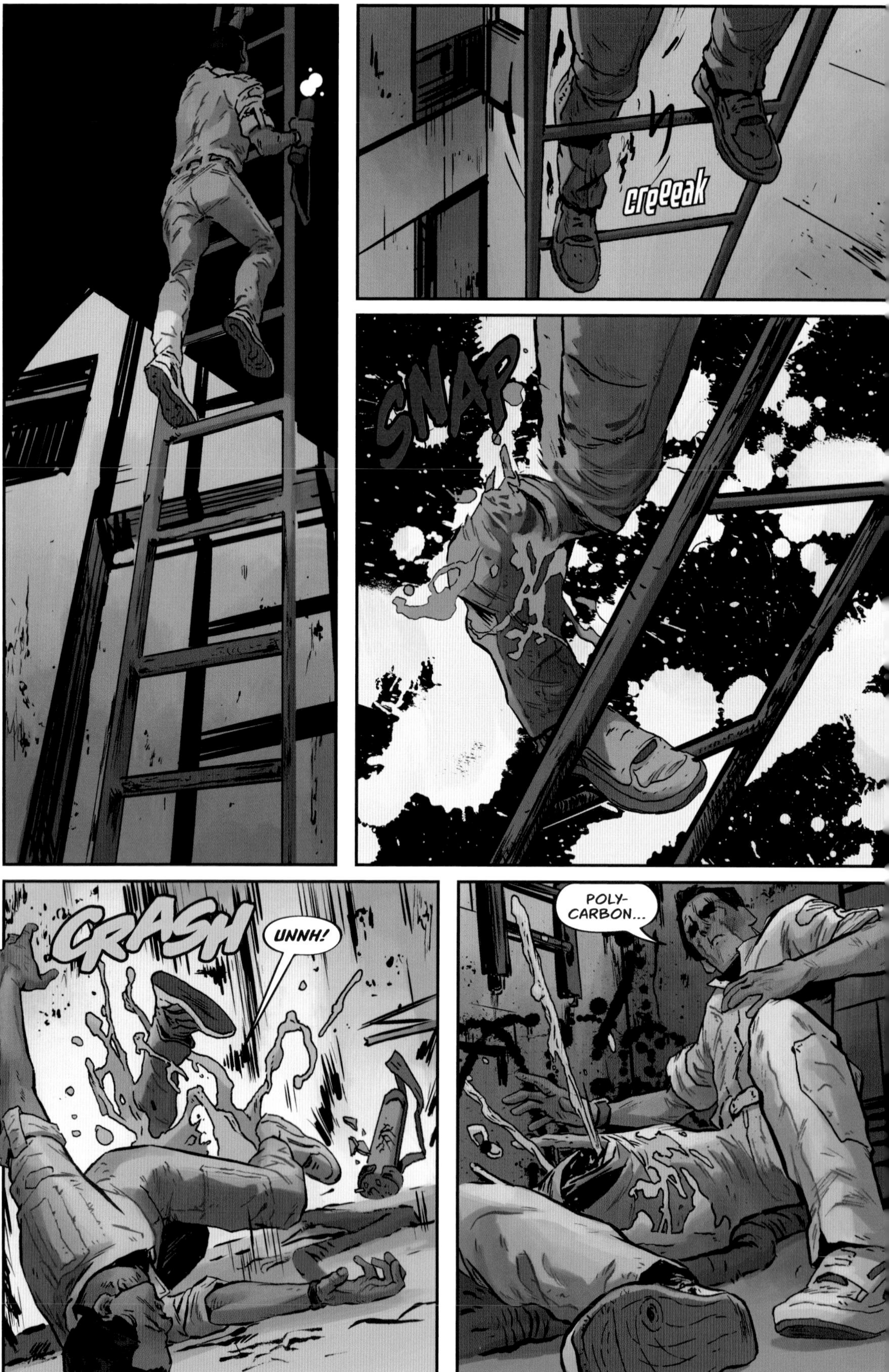
creeeak
SNAP
CRASH
UNNH!
POLY-CARBON...

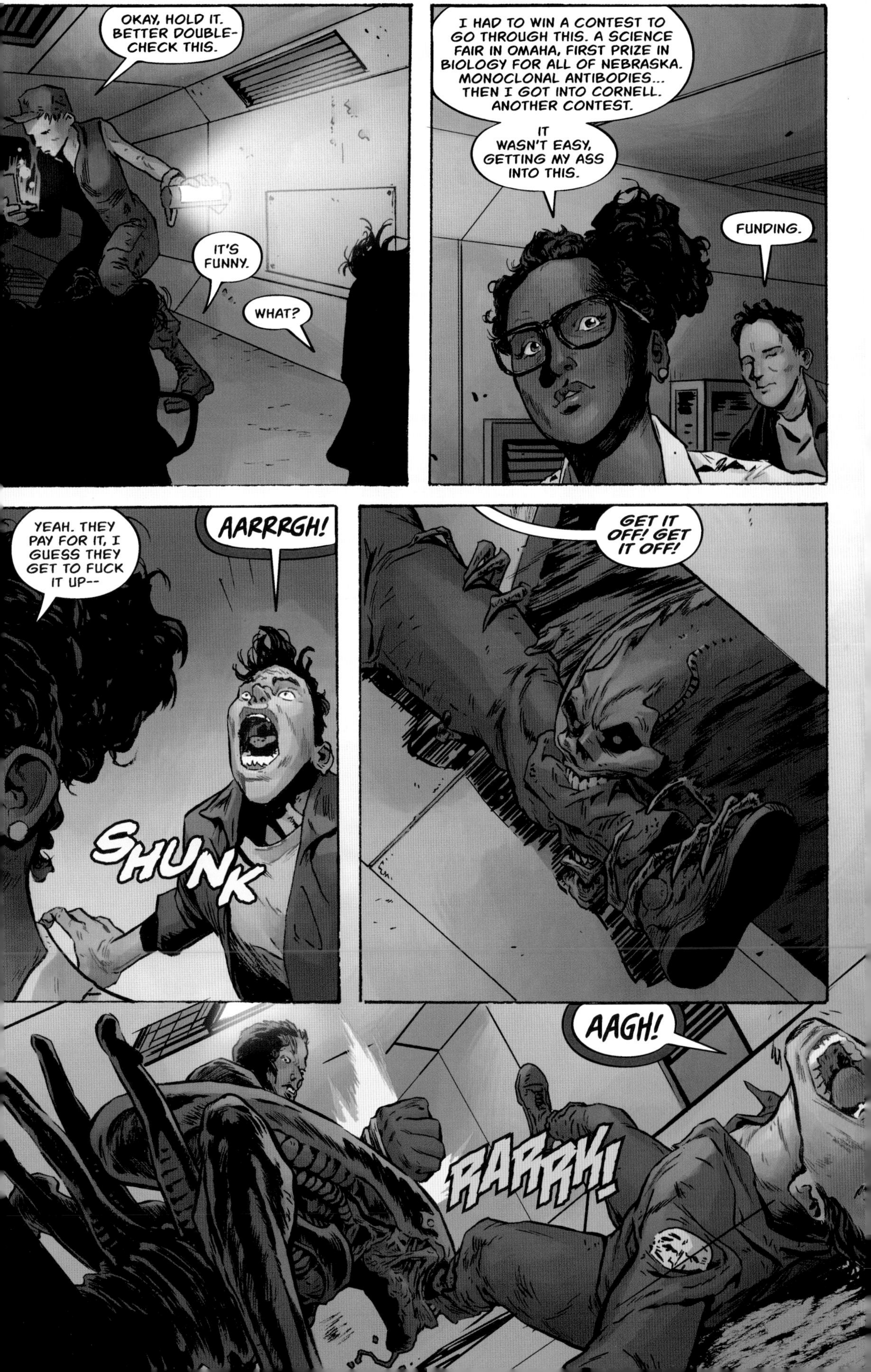
OKAY, HOLD IT. BETTER DOUBLE-CHECK THIS.
IT'S FUNNY.
WHAT?
I HAD TO WIN A CONTEST TO GO THROUGH THIS. A SCIENCE FAIR IN OMAHA, FIRST PRIZE IN BIOLOGY FOR ALL OF NEBRASKA. MONOCLONAL ANTIBODIES... THEN I GOT INTO CORNELL. ANOTHER CONTEST.
IT WASN'T EASY, GETTING MY ASS INTO THIS.
FUNDING.
YEAH. THEY PAY FOR IT, I GUESS THEY GET TO FUCK IT UP--
AARRRGH!
SHUNK
GET IT OFF! GET IT OFF!
AAGH!
RARRK!

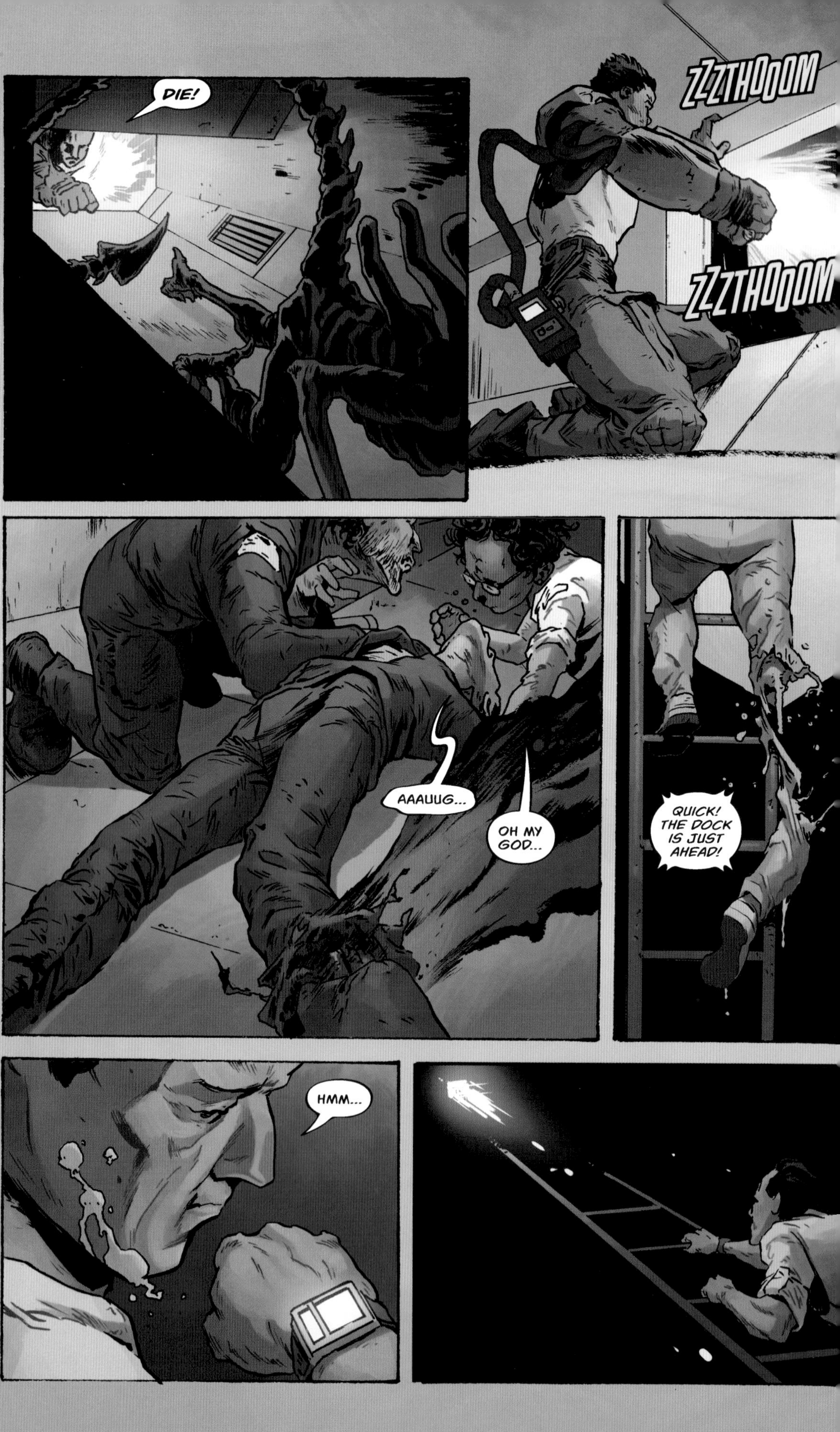
DIE!
ZZZTHOOOM
ZZZTHOOOM
AAAUUG...
OH MY GOD...
QUICK! THE DOCK IS JUST AHEAD!
HMM...

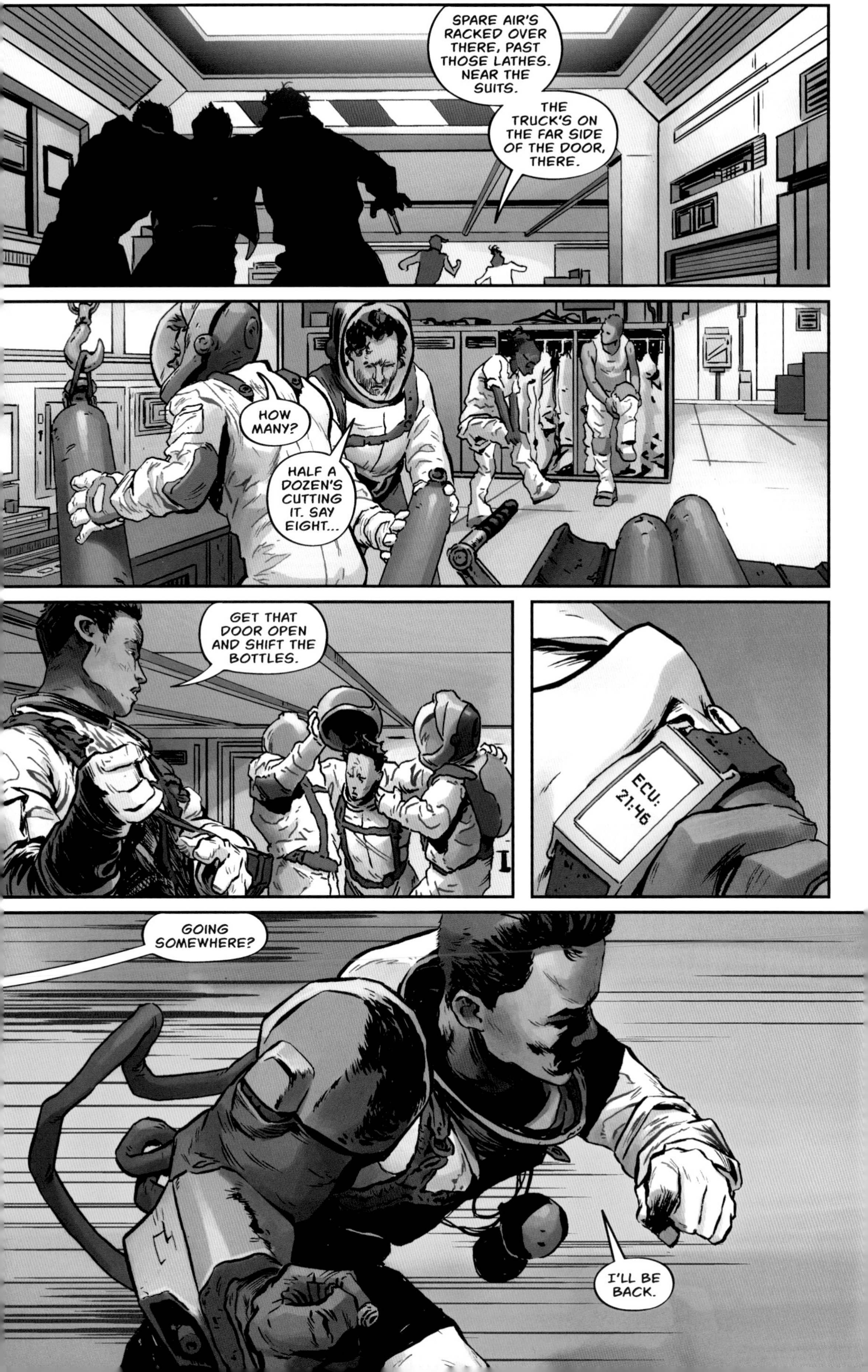
SPARE AIR'S RACKED OVER THERE, PAST THOSE LATHES. NEAR THE SUITS.
THE TRUCK'S ON THE FAR SIDE OF THE DOOR, THERE.
HOW MANY?
HALF A DOZEN'S CUTTING IT. SAY EIGHT...
GET THAT DOOR OPEN AND SHIFT THE BOTTLES.
ECU: 21:46
GOING SOMEWHERE?
I'LL BE BACK.

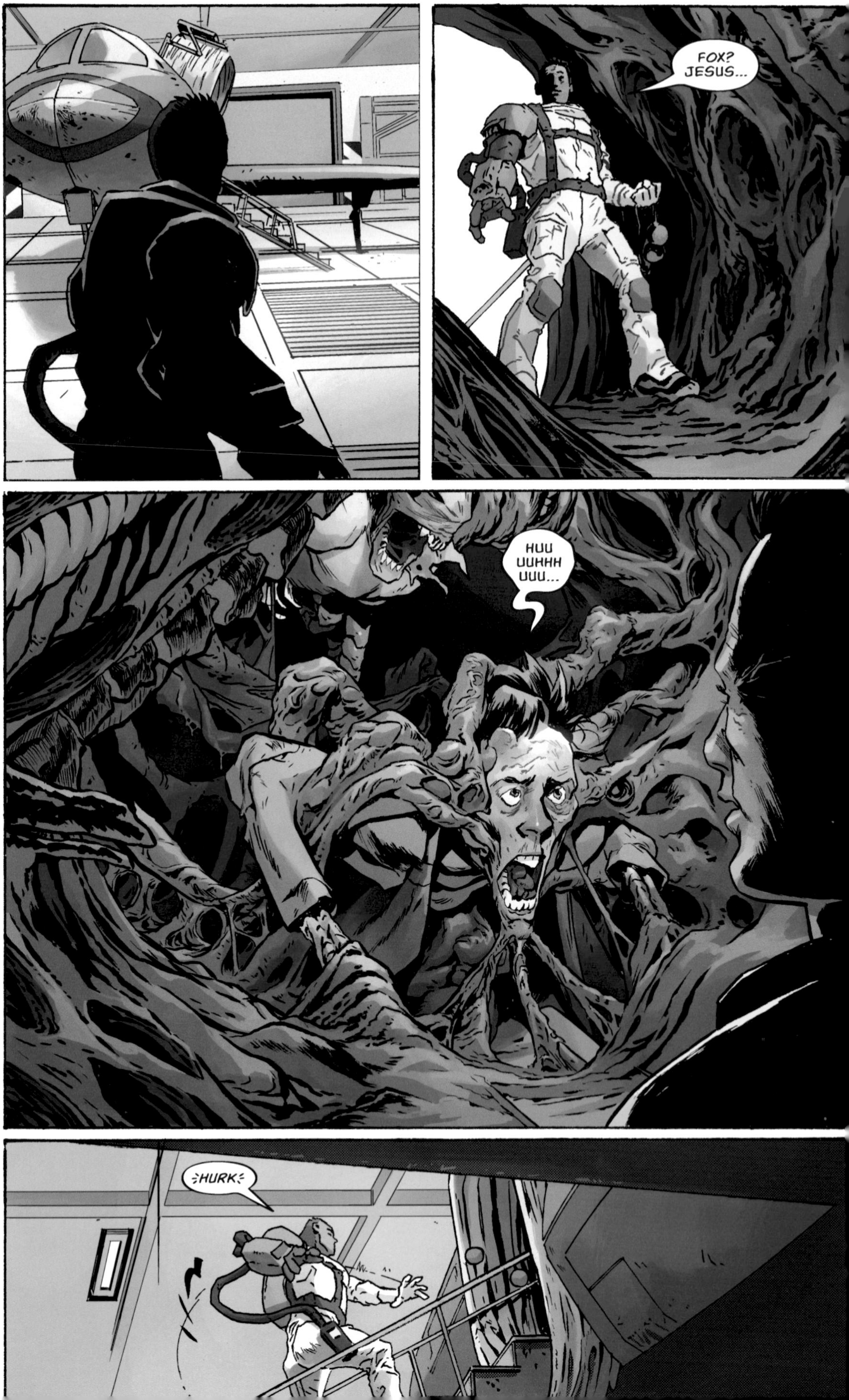
FOX? JESUS...
HUU UUHHH UUU...
HURK

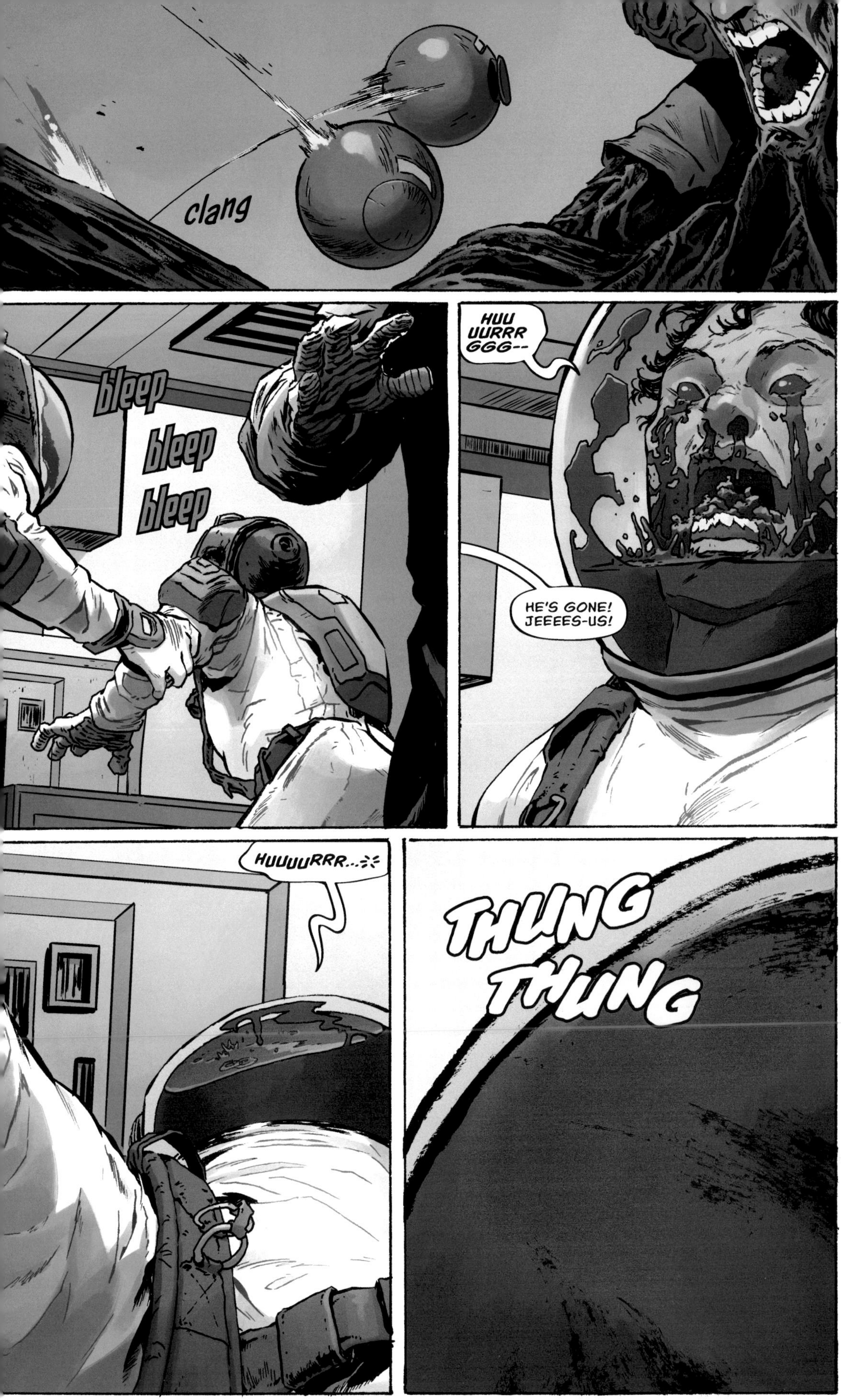
clang
bleep
bleep
bleep
HUU UURRR GGG--
HE'S GONE! JEEEES-US!
HUUUURRR...
THUNG
THUNG

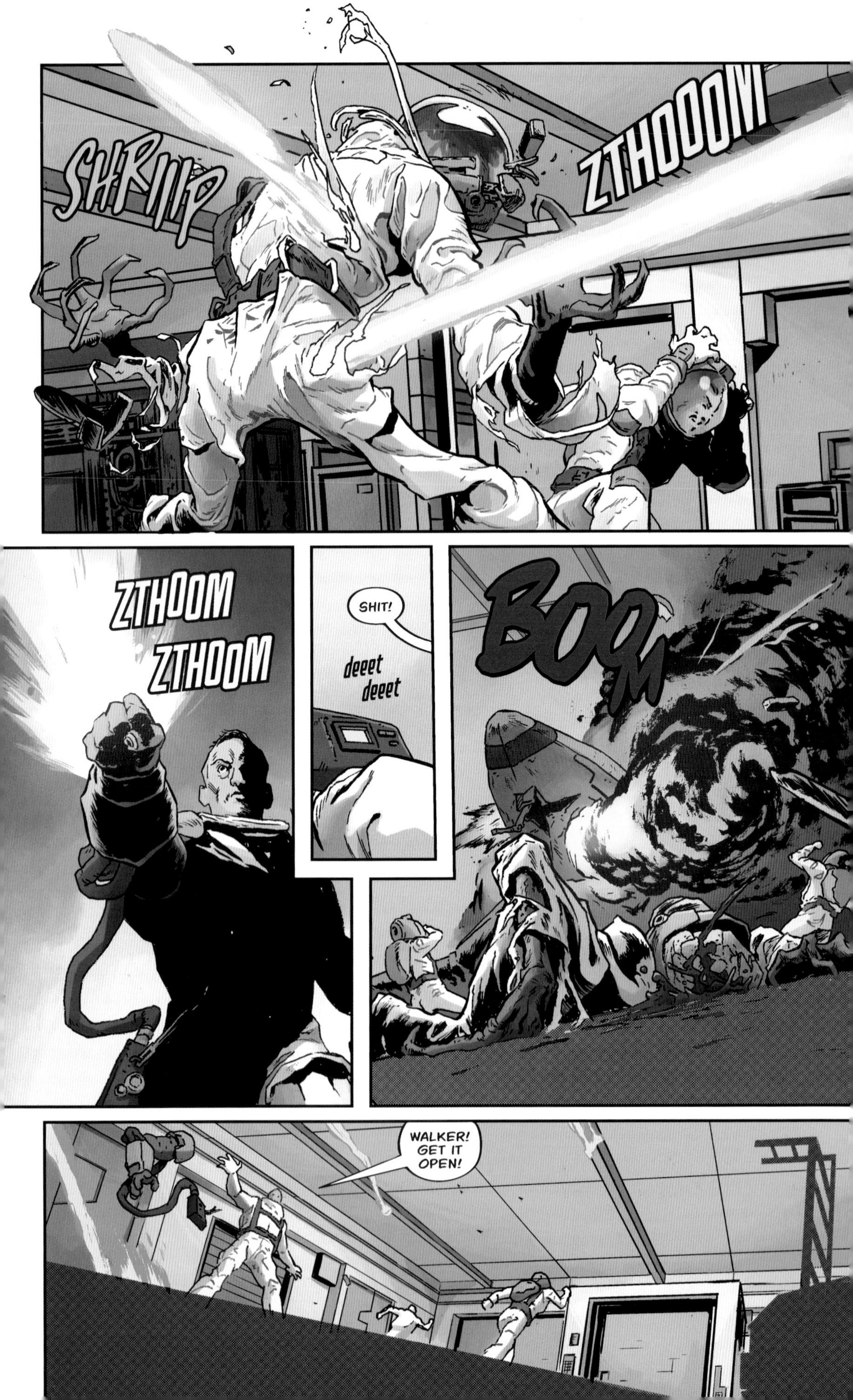
SHRIIIP
ZTHOOOM
ZTHOOM
ZTHOOM
SHIT!
deeet
deeet
BOOM
WALKER! GET IT OPEN!

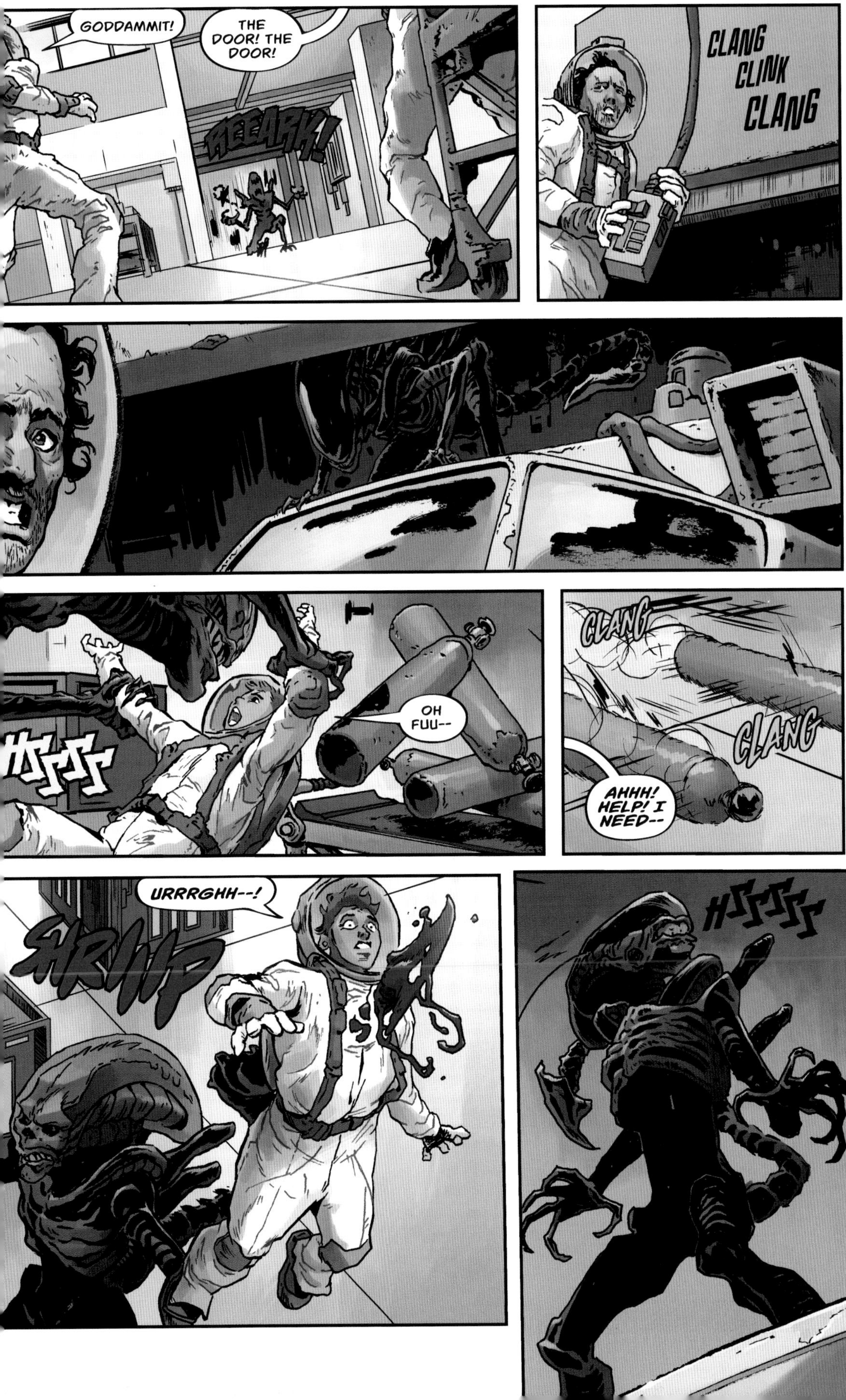
GODDAMMIT!
THE DOOR! THE DOOR!
REEARK!
CLANG
CLINK
CLANG
HSSSS
OH FUU--
CLANG
CLANG
AHHH! HELP! I NEED--
URRRGHH--!
SHRIIIP
HSSSS

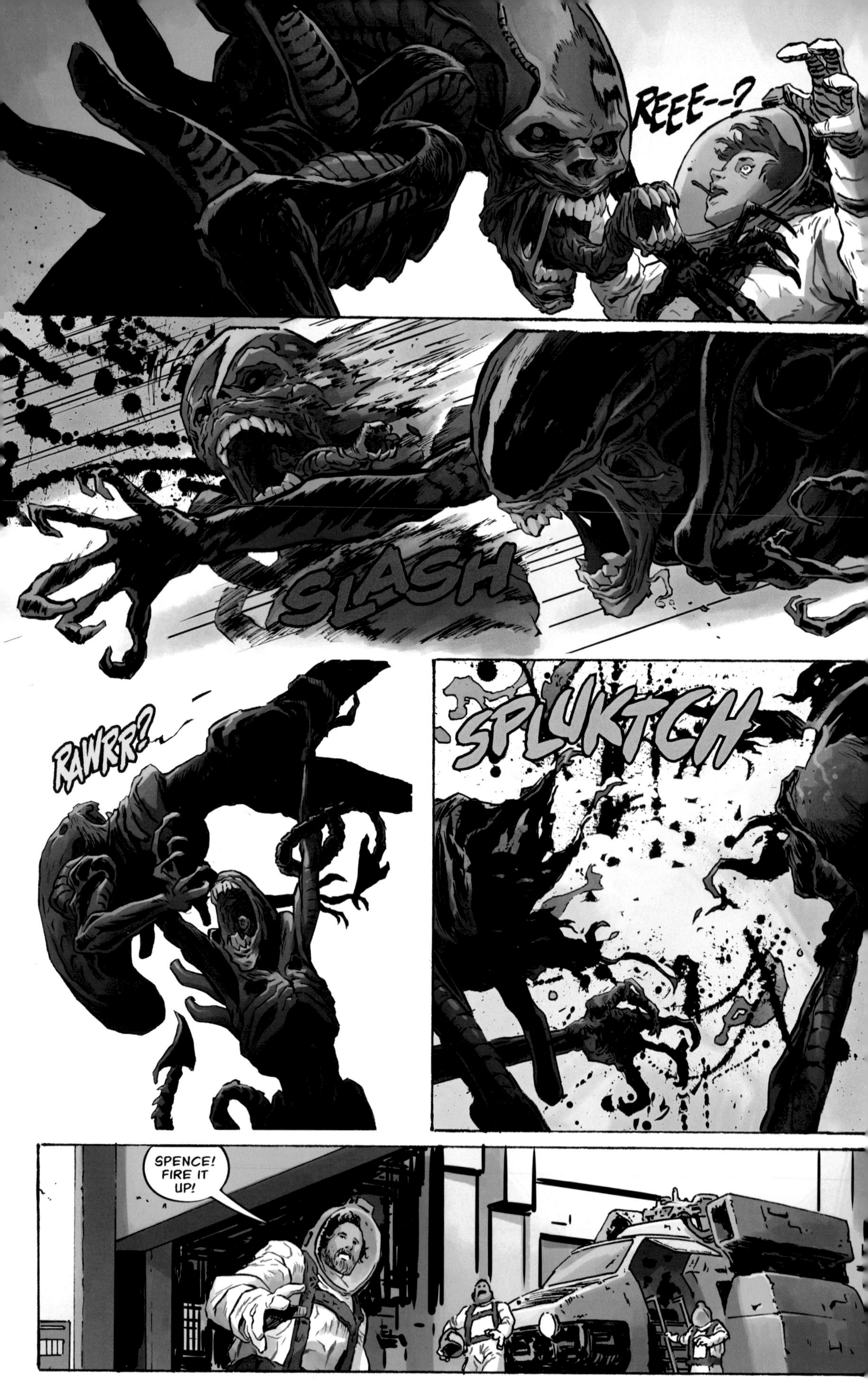
REEE--?
SLASH
RAWRR?
SPLUKTCH
SPENCE! FIRE IT UP!

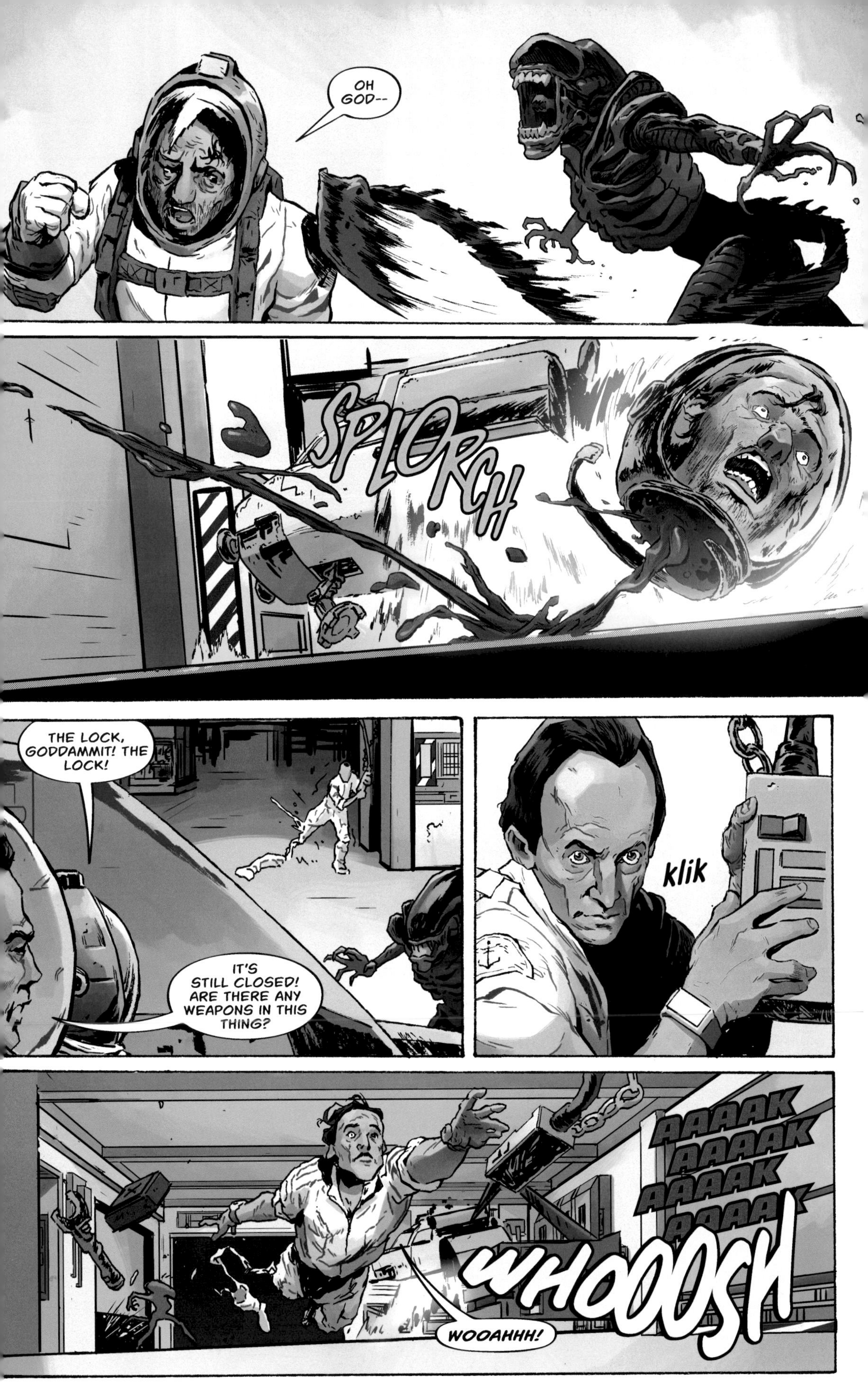
OH GOD--
SPLORCH
THE LOCK, GODDAMMIT! THE LOCK!
IT'S STILL CLOSED! ARE THERE ANY WEAPONS IN THIS THING?
klik
AAAAK AAAAK AAAAK AAAAK
WHOOOSH
WOOAHHH!

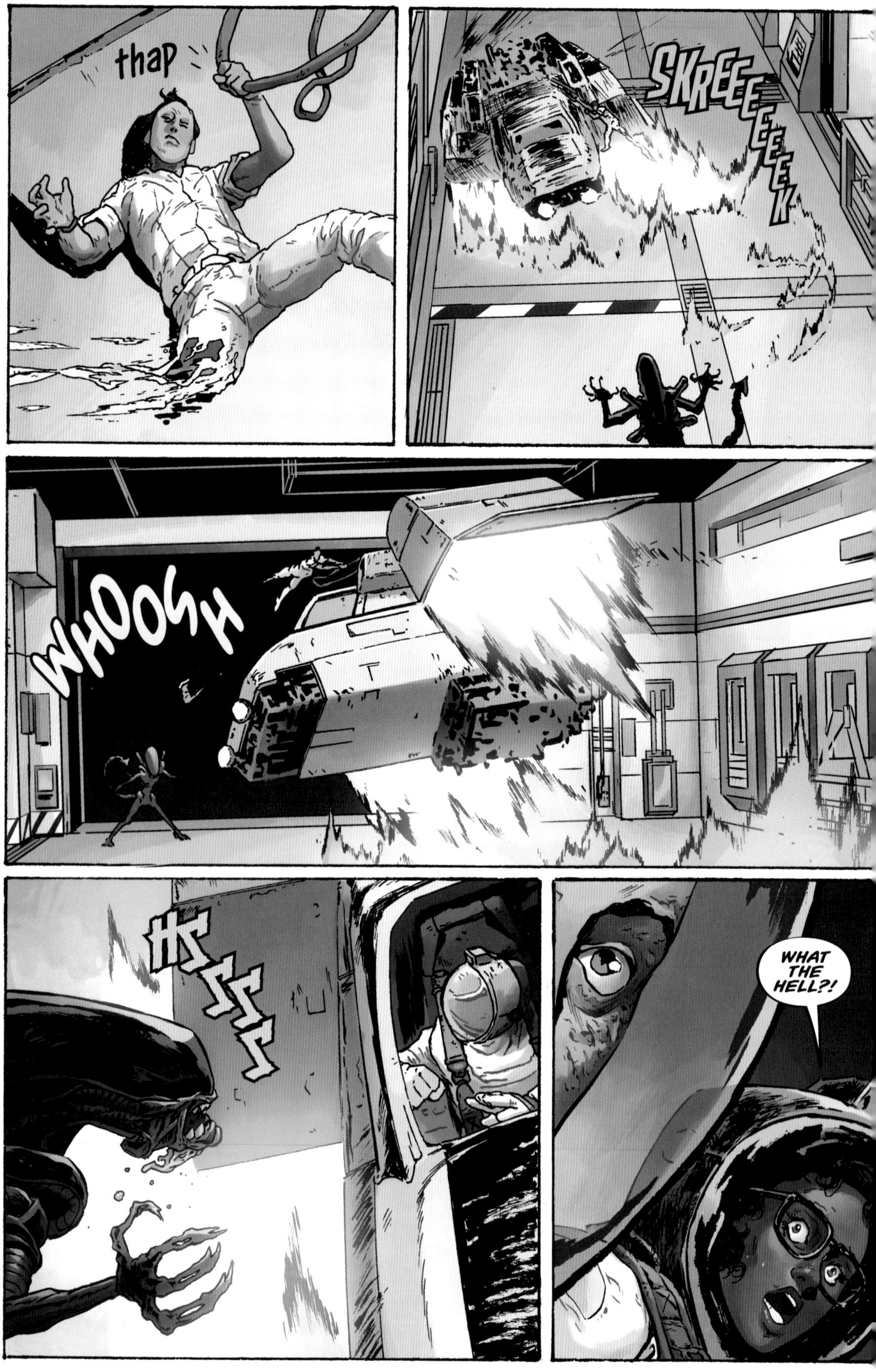
thap
SKREEEEEEK
WHOOSH
HSSS
WHAT THE HELL?!

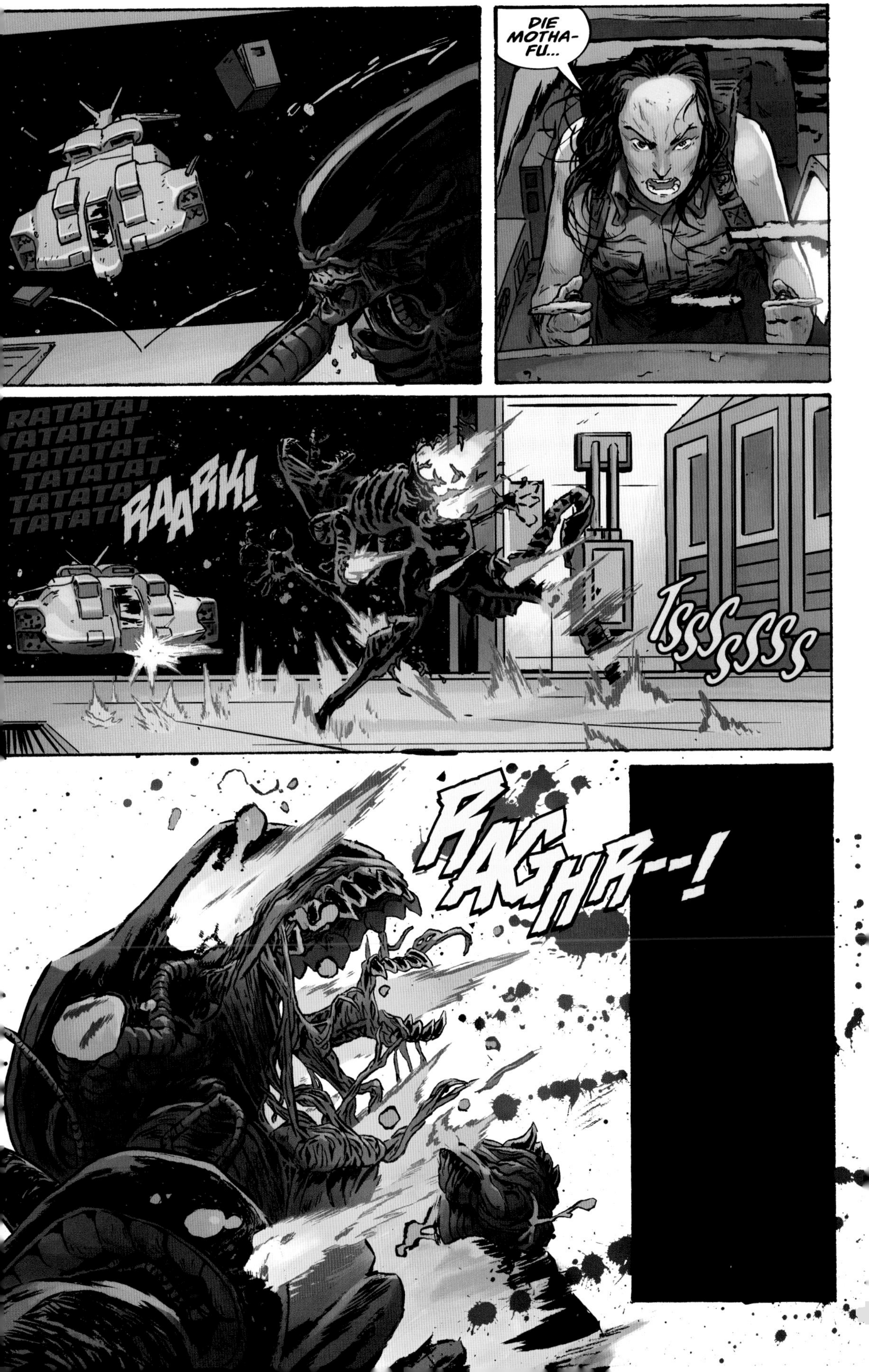
DIE MOTHA-FU...
RATATAT
TATATAT
TATATAT
TATATAT
TATATAT
TATATAT
RAARK!
TSSSSSSS
RAGHR--!

SOON.

deeet *deeet*
deeet

THE OTHER LOAD IS SCHEDULED FOR TWENTY-TWO-FIFTEEN.

TWENTY-TWO-HUNDRED...

deeet
deeet

I THOUGHT YOU MIGHT NEED TIME...

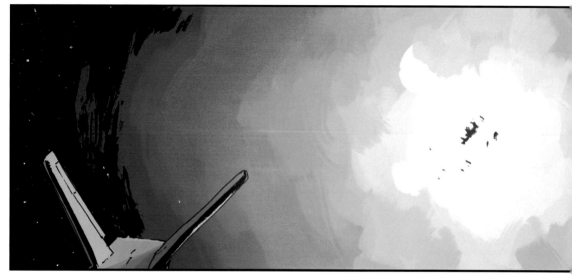

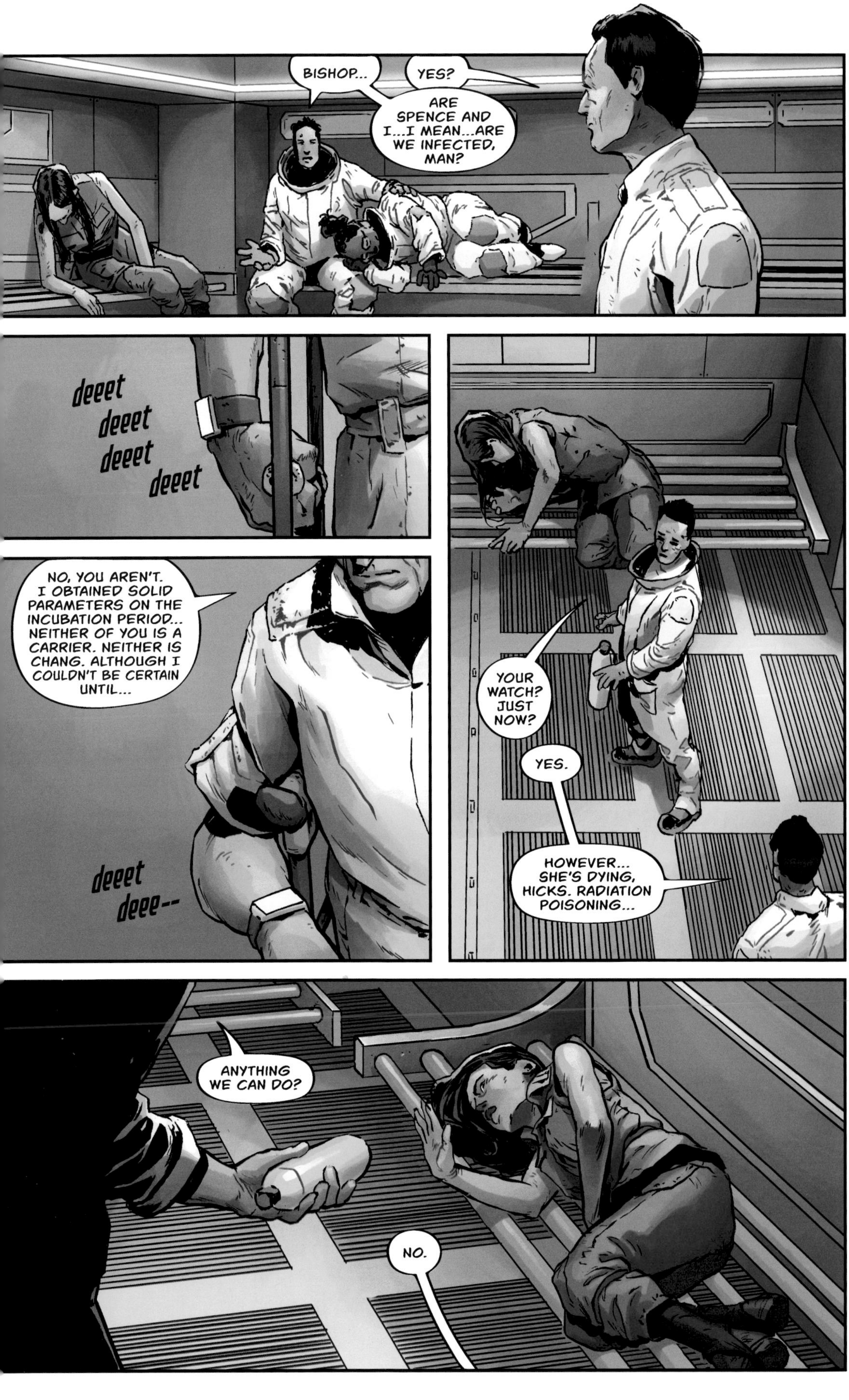
BISHOP...
YES?
ARE SPENCE AND I...I MEAN...ARE WE INFECTED, MAN?
deeet deeet deeet deeet
NO, YOU AREN'T. I OBTAINED SOLID PARAMETERS ON THE INCUBATION PERIOD... NEITHER OF YOU IS A CARRIER. NEITHER IS CHANG. ALTHOUGH I COULDN'T BE CERTAIN UNTIL...
deeet deee--
YOUR WATCH? JUST NOW?
YES.
HOWEVER... SHE'S DYING, HICKS. RADIATION POISONING...
ANYTHING WE CAN DO?
NO.

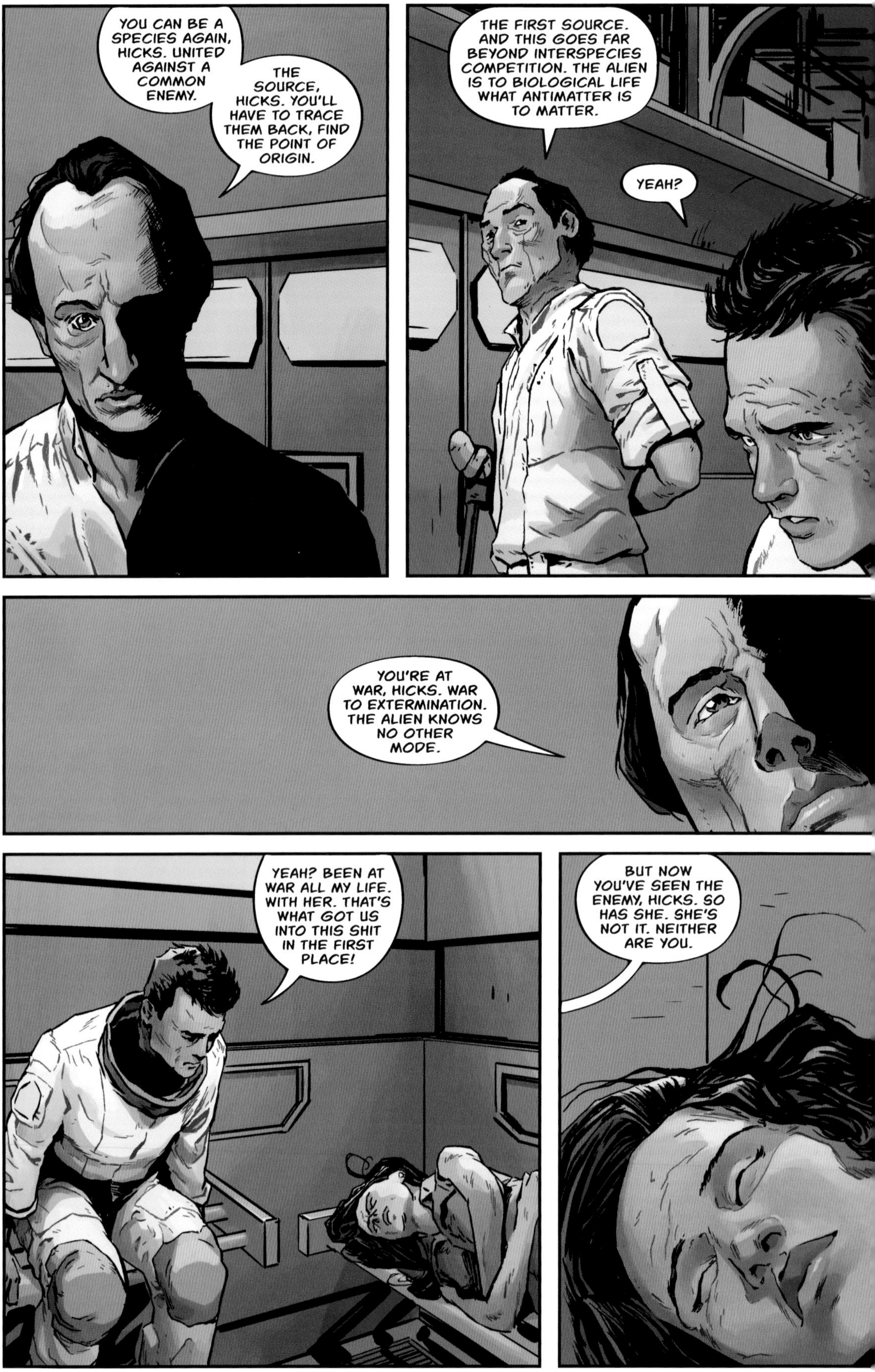
YOU CAN BE A SPECIES AGAIN, HICKS. UNITED AGAINST A COMMON ENEMY.
THE SOURCE, HICKS. YOU'LL HAVE TO TRACE THEM BACK, FIND THE POINT OF ORIGIN.
THE FIRST SOURCE. AND THIS GOES FAR BEYOND INTERSPECIES COMPETITION. THE ALIEN IS TO BIOLOGICAL LIFE WHAT ANTIMATTER IS TO MATTER.
YEAH?
YOU'RE AT WAR, HICKS. WAR TO EXTERMINATION. THE ALIEN KNOWS NO OTHER MODE.
YEAH? BEEN AT WAR ALL MY LIFE. WITH HER. THAT'S WHAT GOT US INTO THIS SHIT IN THE FIRST PLACE!
BUT NOW YOU'VE SEEN THE ENEMY, HICKS. SO HAS SHE. SHE'S NOT IT. NEITHER ARE YOU.

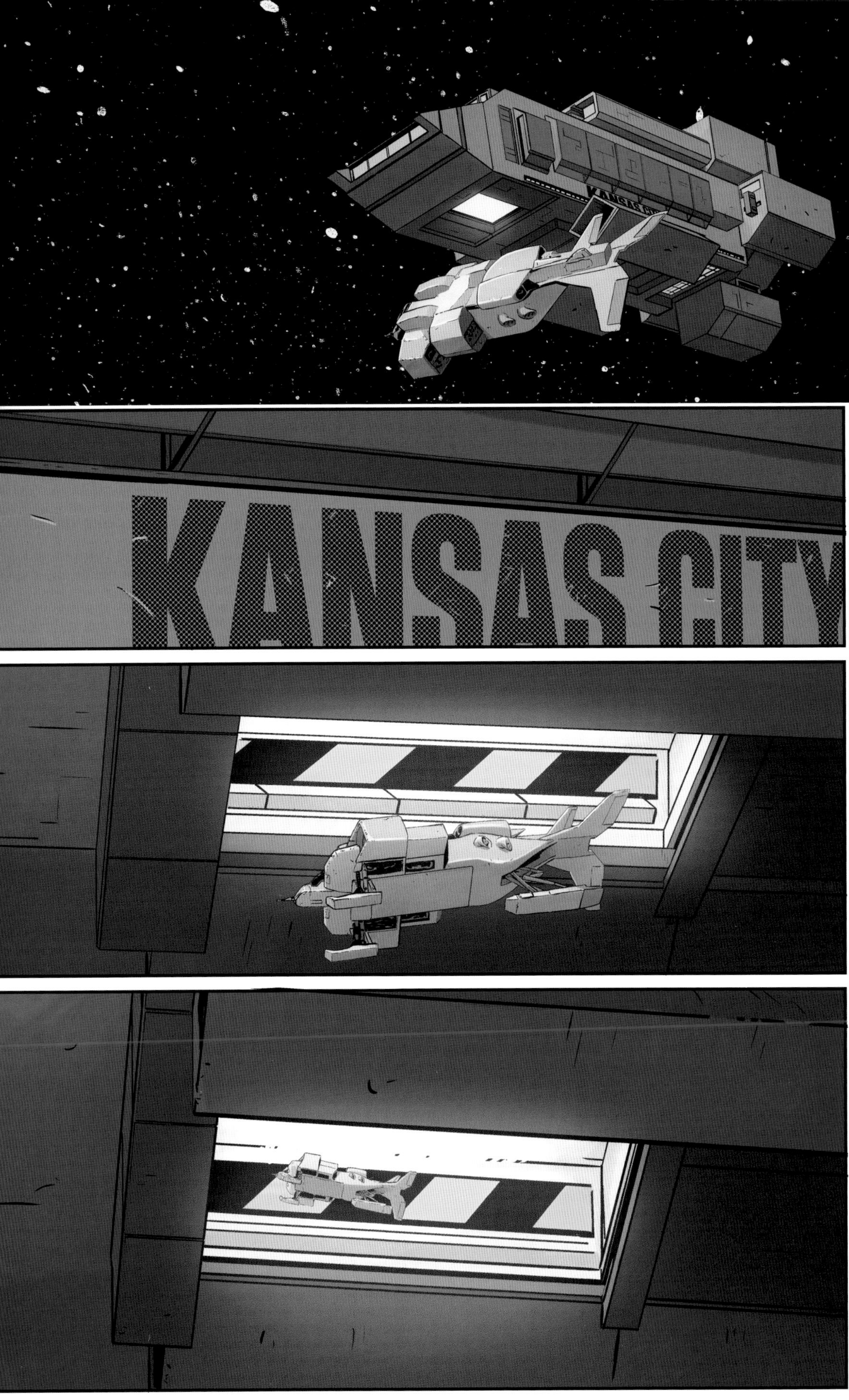
KANSAS CITY

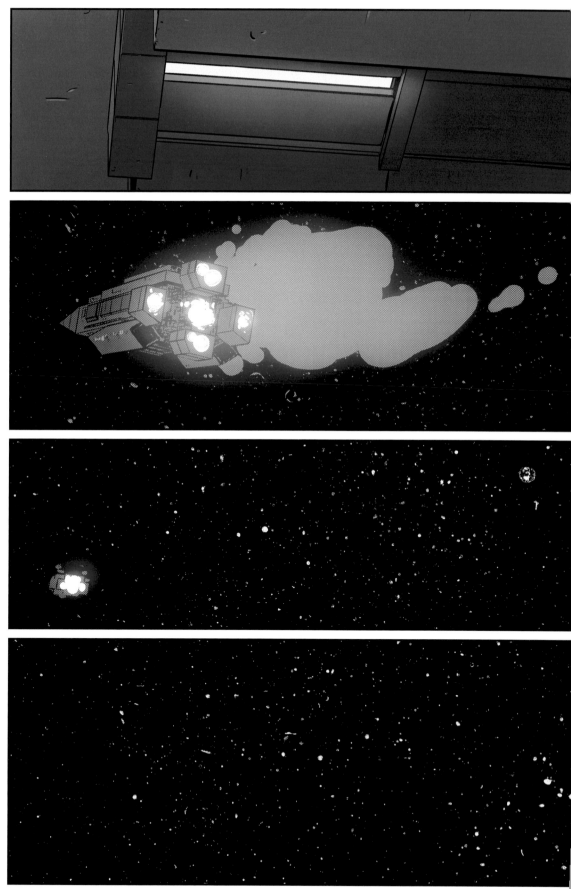

END

ALIEN 3

THE UNPRODUCED SCREENPLAY

SKETCHBOOK

NOTES BY

JOHNNIE CHRISTMAS

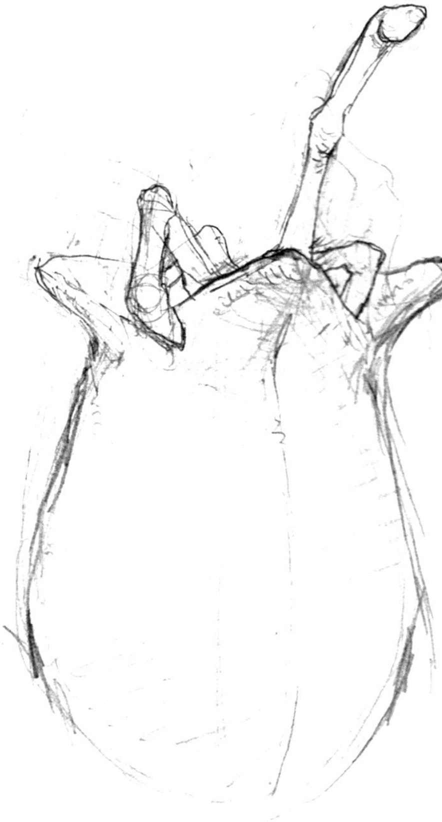

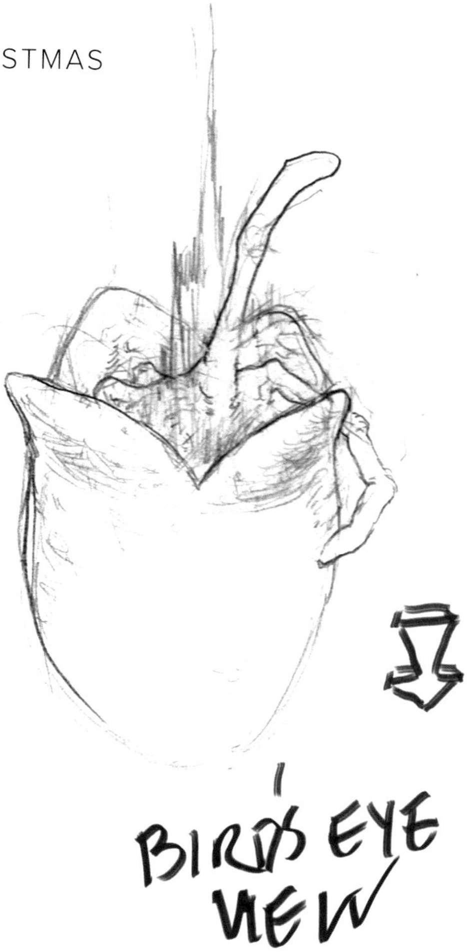
BIRD'S EYE VIEW

Our editor, Daniel Chabon, had the idea of doing vignettes for the series covers. For the first issue's cover (also the cover for this collection) we wanted to have a xenomorph egg to kick it off. This cover came together pretty quickly; I knew what I wanted, but tried a few angles just to make sure.

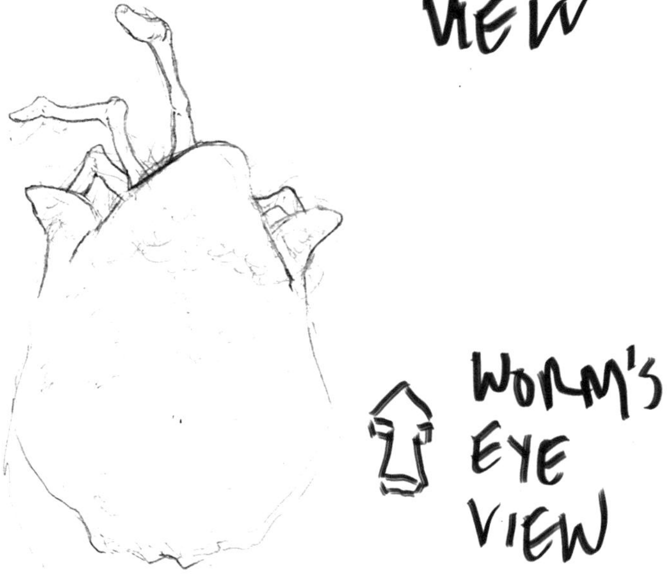
WORM'S EYE VIEW

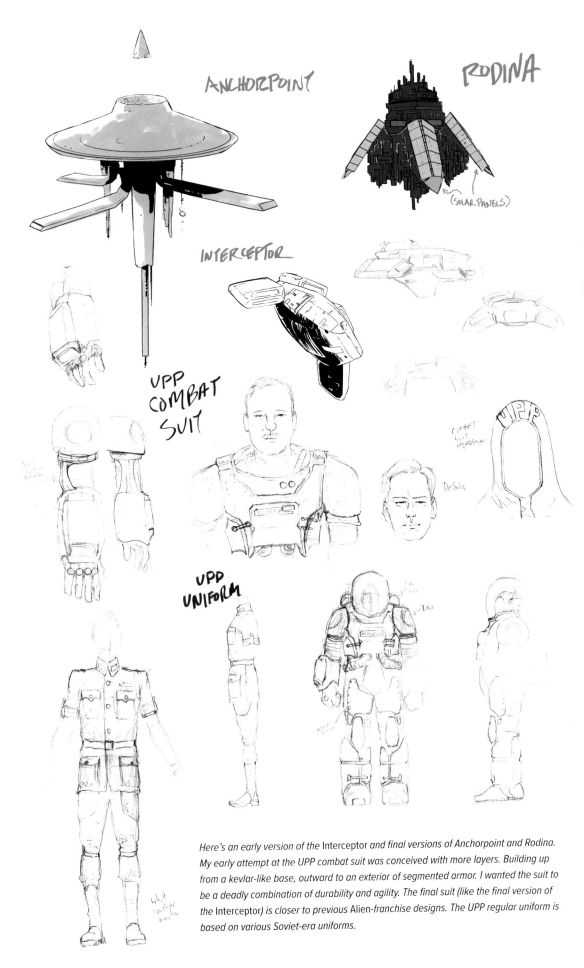

ANCHORPOINT

RODINA

(SOLAR PANELS)

INTERCEPTOR

UPP COMBAT SUIT

COMBAT SUIT HANDGUN

De Salis

UPP

UPD UNIFORM

Here's an early version of the Interceptor *and final versions of Anchorpoint and Rodina. My early attempt at the UPP combat suit was conceived with more layers. Building up from a kevlar-like base, outward to an exterior of segmented armor. I wanted the suit to be a deadly combination of durability and agility. The final suit (like the final version of the* Interceptor*) is closer to previous* Alien-*franchise designs. The UPP regular uniform is based on various Soviet-era uniforms.*

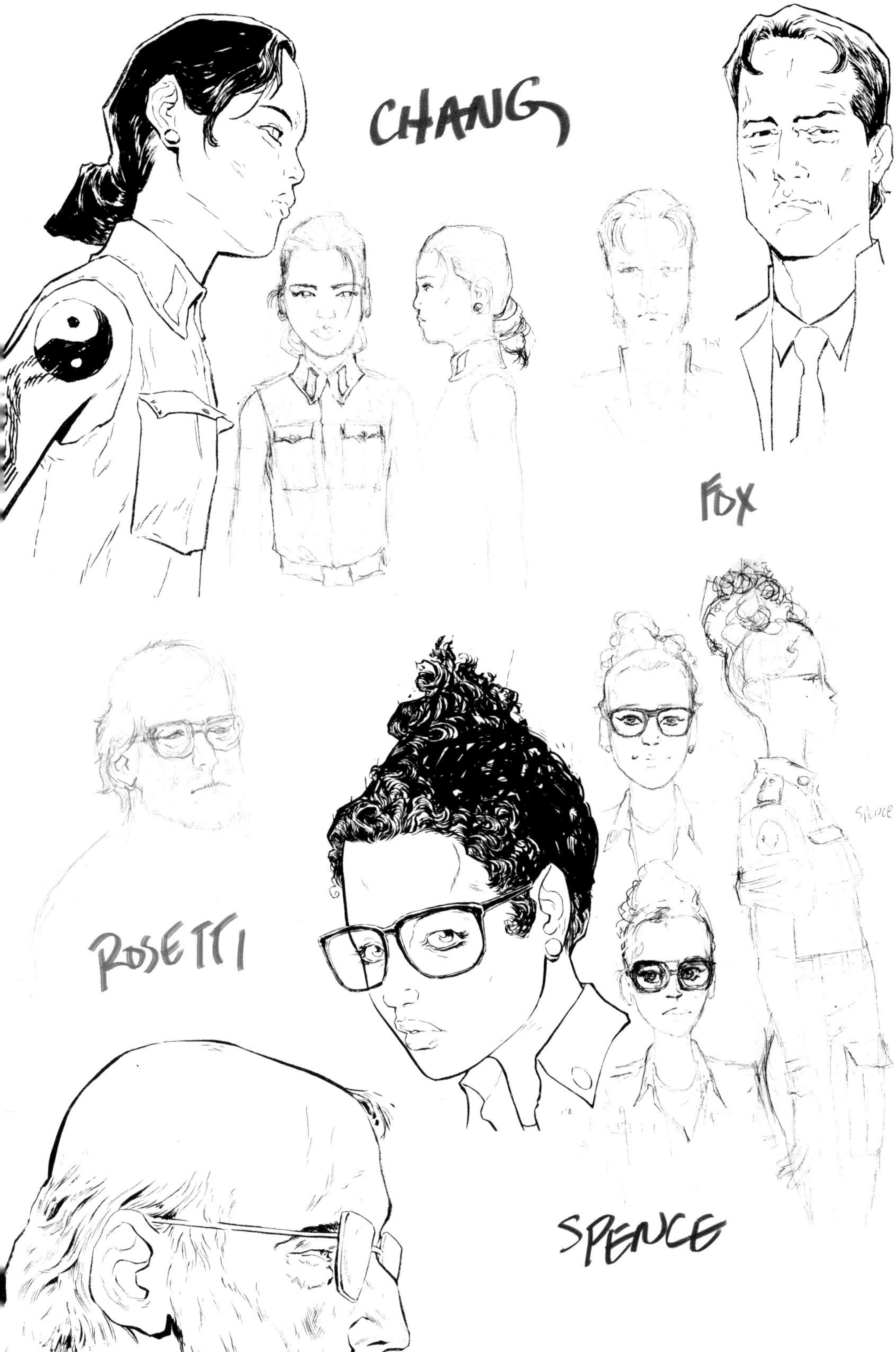
CHANG
FOX
ROSETTI
SPENCE

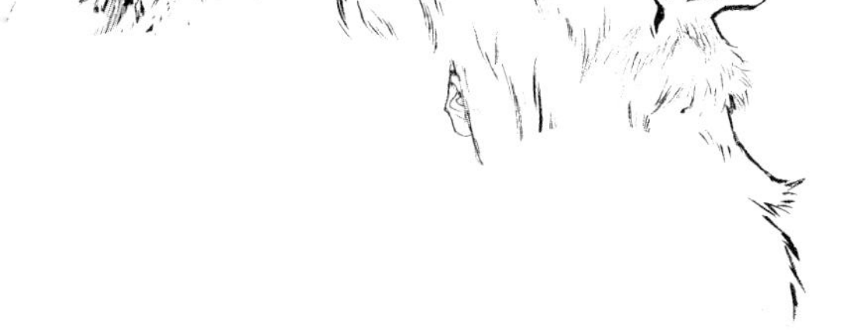

Coming up with visual traits that match our characters' inner (and, obviously, outer) attributes is always a fun process. I love Chang's tattoo.

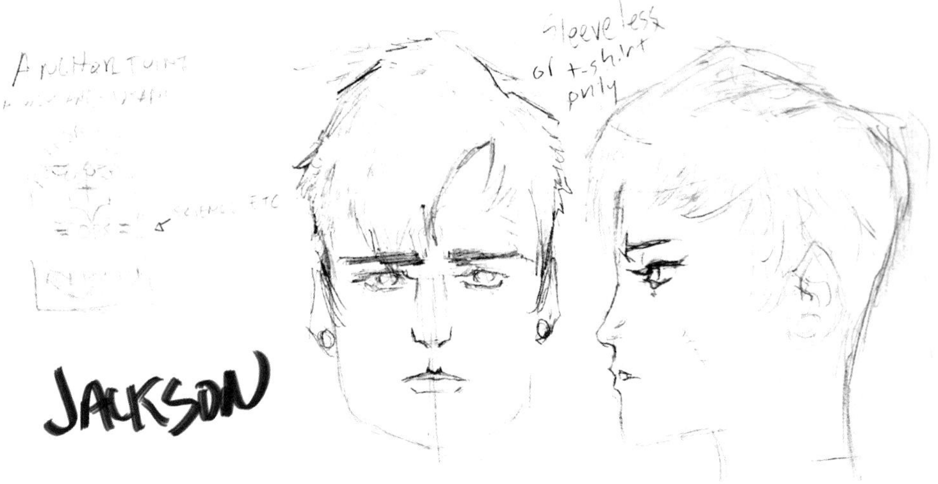
sleeveless or t-shirt only
JACKSON

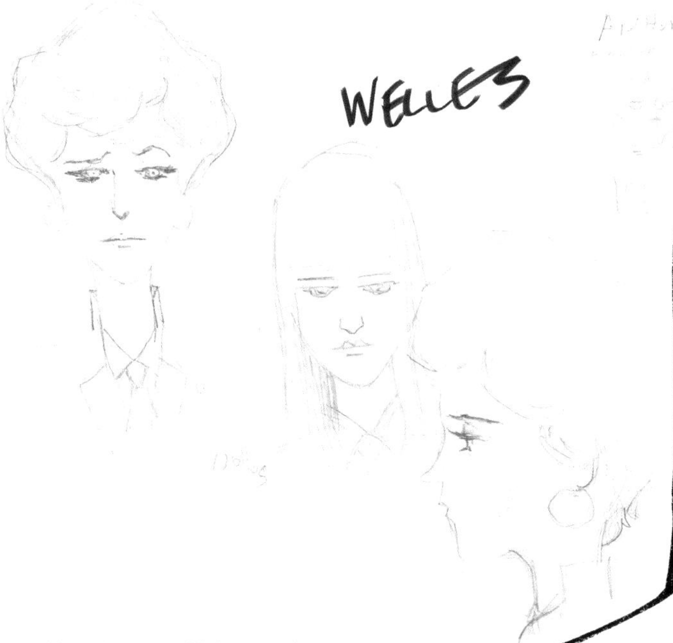
WELLES

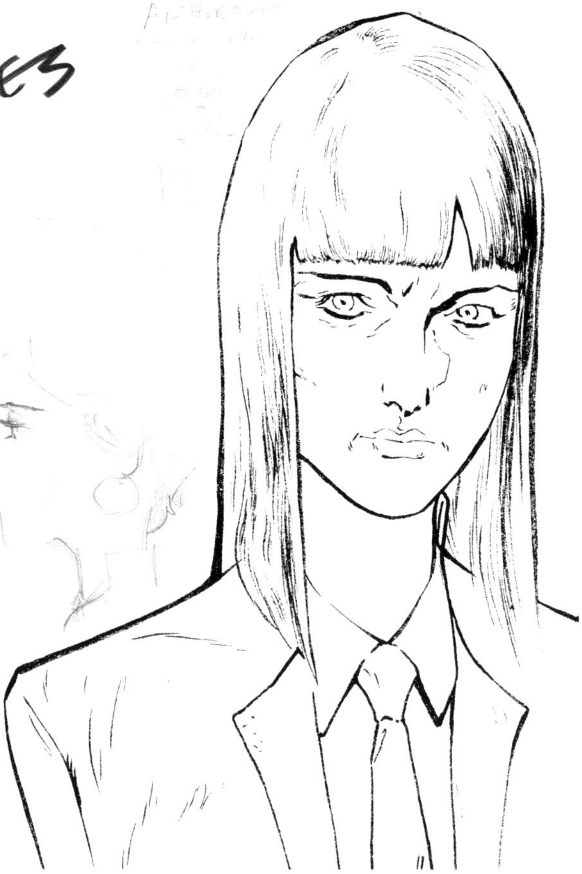

More characters. Welles went from a curly short crop, heavy eyeliner, and earrings to, finally, a simpler, unadorned style.

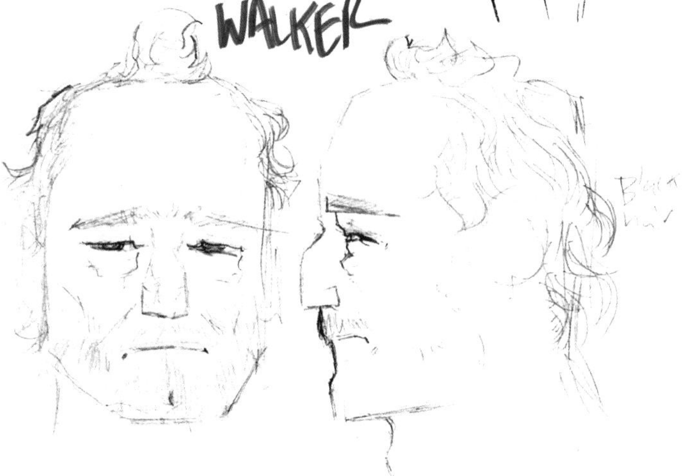
WALKER

Walker and Jackson were two of my favorite character designs.

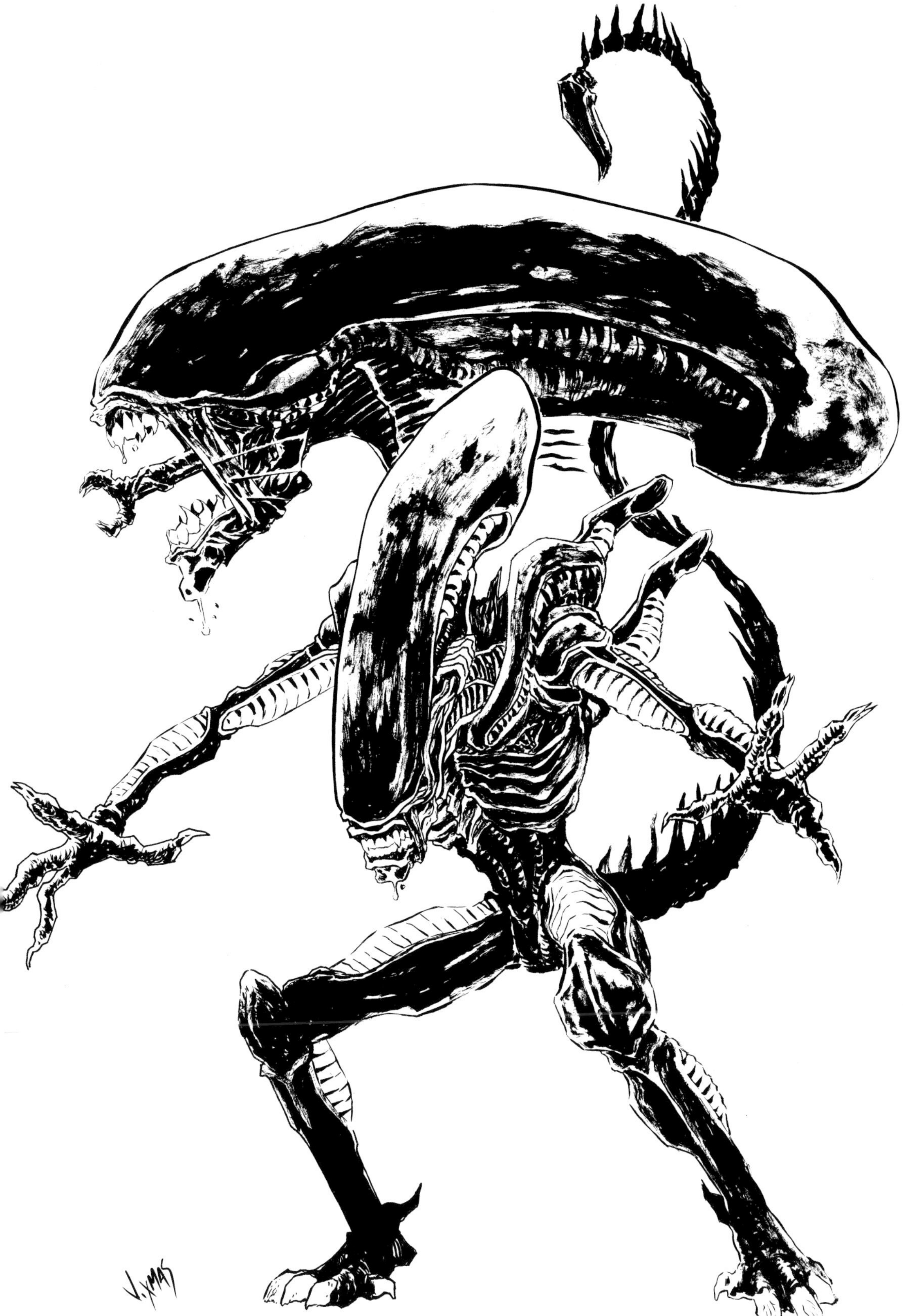

Here's an early xenomorph test.

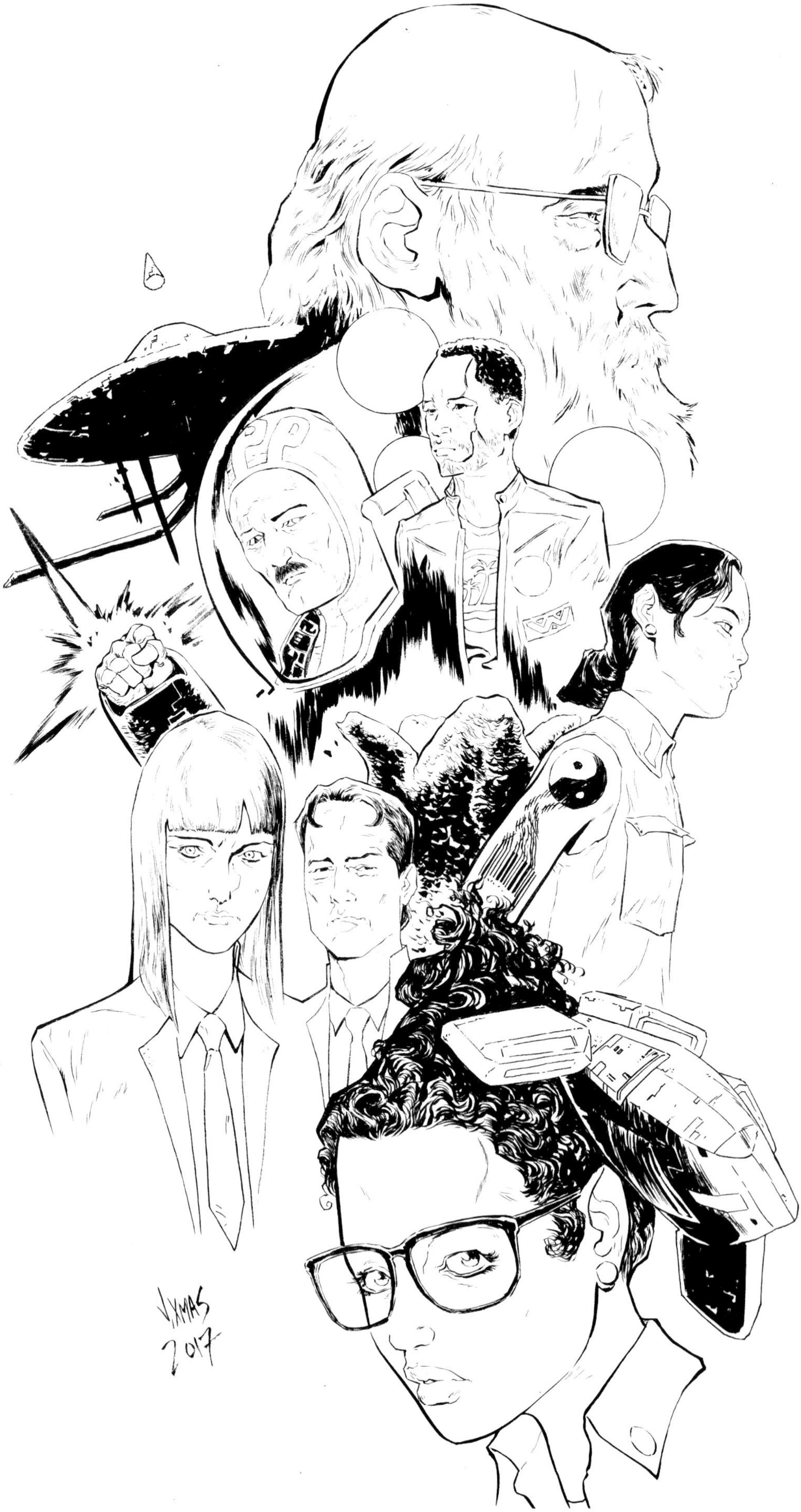
J.XMAS
2017

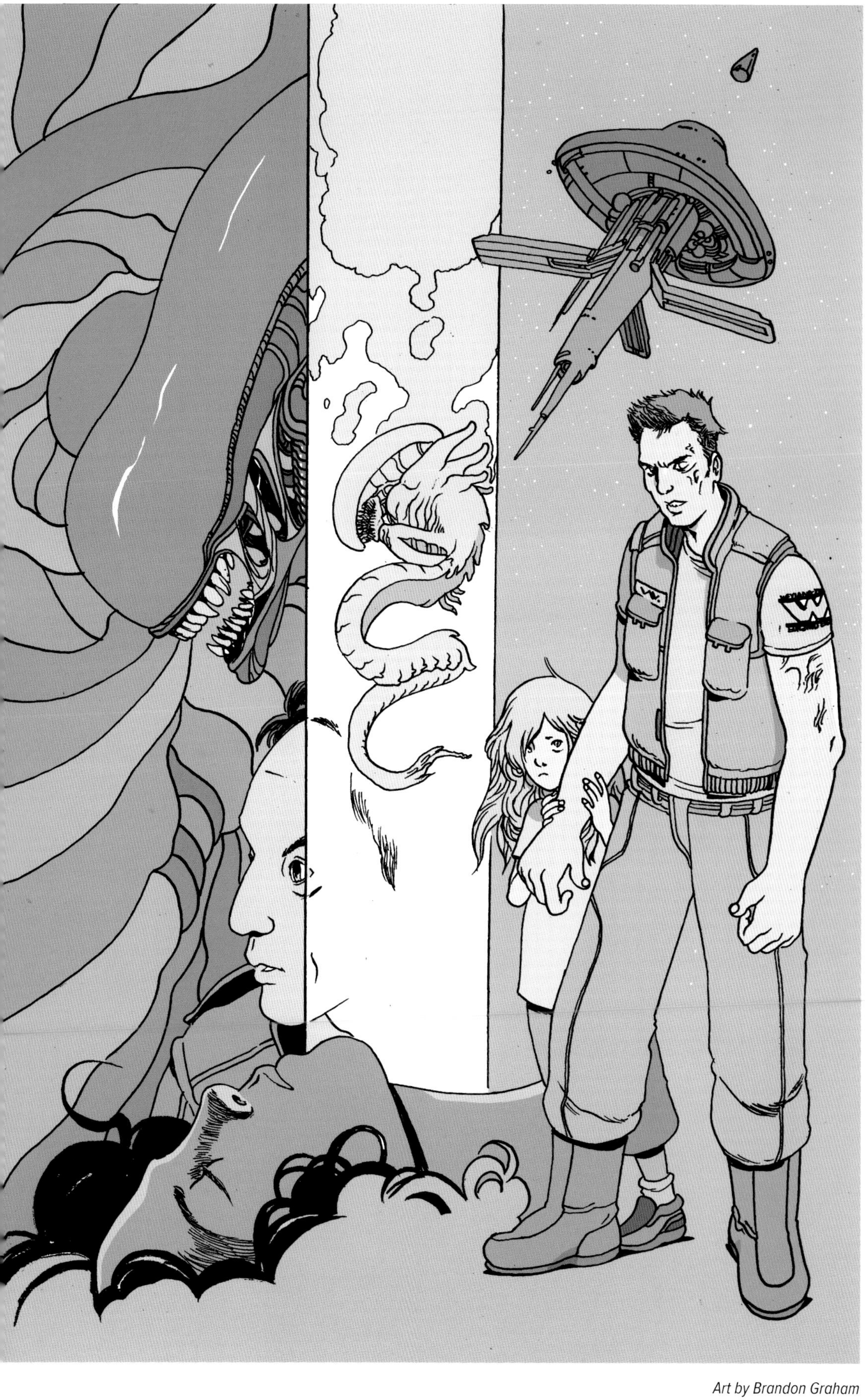

Art by Brandon Graham

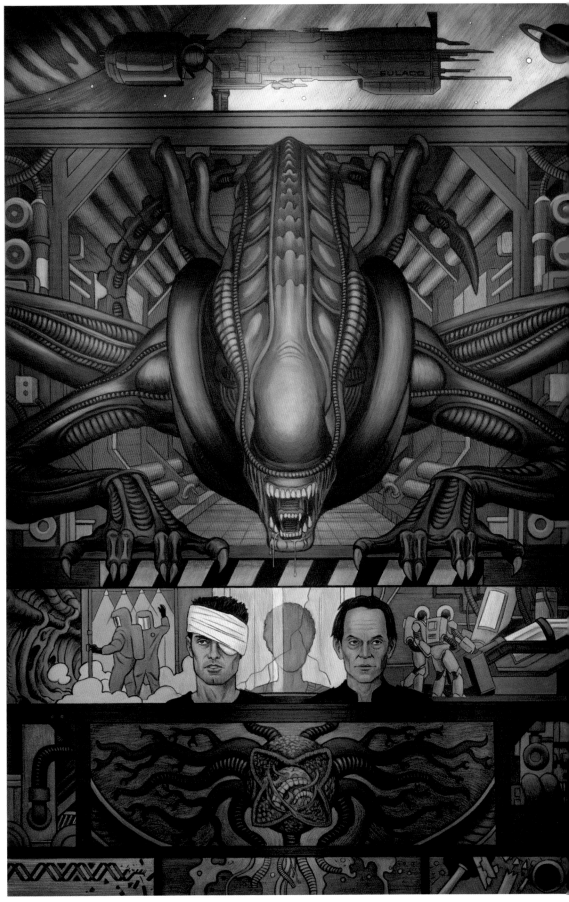

#1 Variant Cover by Paolo and Joe Rivera

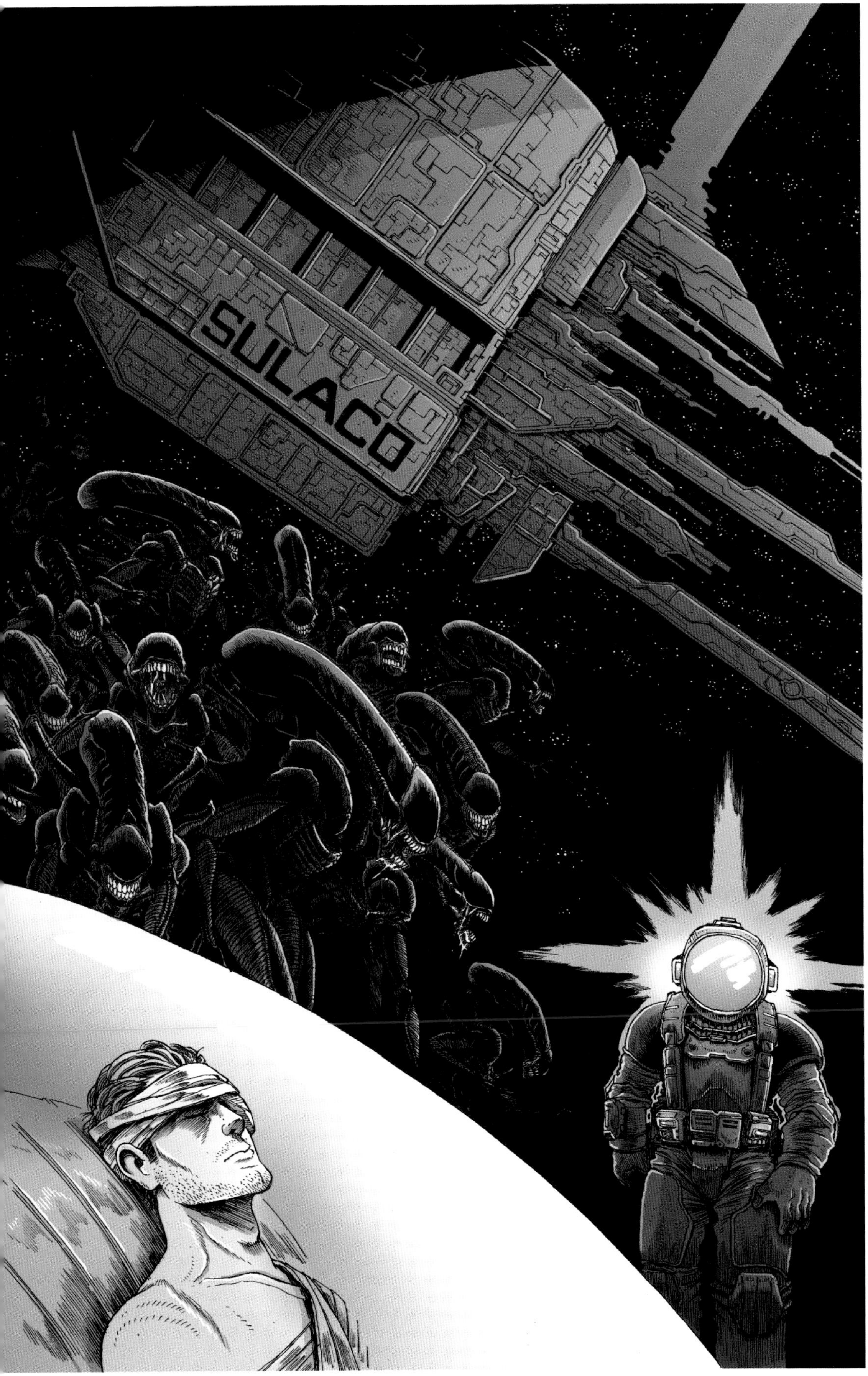

SULACO

Local Comic Shop Day Variant Cover by James Stokoe

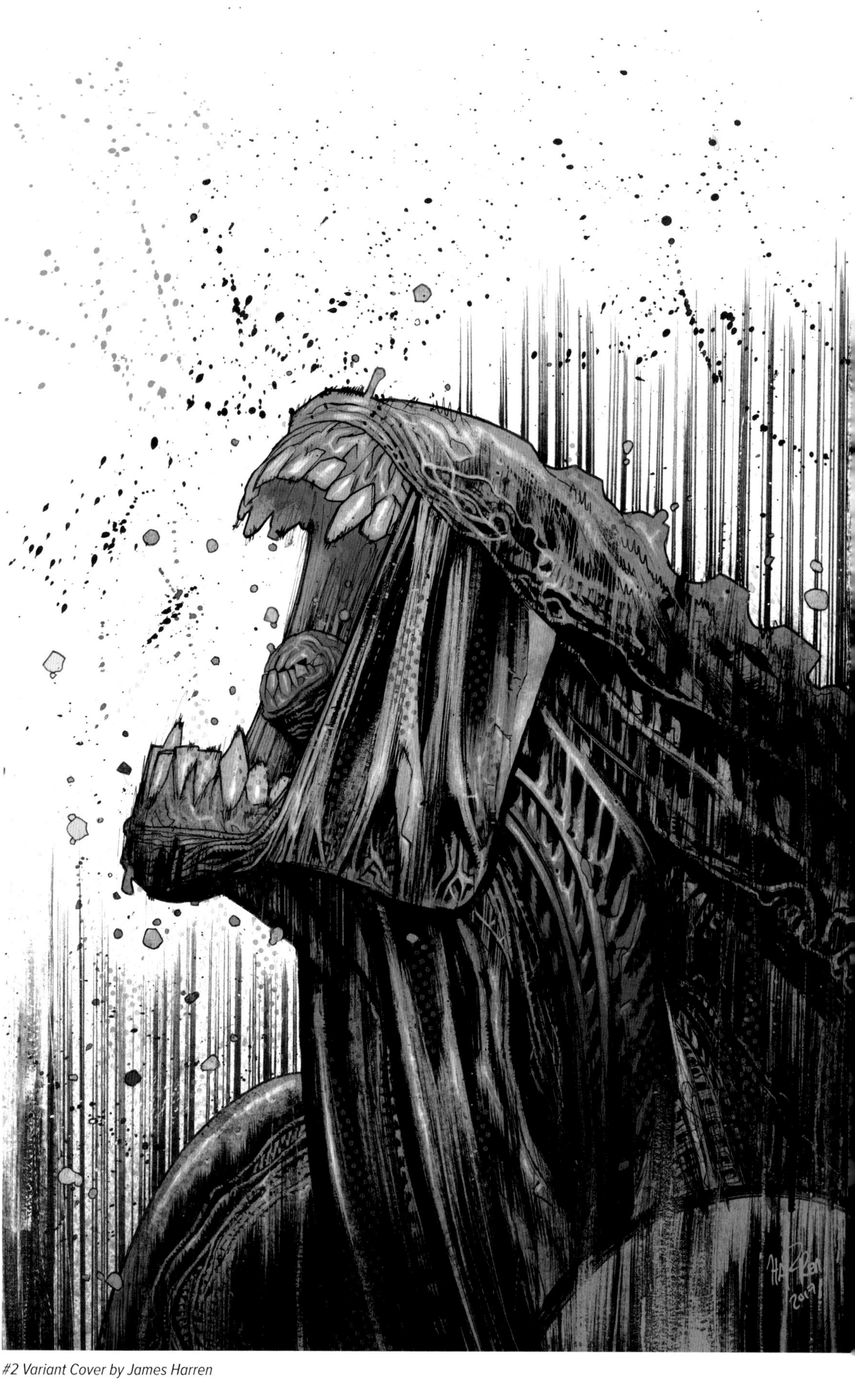

#2 Variant Cover by James Harren

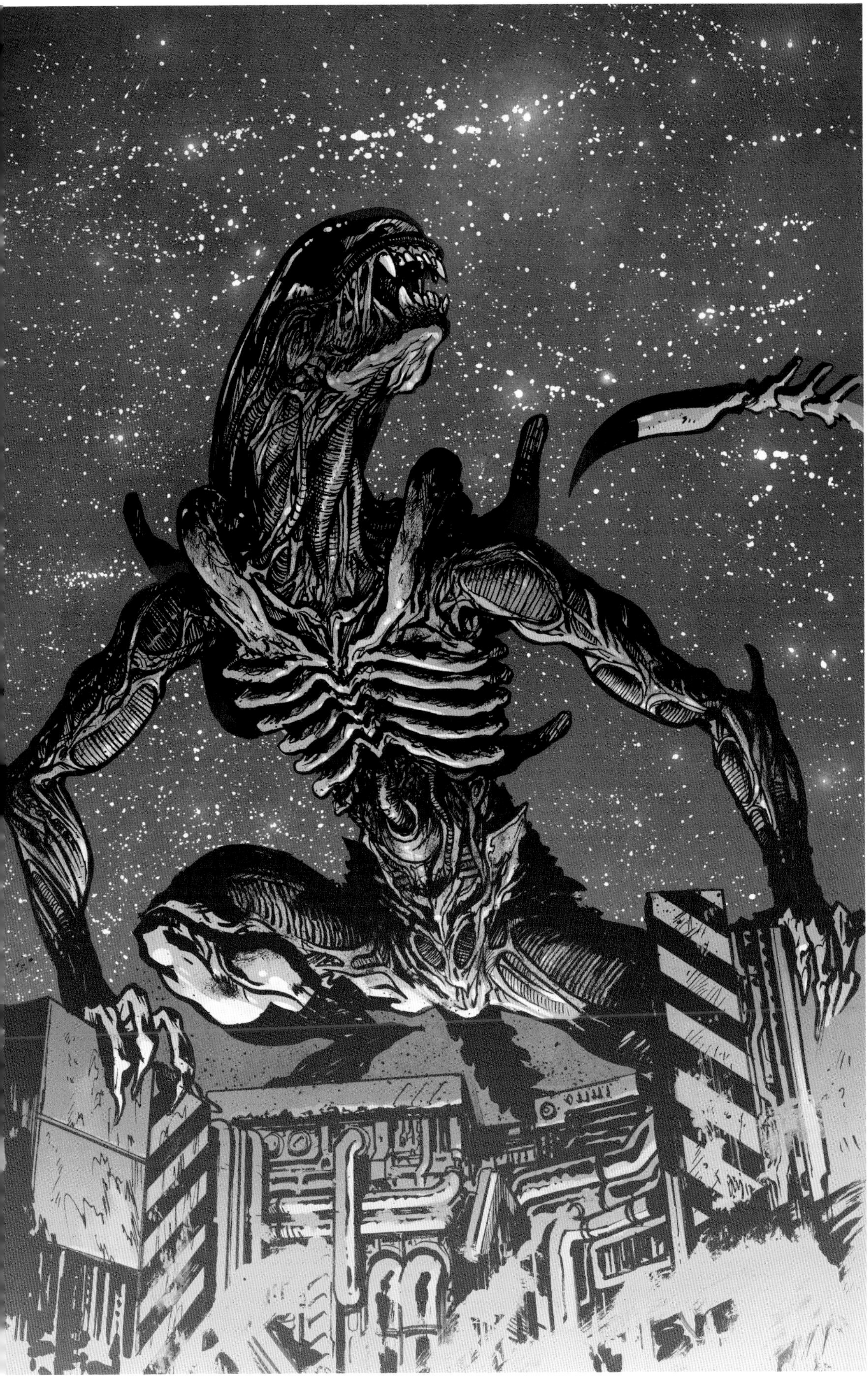

#3 Variant Cover by Daniel Warren Johnson with Mike Spicer

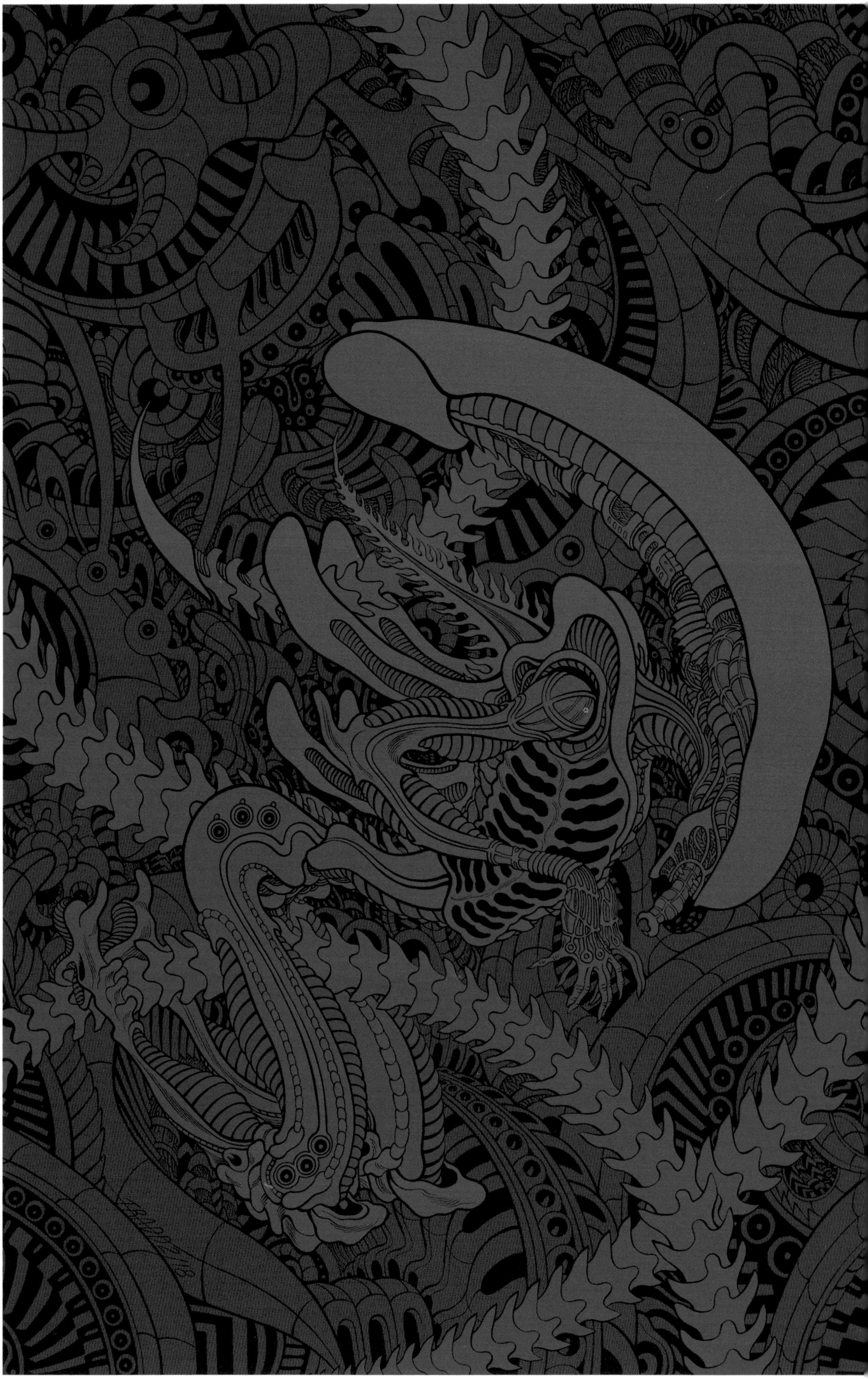

#4 Variant Cover by Tradd Moore

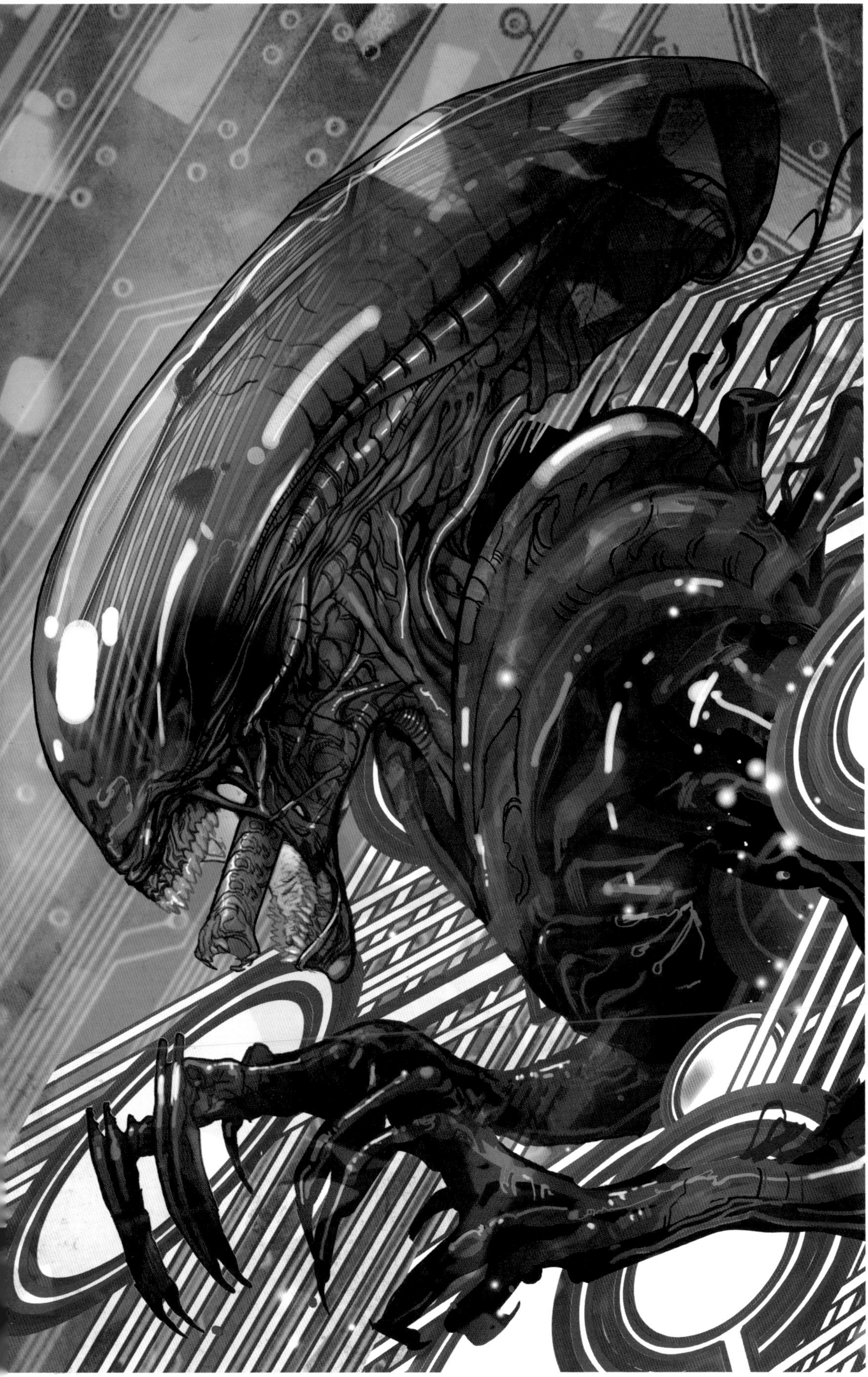

#5 Variant Cover by Christian Ward

ALIENS™

PREDATOR™ PROMETHEUS™ AVP ALIEN VS. PREDATOR™

FIRE AND STONE
ALIENS PREDATOR
PROMETHEUS AVP

ALIENS, PREDATOR, PROMETHEUS, AVP: FIRE AND STONE
The ultimate showdown!
ISBN 978-1-50670-725-9
$24.99 First Time in Paperback!

PROMETHEUS ALIENS AVP PREDATOR
THE COMPLETE
LIFE AND DEATH

ALIENS, PREDATOR, PROMETHEUS, AVP: THE COMPLETE LIFE AND DEATH
The world-hopping sequel to Fire and Stone*!*
ISBN 978-1-50670-678-8
$49.99 Deluxe Hardcover

ALIENS
DEAD ORBIT
JAMES STOKOE

ALIENS: DEAD ORBIT
James Stokoe's exploration of terror!
ISBN 978-1-50670-333-6
$17.99 Trade Paperback

OVERSIZED EDITION
ISBN 978-1-50670-992-5
$34.99 Deluxe Hardcover

ALIENS
DEFIANCE

ALIENS: DEFIANCE VOL. 1
Brian Wood introduces heroine Zulu Hendrix!
ISBN 978-1-50670-126-4
$19.99 Trade Paperback

ALIENS
DEFIANCE

ALIENS: DEFIANCE VOL. 2
Zulu Hendrix is the new hero of the Aliens universe!
ISBN 978-1-50670-168-4
$19.99 Trade Paperback

ALIENS
GABRIEL HARDMAN

ALIENS: DUST TO DUST
A bloodcurdling coming-of-age story by master storyteller Gabriel Hardman!
ISBN 978-1-50670-792-1
$17.99 Trade Paperback

DARK HORSE BOOKS
DarkHorse.com

AVAILABLE AT YOUR LOCAL COMICS SHOP OR BOOKSTORE
To find a comics shop in your area, consult www.comicshoplocator.com
For more information or to order direct: On the web: darkhorse.com | E-mail: mailorder@darkhorse.com | Phone: 1-800-862-0052
Mon.–Fri. 9 a.m. to 5 p.m. Pacific Time.

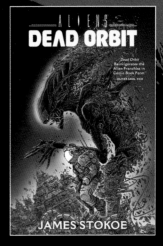